# Philip Roth Revisited

## Twayne's United States Authors Series

Frank Day, Editor

*Clemson University*

TUSAS 611

PHILIP ROTH
*Photograph © Nancy Crampton*

# Philip Roth Revisited

Jay L. Halio

*University of Delaware*

Twayne Publishers • New York
Maxwell Macmillan Canada • Toronto
Maxwell Macmillan International • New York  Oxford  Singapore  Sydney

*Philip Roth Revisited*
Jay L. Halio

Twayne Publishers
Macmillan Publishing Company
866 Third Avenue
New York, New York 10022

Maxwell Macmillan Canada, Inc.
1200 Eglinton Avenue East
Suite 200
Don Mills, Ontario M3C 3N1

Macmillan Publishing Company is part of the Maxwell Communication Group of Companies.

10 9 8 7 6 5 4 3 2 1

The paper used in this publication meets the minimum requirements of American National Standard for Information Sciences—Permanence of Paper for Printed Library Materials. ANSI Z3948-1984. ∞™

Printed in the United States of America

**Library of Congress Cataloging-in-Publication Data**

Halio, Jay L.
    Philip Roth revisited / Jay L. Halio.
        p.    cm. — (Twayne's United States authors series ; TUSAS 611)
    Includes bibliographical references and index.
    ISBN 0-8057-3962-9
    1. Roth, Philip—Criticism and interpretation.    I. Title.
II. Series.
PS3568.0855Z69    1992
813'.54—dc20                                          92-12173
                                                        CIP

# *Errata*

| Page | For | Read |
|------|-----|------|
| xi, line 4 | Newark College, Rutgers University | Newark College of Rutgers University |
| xi, line 30 | 1965-80 | 1965-77 |
| xii, line 10 | *Add*: Visits Prague for first time. | |
| xii, line 11 | *Delete:* Visits Prague. | |
| xii, line 17 | 1975-80 | 1975-89 |
| xii, line 25 | Undergoes surgery and suffers a serious nervous breakdown. | Undergoes knee surgery and suffers a Halcion-induced depression. |
| xii, line 26 | *Add*: Wins National Book Critics Award. | |
| xii, line 28 | quintuple heart surgery | quintuple by-pass surgery |
| xii, line 31 | *Add:* Wins National Book Critics Award. | |
| xv, line 16 | Bessie | Besse |
| xvi, line 5 | a child | two children |
| xvi, line 25 | children | a child |
| xvi, line 31 | 1980 | 1977 |
| xvii, line 10 | 1975 | 1971 |
| xvii, line 17 | nervous breakdown | Halcion-induced depression |

For
June, Brian,
and Amy

# Table of Contents

# Acknowledgments

Many people helped in the writing of this book. For reading all or parts of the manuscript in various stages of composition and making many useful comments, I am grateful to Richard Davison, Frank Day, June Halio, Marcia Halio, and Jerzy Limon. Melvin J. Friedman, Ben Siegel, and Daniel Walden helped by sending me various materials in timely fashion. Thanks are due, also, to the editors at Twayne Publishers: Liz Fowler, who before leaving the company encouraged submission and arranged for a contract; and Jacob Conrad, who helped edit the book and see it through the press. The Center for Advanced Study at the University of Delaware generously awarded me a grant for the academic year 1989–90 that provided much valuable time and made completion of the book possible. While I extend thanks to each and every one, I reserve the right to claim sole responsibility for any errors or misjudgments that may remain in my work.

# Chronology

1933    Philip Roth born on 19 March to Herman and Bess (Finkel) Roth, in Newark, N.J.

1946–1950    Attends Weequahic High School, Newark.

1950–1951    Attends Newark College, Rutgers University.

1951–1954    Attends Bucknell University. B.A. in English, magna cum laude; Phi Beta Kappa. Edits and helps found Bucknell literary magazine, *Et Cetera,* which publishes first stories. "The Day It Snowed" published in *Chicago Review.*

1955    Graduate study at University of Chicago. M.A. in English. Enlists in army; discharged within a year because of injury.

1956–1958    Ph.D. study at University of Chicago (1956–57) and instructorship there. "The Contest for Aaron Gold," published in *Epoch* in 1955, chosen for Martha Foley's *Best American Short Stories of 1956.*

1959    Marries Margaret Martinson Williams on 22 February. *Goodbye, Columbus.* Houghton Mifflin Literary Fellowship; National Institute of Arts and Letters grant; Guggenheim Fellowship. Stories win various awards.

1960    *Goodbye, Columbus* wins National Book and Daroff awards. Joins faculty of the University of Iowa Writers Workshop.

1961    "Writing American Fiction" published in *Commentary.*

1962    *Letting Go.* Writer in residence, Princeton University, 1962–64. Ford Foundation grant in playwriting.

1963    Legally separated from Margaret Martinson Roth on 1 March.

1964    *The Nice Jewish Boy* (unpublished) read as workshop exercise at American Place Theater with Dustin Hoffman in title role.

1965    Teaches one semester a year at University of Pennsylvania, 1965–80.

1966   Rockefeller Fellowship.

1967   *When She Was Good,* "Whacking Off," and "Jewish Patient Begins His Analysis."

1968   Margaret Martinson Roth killed in car accident on 19 May.

1969   *Portnoy's Complaint.* Paramount film of *Goodbye, Columbus.*

1970   Elected to National Institute of Arts and Letters. "On the Air" and "Salad Days."

1971   *Our Gang.* Larry Arrick's dramatization of "Epstein," "Defender of the Faith," and "Eli, the Fanatic" produced in New York under the title *Unlikely Heroes.*

1972   *The Breast.* Visits Prague.

1973   *The Great American Novel,* "'I Always Wanted You to Admire My Fasting'; or, Looking at Kafka," and "Marriage a la Mode."

1974   *My Life as a Man.*

1975   *Reading Myself and Others.* General editor of "Writers from the Other Europe," 1975–80.

1977   *The Professor of Desire.*

1979   *The Ghost Writer.*

1981   *A Philip Roth Reader* and *Zuckerman Unbound.* Mother dies.

1983   *The Anatomy Lesson.*

1984   *The Ghost Writer* produced on PBS's "*American Playhouse.*"

1985   *Zuckerman Bound;* includes *The Ghost Writer, Zuckerman Unbound, The Anatomy Lesson,* and *Epilogue: The Prague Orgy.*

1987   Undergoes surgery and suffers a serious nervous breakdown. *The Counterlife.* Father ill with brain tumor.

1988   *The Facts: A Novelist's Autobiography.*

1989   Undergoes emergency quintuple heart surgery in August. Father dies in October.

1990   *Deception.* Marries the actress Claire Bloom on 29 April.

1991   *Patrimony: A True Story.*

Truth is like castor oil: the taste
is bitter and people don't like it;
so you make them laugh, and when their
mouths are open, you pour it in.

—Harold Clurman

# Philip Roth: A Biographical Sketch

When Philip Roth grew up in Newark, New Jersey, where he was born in 1933, the city was quite different from the way it is now. Roth's neighborhood was predominantly Jewish, and he had many friends and relatives who lived there. The Hebrew school he attended in the afternoons is reflected in such stories as "The Conversion of the Jews" and "'I Always Wanted You to Admire My Fasting'; or, Looking at Kafka." He graduated from Weequahic High School, at that time predominantly Jewish as well, and spent a year, like Neil Klugman in "Goodbye, Columbus," at Newark College of Rutgers University. But when he visited Bucknell and fell in love with the school, his father determined to send him there, despite the sacrifices it would cost the family to do so.

Tight-knit family life is reflected in many of Roth's stories and novels, though one has to be careful to avoid one-to-one equivalences. For example, while hardworking Jack Portnoy bears some resemblances to Philip's father, Herman Roth, Sophie Portnoy is very distant from Philip's beloved mother, Bessie, whose quiet competence and efficiency as mother and housekeeper Roth praises in *Patrimony*. Again, *Patrimony* reveals the close relationship, especially later in life, between Philip and his father, although in his teens Philip felt the usual kinds of between-generations antagonisms that were prevented from becoming more serious by his move to Bucknell and later the University of Chicago, where he did graduate work in English. Unlike old Dr. Zuckerman in *Zuckerman Bound,* who became furious with his son for publishing *Carnovsky,* Herman Roth always took pride in Philip's accomplishments and fully supported his son.

At Bucknell Philip became interested in writing and helped found and edit *Et Cetera,* the literary magazine that published his first stories. Other stories began appearing in *Epoch,* the *Chicago Review,* and later *Commentary,* the *Paris Review,* and *Esquire.* When five of them were collected for publication along with the title story in *Goodbye, Columbus* (1959), Roth was well on his way to an outstanding career as a fiction writer. While the military draft was still on, he enlisted in the army (1955), from which he was discharged several months later after receiving a back injury during basic training. In 1960 *Goodbye, Columbus* won the National Book

Award, along with several other prestigious awards, and earned Roth a number of fellowships and grants.

During his days as a graduate student at the University of Chicago and later as an instructor of English there, he met and married Margaret Martinson Williams, a divorcée with a child from a previous marriage. Their marriage, an unhappy one, is fictionalized in *My Life as a Man* and recounted again in Roth's autobiography, *The Facts*. With Margaret, Roth went to Iowa as a faculty member in the Writers Workshop and continued writing. His second book and first full novel, *Letting Go* (1962), is set partly in Iowa and Chicago. As writer in residence at Princeton University and with a Ford Foundation grant under his belt, Roth tried playwriting, but though he produced several scripts and at least one had a reading in New York, with Dustin Hoffman in the leading role, none has ever been produced professionally. On the other hand, Larry Arrick adapted some of Roth's early stories in *Unlikely Heroes,* which opened in New York in 1971, and later *The Ghost Writer* was made into a screenplay and performed on PBS's "American Playhouse" in 1984. Two of his other works, *Goodbye, Columbus* and *Portnoy's Complaint,* have been made into films.

In 1963 Roth finally secured a legal separation from his wife, Margaret, who refused to agree to a divorce. For a long time thereafter, Roth lived alone or with someone else more compatible. He refused to remarry until 1990, when he married the British actress Claire Bloom, with whom he had been sharing his home in Connecticut and hers in London for many years. Claire Bloom has children from a previous marriage, but Roth has never been a father.

*When She Was Good* (1967) was Roth's second full-length novel and, untypically, has not a Jew in it. It is written out of Roth's experience of living in the Midwest. By this time Roth had begun teaching one semester a year at the University of Pennsylvania, work he apparently enjoyed and continued until 1980. More recently, since moving to New York, he has taught at Hunter College of the City University of New York. In May 1968 Margaret Martinson Roth was killed in an automobile accident in Central Park, New York, freeing Roth at last from crippling alimony payments and Margaret's legal hectoring.

The publication of *Portnoy's Complaint* in 1969 brought Roth increased fame and fortune and also a great deal of antagonism from Jewish groups, which earlier had objected to much of the material in his first book, *Goodbye, Columbus.* Roth's defense of his work was carried on through public lectures and essays, several of them collected in *Reading Myself and*

*Others* (1975). He had started publishing excerpts from his novels in progress, such as "Whacking Off" in the *Partisan Review,* and this practice became a regular form of publication and source of income. The death of his first wife and the success of *Portnoy's Complaint* released great creative energy, but Roth admits to having had serious difficulty fictionalizing his marriage in what finally became one of his best novels, *My Life as a Man* (1974).

Meanwhile, he became active as a political and cultural satirist, as *Our Gang, The Great American Novel,* and many of his fugitive articles and stories reveal. After his visit to Prague in 1975, he became deeply interested in Eastern European writers and began editing a series for Penguin Books, "Writers from the Other Europe," which published English translations of such novelists as Milan Kundera. But Roth's major work was and remains in the form of the Jewish-American novel, if there is such a genre, and more recently he has taken to fictionalizing his experience as a famous, or notorious, writer, in such novels as those that constitute the trilogy *Zuckerman Bound* (1985). Serious illness and a nervous breakdown have led to more reflective autobiographical books, *The Facts* (1988) and *Patrimony* (1991), in which Roth has tried to set the record straight regarding certain aspects of his life, particularly his first marriage to Margaret and his relationship with his father. *Deception* (1990) shows his willingness still to experiment with forms of fiction and to take greater chances in connecting fiction with autobiography.

## Chapter One

# Introduction:

### The Comedy of Philip Roth

Often misleadingly grouped with Saul Bellow and Bernard Malamud as one of the three leading Jewish-American writers since World War II[1]— the Hart, Schaffner, and Marx of contemporary American literature, as Bellow once quipped—Philip Roth has by the 1990s achieved a substantial body of fiction that easily stands on its own merits. He requires the support of neither figurative bookends nor sophisticated literary analysis, though invariably he gets both, as an enormous body of critical commentary attests (see, for example, Bernard Rodgers's *Bibliography,* expanded second edition, 1984). This book is not just another attempt to add to that still-growing body of criticism; rather, it is an attempt to define and to demonstrate Roth's abilities as a specifically comic writer, one whose wit and humor are as varied and effective as they are funny and illuminating.

Like any good writer, Roth will not stand pigeonholing. He rarely repeats himself, and although he has arguably the best ear of any novelist writing in the past 50 years, he does not depend on a single voice or set of voices. His dialogue, like his comedy, ranges broadly. It is, moreover, unique, peculiar to himself. Although comparisons to Malamud, Bellow, and others are natural enough, the differences among them are more important, particularly in the kinds of comedy they create—the subjects they choose, the characters and their milieus, and the humor that pervades their fiction.

Like Malamud, for example, Roth is an easterner, born and brought up in Newark, New Jersey, the focus for much of his fiction. But as any native knows, Newark is not New York, and there some of the differences between Malamud and Roth begin. And Newark certainly is not Chicago, the locus for much of Bellow's fiction. Roth delights in portraying his old hometown, all but obliterated now by the disruptions of ethnic and other kinds of change. His Weequahic neighborhood is, moreover, miles away from Brooklyn, where Morris Bober runs his little grocery

1

store in Malamud's *The Assistant*. And as the neighborhoods differ, so do the characters and the kinds of comedy Roth and Malamud write through and about them. Unlike Malamud's mordant humor, Roth's is infused with a vivacity that clearly derives from the stand-up comedians to whom he has often been compared.[2] Whereas Malamud deftly uses the accents and attitudes of immigrant parents and first-generation Jews, Roth's characters are second- or third-generation men and women, struggling in different ways to come to grips with their Jewish heritage and the American environment that constantly impinges on it. Alexander Portnoy and his family thus are far different from the characters that people Malamud's stories in *The Magic Barrel* or *Idiot's First*. Although Roth's comedy sometimes takes flight into fantasy, as in *The Great American Novel*, nothing in his fiction remotely resembles Malamud's "The Jew Bird" or "Have Pity." Stories like those link Malamud more closely to Isaac Bashevis Singer and earlier Jewish writers than to Philip Roth.

Similarly, the "whirling" world of Chicago, as in Bellow's *The Dean's December*, is far distant from the streets of Newark in the 1950s that Roth depicts. Or, since Roth too writes about Chicago, as in *Letting Go*, perhaps finer distinctions must be made. Both Bellow and Roth know the University of Chicago; Bellow was an undergraduate anthropology major there in the 1940s, Roth a graduate student in English in the 1950s, and later each taught there. But their experiences, which have something to do with their age difference, were as different as their temperaments. Although he was born in Montreal, Bellow grew up in Chicago and writes with the knowledge and perceptions of a native Chicagoan. Roth, on the other hand, writes of Chicago as seen through the eyes of a transient, a visitor: Gabe Wallach is no more a Chicagoan than Augie March is a New Yorker. If Augie has the breeziness of the young adventurer and the wanderlust of the picaresque hero, Wallach has the sophistication and urbanity of the eastern intellectual. The comedy that each becomes involved in is accordingly distinctive and serves different purposes.[3]

These may be only superficial differences, but they point in the right direction. All three novelists, however, recognize the value of wit and humor to illuminate aspects of the human condition that, were it not for the comic perspective, might otherwise become too dispiriting, too depressing. Here irony is a frequent instrument for pointing up the incongruities that make us laugh but also help us see what life is really like. Bellow recognizes the flawed nature of many of his characters but nevertheless tries to find their saving manhood or nobility (Cohen, 6). Malamud in *The Fixer* with bitter irony shows the disastrous consequences that befall Yakov Bok's attempt to escape his Jewishness in czarist Russia, but the novel ends on a strong note of triumph. In these ways both Bellow and Malamud are humanists, exploring the existential situation and (more assuredly in Bellow) reaffirming the worth of human existence. Roth too explores the existential situation, mainly by placing his characters in nearly hopeless predicaments and requiring them to search for answers, resolutions, or solutions, regardless of whether any are possible. Much of his comedy derives from such situations, often broader and more obviously funny than comparable situations in Bellow's fiction or Malamud's. The closest Malamud comes to farce, for instance, is in some of the Fidelman stories, but it is recurrent in Roth, from the wedding scene in *Goodbye, Columbus* to the hijacking episode in *The Counterlife*. None of this denies his underlying seriousness, which is, like the others', to discover and, if possible, reaffirm values in our common human existence.

Take, for example, the predicament of Alexander Portnoy, Roth's most famous and nearly archetypal "hero." Portnoy's inner conflict rages between his moral self and his powerful hedonistic urges, or, in Freudian terms (since the novel is a series of psychoanalytic sessions), between his superego and his id. Caught in the conflict, his ego, the poor struggling "I," pleads with his therapist for help. Portnoy wonders if what he experiences is the "Jewish suffering" he used to hear so much about, descended from persecutions and pogroms. "Oh my secrets, my shame, my palpitations, my flushes, my sweats!" he cries. "Doctor, I can't stand any more being frightened like this over nothing! Bless me with manhood! Make me brave! Make me strong! Make me *whole!*"[4]

Portnoy is indeed in a bad way. Why, then, do we laugh? What's so funny? Is it his manner of speaking, his inveterate tendency to excess, to melodrama, inherited from his parents, his mother especially? It is all that—and more—that makes him appear comic. But underlying his cries for help is a truly agonized soul. Portnoy's seeing the humor himself only enhances the comedy, but it should not obscure the very human problems he confronts. By magnifying and so distorting them, Roth not only creates comic situations that are hilarious but helps us see the issues involved more clearly and prepares us to accept them. The Elizabethans found freaks and mad people funny; today we recognize their essential humanity and feel compassion. And so we should for Alexander Portnoy, Peter Tarnopol, David Kepesh, and Nathan Zuckerman. The compassion does not invalidate the comedy; it deepens it.

Roth's ability to treat complex characters and situations has grown considerably during his career as a novelist. Compare his early protagonists, Neil Klugman and Gabe Wallach, with Peter Tarnopol or Nathan Zuckerman to see the differences. In an interview, "After Eight Books," Roth has said that "Sheer Playfulness and Deadly Seriousness are my closest friends. . . . I am also on friendly terms with Deadly Playfulness, Playful Playfulness, Serious Playfulness, Serious Seriousness, and Sheer Sheerness," although he confesses that from the last he gets nothing; "he just wrings my heart and leaves me speechless" (*RMAO,* 111). The others apparently do not, and despite the playful wit the point comes through: Roth's comedy is neither simple nor univocal. It often involves forms of "parody, burlesque, slapstick, ridicule, insult, invective, lampoon, wisecrack, . . . nonsense, . . . levity" (*RMAO,* 31)—in short, *play.* It also incorporates the contradictions, incongruities, paradoxes, and ironies of which high comedy consists—precisely the kind that makes us think even as it makes us laugh.

## Roth's "Jewish" Humor

Roth's humor is often described as "Jewish," and there is no denying the specifically Jewish humor in much, though by no means all, of his fiction (*The Great American Novel* is the major exception). Regardless of how we define "Jewish humor"—and some, like Allen Guttman, reject the phrase[5]—common elements often appear in the work of Jewish writers and comedians. The most salient feature is, of course, a self-deprecating attitude that at once endears the teller and the tale, as in so many of I. B. Singer's stories. Reassured that many people talk to themselves and he shouldn't worry, a doctor's patient replies, "Yes, but you don't know what a *nudnik* I am!"[6] Often jokes contain a self-reflexive irony, as in the story of the vacationing New Yorker who complains about the poor quality of food at a resort, adding, "And such small portions, too!"

The humor is also often defensive, a means of shielding Jews from the harsh conditions of existence. Or, as Stephen J. Whitfield says, it became "an opiate of the Jewish masses, a pain-killer for the incongruities of an exilic past."[7] Aware of the absurdities of life that surrounded them, ghetto Jews found a means of dealing with those absurdities through the comic invention of the *schlemiel* who, however dim-witted or unlucky, managed to survive and sometimes even prosper. But as Ruth Wisse notes, the incarnation of the schlemiel character in American fiction shows a new emphasis on intensity, on suffering as an indicator of vital life. Citing Saul Bellow's *Dangling Man,* she defines the schlemiel in American literature as "a cultural reaction to the prevailing Anglo-Saxon model of restraint in action, thought, and speech." If the Yiddish schlemiel was "an expression of faith in the face of material disproofs," the American schlemiel "declares his humanity by loving and suffering in defiance of the forces of depersonalization and the ethic of enlightened stoicism."[8]

Many of Roth's protagonists are thus easily identified, not only Alexander Portnoy, perhaps the clearest example in his fiction of the American schlemiel (Wisse, 118–23), but Neil Klugman and Gabe Wallach as well. Despite (or perhaps because of) their sophistication and wit, they are unable to find a clear path to happiness and easy contentment, apparently preferring a life of agonizing introspection and self-doubt instead. Neil foolishly forces a situation on Brenda, the girl he thinks he loves, that precipitates the end of their affair and leaves him lonely and lost, as Gabe Wallach is at the end of *Letting Go.* Neither their college education nor their native intelligence is sufficient, it seems, to stave off the disasters that befall them and, in Wallach's case, that he causes others even as he tries to help. But in some ways Nathan Zuckerman of *Zuckerman Bound* is Roth's best exemplar of the sophisticated schlemiel. His three marriages all end in divorce, although every one of his wives is a deserving woman whose only fault, if we can judge from the third one, Laura, is that she ultimately became "boring."[9] Obviously, Zuckerman, like Roth's other protagonists, prefers suffering to "the good life," which looms as something stultifying, not stirring. "Trouble," Joseph says in *Dangling Man,* "like physical pain, makes us actively aware that we are living" (Wisse, 82), and Roth's protagonists, like Bellow's, are nothing if not alive and in trouble.

One feature of their liveliness is their rich fantasy life, another source of humor in the novels. Roth endows all of his major characters with the ability to imagine life not as it is but as it might be—usually more horrible than the difficulties they are already experiencing. The chasm that opens between the fantasy and reality may be great or small, but it is invariably funny. Neil Klugman imagines he creates a fiasco at Patimkin Kitchen and Bathroom Sinks; Alex Portnoy imagines he goes blind after he ejaculates into his eye; Nathan Zuckerman imagines his mother has been kidnapped by an extortionist from her apartment in Miami Beach. Zuckerman's impersonation of the critic Milton Appel as a porn king in *The Anatomy Lesson* is one of the wildest fantasies in the novels, rivaled only by his earlier fantasy in *The Ghost Writer* of Amy Bellette as Anne Frank, miraculously rescued from the death camps. On the other hand, as *Our Gang* and *The Great American Novel* demonstrate, there seem to be no limits to the range of Roth's own imagination once he lets it loose. In this respect, at least, he is at one with his characters.

If, as the commentators say, the aim of Jewish humor is to take some of the sting out of bitter reality, [10] the reverse is also true: through humor we come to grips with that reality, or at least begin to recognize what it is. The conflict between fantasy and reality reveals the essential qualities of both. But humor, Stephen Whitfield reminds us, is also one of "the needle trades" (Whitfield, 124); much of it is tendentious, as Freud showed in *Wit and Its Relation to the Unconscious*. Zuckerman's impersonation of Milton Appel the porn king is thus more than a comic send-up of Irving Howe, and Neil Klugman's quips repeatedly cause Brenda such discomfort that she has to ask him to stop being "nasty." The hostility and aggressiveness of Jewish jokes, again, are a measure of their defensive nature; behind the shield of wit one may more safely launch an attack. If cruelty, then, is "rarely far below the surface in comedy" (Whitfield, 125), in Roth's fiction comedy is rarely far below the surface of such cruel experiences as Paul Herz's in *Letting Go* and even Lucy Nelson's in *When She Was Good*. Or, if not below the surface, then hugging its perimeter, at times impinging on the center. Roth has spoken of the "sit-down" comedy of Franz Kafka as an influence on his work as opposed to the "stand-up" comedy of comedians with whom he has often been compared (*RMAO*, 21–22), and there is much justice in his remarks, as these novels reveal. When Paul brings his wife, Libby, home after her abortion, a scene of frenzied farce occurs in their presence between Levy and Korngold over some stolen underwear. Lucy's stringent morality does not save her from becoming pregnant and then marrying Roy Bassart, whom she does not even like. Alexander Portnoy's or Nathan Zuckerman's predicament, however, is more typical: beneath their comic exclamations beats a heart truly in pain.

Roth's vivid representations of Jewish men and women inevitably brought him under attack by the Jewish establishment—the rabbis, neo-conservatives, apologists, and so forth—who complained loud and long that he was defaming the Jewish people. They evidently gibed at Roth's social satire and misunderstood its intent. At first startled by their response, Roth fought back, using the traditional arguments of fiction and artistic truth to defend what he had written. Many of his essays from that period, such as "Writing about Jews," are collected in *Reading Myself and Others*. Although they seem to have been largely ineffectual in quieting his critics, who continued to accuse him of Jewish self-hatred, if not blatant anti-Semitism, his arguments are trenchant, witty, and utterly sensible. For example, he argues that far from affirming the principles and beliefs that everybody holds, fiction "frees us from the circumscriptions that society places upon feeling" and "allows both the writer and the reader to respond to experience in ways not always available in day-to-day conduct" (*RMAO*, 151). Elsewhere in the essay Roth defends himself against an alleged ignorance of Jewish tradition—an irrelevance, he claims: "The story of Lou Epstein stands or falls not on how much I know about tradition but on how much I know and understand about Lou Epstein" (*RMAO*, 154). If the attacks have diminished in recent years, it may be, as Roth suggests, that either he has become less irritating than the Zuckerman he depicts or "the Jewish generation that didn't go for me is by now less influential and the rest are no longer ashamed, if they ever were, of how Jews behave in my fiction."[11]

Roth as a social satirist has scarcely disappeared, however. The early stories and novels may have focused sharply on Jewish inconsistencies, hypocrisies, contradictions, or, rather, the kinds of Jews who demonstrate such attributes; later, though, Roth undertook to satirize the follies and foibles of other Americans and of other nationalities. *The Great American Novel* is about more than baseball; in it Roth attacks the greed, materialism, religious dogma, phony patriotism, and other failings in American society. In *Zuckerman Unbound* the high life of film and media stars is satirized through Caesara O'Shea. In *The Counterlife* and *Deception* British anti-Semitism in both its blatant and its more subtle forms come in for scrutiny, and in *The Counterlife* Israelis receive fuller treatment than in *Portnoy's Complaint*. Roth has also indulged in political satire, preeminently in *Our Gang*, in which he pillories Richard Nixon and his administration. Significantly, Roth wrote that book *before* Watergate broke, beginning with a series of stories or sketches, later collected and expanded into his novel. Like his great forebear Jonathan Swift in the eighteenth century, Roth realized how effectively fantasy could be pressed into the service of satire.[12]

## Autobiography and Fiction

Self-satire is another of Roth's fictional modes, perhaps his most important one, certainly in his later fiction, wherein he has repeatedly exploited autobiography for the purposes of his fiction. The attacks levied against him for his depiction of Jews provided Roth with a subject he has used to comic advantage,[13] best of all in the trilogy *Zuckerman Bound*. But like any other writer, perhaps more than most, Roth has used personal experiences in much of his other fiction, turning them into what Mark Shechner calls his "fables of identity." As "variations on the theme of the self designed to heighten and refine essential elements, highlight basic terms of being, and dramatize recurring conflicts," these "myths of self" are vital to Roth.[14] They are important in the same way that his "useful fictions" are important to Peter Tarnopol in *My Life as a Man*. Or, as Roth puts it, "This mythology, this legend of the self (the useful fictions frequently mistaken by readers for veiled autobiography), is a kind of idealized architect's drawing for what one may have constructed—or is yet to construct—out of the materials actuality makes available" (*RMAO*, 106). The mythology also allows Roth to criticize tendencies in himself by extending them further than he actually might, as in Zuckerman's impersonation of Milton Appel. Roth's sense of moral indignation becomes highly comic, moreover—for example, in Peter Tarnopol's diatribes against his undivorcing and undivorceable wife, Maureen, and the laws of New York State in the 1960s.

But throughout his work, especially in the Zuckerman novels, which came closer to autobiography than any others (except *My Life as a Man*), careful differentiations are necessary to distinguish between Roth and his alter ego, between what actually happened to the author and what happens to Zuckerman, his "useful fiction." One needs to penetrate behind the veil, or risk seriously mistaking fiction for fact. This is what happens to readers of Zuckerman's *Carnovsky* and is presumably what happened to readers of Roth's *Portnoy's Complaint*. In *Zuckerman Unbound* many people reading or just hearing about Zuckerman's novel immediately concluded that Nathan Zuckerman was Gilbert Carnovsky. "They had mistaken impersonation for confession," Zuckerman laments, trying to ignore greetings from strangers, "and were calling out to a character who lived in a book."[15] Roth's parents did not make that mistake and took pride in their son's achievements and his growing fame, quite unlike "Doc" Zuckerman, whose dying word, uttered into the eyes of his "apostate" son, is "Bastard" (*ZU*, 373).

Zuckerman's brother, Henry, never forgives Nathan for what he has done to the family by writing the book, and after their father's funeral they become estranged. All of this is fictitious; in actuality, Roth's father lived for many years after *Portnoy's Complaint* appeared, and Roth's brother Sandy seems to have borne no family grudge. Why, then, has Roth drawn so closely on personal experience, only to alter it in significant but occasionally baffling ways? I suggest that part of the continuing comedy Roth enjoys is playing with autobiography, a playfulness that in his most recent novel, *Deception,* he practically admits. There he drops Zuckerman as an alter ego and lets his main character go by the name Philip. Allusions to actual events and books "Philip" has written occur frequently, but the title of the novel is the surest warning that Roth is again playing games with autobiography. As he says at one point, "I write fiction and I'm told it's autobiography, I write autobiography and I'm told it's fiction, so since I'm so dim and they're so smart, let *them* decide what is or what isn't."[16]

## Parody and Wit

Parody is akin to satire; in fact, it is one of its most useful instruments. From his earliest years Roth has been an exceptionally good mimic, and mimicry is the stuff of parody. It can be employed for its own sake or in the service of satire, as in Roth's parodies of Ernest Hemingway in *The Great American Novel* and Richard Nixon, first in *Our Gang* and later in "The President Addresses the Nation" (*RMAO,* 59–64). In *Goodbye, Columbus* Roth parodies the all-American jock in Brenda's brother, Ron Patimkin, revealing not only the shallowness of such men but their essential passivity. In Alvin Pepler, the Jewish ex-marine and erstwhile quiz-show contestant in *Zuckerman Unbound,* Roth parodies someone who proudly displays his phenomenal memory for trivia, as Pepler reels off all the "Hit Parade" winners for the 1940s and 1950s. In a more serious vein, Roth imaginatively captures the life of Anne Frank as it must have been in the camps and as it might have been, had she really survived. In one important sense, *When She Was Good* is a long parody of lower-middle-class, midwestern attitudes as enacted in the behavior and speech not only of Lucy Nelson but of her family and her husband as well.

Burlesque is an extreme form of parody, and Roth uses it sparingly, except in *The Great American Novel,* in which the speech, antics, and aspirations of baseball players become grist to his grindings. Not for nothing did he listen to the recordings of ballplayers in the Baseball Hall of Fame in Cooperstown, New York. The baseball game between the Mundys and the inmates of the mental hospital near Asylum, Ohio, is more than a travesty of the sport. Its burlesque explodes repeatedly into hilarity as Roth epitomizes the neurotic behavior of players on both sides, including the Mundys' exultation after winning the meaningless exhibition game against opponents even more inept than they. In *The Counterlife* Roth burlesques a hijacking attempt aboard an El Al airliner, parodying the superseriousness of the security guards who jump Zuckerman along with Jimmy Ben-Joseph and then preach to them about Zionism as they manhandle and otherwise terrify them.

A sometime college professor and a very well read writer, if not a professional scholar, Roth writes novels filled with literary allusions, parodies, and analyses that form a special category of humor. Examples of his "lit. wit" abound, perhaps most of all in *The Professor of Desire,* in which the principal character, appropriately, is a student of literature. David Kepesh as a young man travels to England on a Fulbright scholarship to study Arthurian legends and Icelandic sagas, but he finds himself more interested in the erotic life of London. Within a few days of his arrival, he has his first encounter with a prostitute, a woman somewhat older than himself. As he revels in her sensuality, he realizes "with an odd, repulsive sort of thrill" that this woman was probably born "before the publication of *Ulysses.*"[17] Years later, David (now Professor) Kepesh learns why his colleague, the poet Baumgarten, has never written about his family. The reason has much to do with Baumgarten's revulsion against the Jewish family saga (see *Portnoy's Complaint*), *menschlichkeit,* "the baffled quest for dignity," and "goodness." Baumgarten derides "the Jewish literature of goodness" and expects any day to find a work on "conviviality in Joyce, Yeats, and Synge" or an article by "some good old boy from Vanderbilt on hospitality in the Southern novel: 'Make Yourself at Home: The Theme of Hospitality in Faulkner's "A Rose for Emily"'" (*POD,* 138). It does not require much knowledge of criticism or fiction to get the point of Baumgarten's remarks, though such knowledge helps, especially in understanding what the word *hospitality* means in reference to Faulkner's *A Rose for Emily.*

Examples of lit. wit in Roth's novels are rivaled only by allusions to Freudian psychoanalysis, usually in the context of comic situations. Sometimes these allusions combine with lit. wit, as in "Courting Disaster," one of the "Useful Fictions" in *My Life as a Man.* While at the University of Chicago, Nathan Zuckerman seeks help for persistent migraines. He winds up at a North Shore clinic, under the direction of an eminent Freudian analyst, because the questions Zuckerman had asked his neurologist (who referred him to the clinic) bore what he took to be a "Freudian orientation":

I did not know [Zuckerman says] that it was a Freudian orientation so much as a literary habit of mind which the neurologist was not accustomed to: that is to say, could not resist reflecting upon my migraines in the same supramedical way that I might consider the illnesses of Milly Theale or Hans Castorp or the Reverend Arthur Dimmesdale, or ruminate upon the transformation of Gregor Samsa into a cockroach, or search out the "meaning" in Gogol's short story of Collegiate Assessor Kovalev's temporary loss of his nose. Whereas an ordinary man might complain, "I get these damn headaches" . . . I tended, like a student of high literature or a savage who paints his body blue, to see the migraines as *standing for something,* as a disclosure or "epiphany."[18]

Of course, *Portnoy's Complaint* is the novel that excels in Freudian or psychoanalytic humor, beginning with Roth's epigraph, a definition of "Portnoy's Complaint" in pseudoscientific, psychoanalytic jargon. In *My Life as a Man* Dr. Spielvogel reappears, this time as Peter Tarnopol's therapist, and plays a much more active role. At one point he and Tarnopol become enmeshed in a prolonged conflict as the result of an article Spielvogel publishes entitled "Creativity: The Narcissism of the Artist," which includes a thinly veiled description of Tarnopol and his problems. Tarnopol becomes incensed and argues that Spielvogel had no right to write as he did about his patient, especially since he gets so much wrong. He maintains that a vast difference exists between a writer of fiction, like himself, and a scientist. "Why, to substantiate your 'ideas,'" he asks his therapist, "do you want to create this fiction about me and my family, when your gift obviously lies elsewhere? Let *me* make up the stories—you make sense!" (*MLAM,* 242). Their contretemps continues fruitlessly until Spielvogel at last suggests the therapy should end. In true comic fashion, however, Tarnopol rejects the suggestion; he can't leave Spielvogel, he says, "Because I'm scared to be out there alone. But also because I *am* stronger—things in my life *are* better" (*MLAM,* 248). Flawed therapist and anguished patient go on, until after further complications in his life Tarnopol finally retreats to the writers' colony at Quahsay. There he writes his "True Story," recognizing that it "remains to be seen whether his candor, such as it is, can serve any better than his art (or Dr. Spielvogel's therapeutic devices) to demystify the past and mitigate his admittedly uncommendable sense of defeat" regarding his obsession with his now-deceased wife, Maureen Johnson Tarnopol (*MLAM,* 100–101).

In his later work Roth seems to have abandoned the framework of psychoanalysis, as Shechner remarks, but he has stayed with its "basic morality." The basic morality of *The Anatomy Lesson,* for example, is "the morality of striking deep, diving to the floor of the imagination and searching for insight and health, like pearls, in the darkest recesses" (Schechner, 237). If in the process of diving deep Roth's humor darkens, the range of his comedy expands, as *The Counterlife* and *Deception* show, for as he comes more and more to grips with the absurdities of existence, they continue to feed his sense of the comic. Or, as Lawrence E. Mitz says, "Philip Roth's literary applications of humor span the entire range, from playful fun with language and description, to ironic assessment, to scathing ridicule and expression of anger disguised and contexted as humor. As a comic novelist he reaches still further, to complex, sophisticated appreciation of the nature of human life as fundamentally incongruous and to the assertion that the understanding of this comic truth is a prolegomenon to coping, to transcending and achieving self-understanding and a modicum of self control."[19]

In the chapters that follow, Roth's work is considered in more or less chronological order of publication. The chief exception is the discussion of *The Breast,* which is treated as a sequel to *The Professor of Desire,* although it was written and published earlier. Discussion of Roth's nonfiction (the essays in *Reading Myself and Others, The Facts: A Novelist's Autobiography,* and *Patrimony*) appears midway in chapter 6, where it may provide a useful perspective for the "autobiographical" novels, such as *My Life as a Man* and the trilogy *Zuckerman Bound.* A number of Roth's minor works, such as the uncollected stories and fugitive magazine articles, are not included, not because they are insignificant or insufficiently comic but because of space limitations.

# Chapter Two

# Nice Jewish Boys:

## The Comedy of "Goodbye, Columbus" and the Early Stories

Roth's most famous protagonist, Alexander Portnoy, complains that he is living inside a Jewish joke and pleads with his psychiatrist, Dr. Spielvogel, to help get him out of it. Though at first he seems oblivious of it, Neil Klugman in "Goodbye, Columbus" lives inside a burlesque-show joke—a sexual tease that from the opening paragraph sets his hormones pumping wildly. He describes his first sight of Brenda Patimkin at the country club swimming pool, when she asks him to hold her glasses. After her dive, as Neil returns her glasses he gazes after her: "I watched her move off. Her hands suddenly appeared behind her. She caught the bottom of her suit between her thumb and index finger and flicked what flesh had been showing back where it belonged. My blood jumped."[1] Without any kind of formal introduction, Neil calls her that very evening for a date. Thus their affair begins.

That Neil is a "nice Jewish boy" who quickly captures the reader's sympathy is manifest from his background, his education, his current job, and his warm family relationships. Educated at the Newark Colleges of Rutgers University with a degree in philosophy, he makes no apologies for not having gone to an Ivy League school or anything so prestigious (Brenda is a Radcliffe undergraduate). An only child, he lives with his aunt and uncle and their daughter in a Jewish neighborhood of Newark, because his mother and father, afflicted with asthma, have immigrated to the aridity of Arizona. Neil is devoted to his surrogate family, especially his Aunt Gladys who, like any Jewish mama, worries about his food, his social behavior, and anything else that affects her loved ones. Like many nice Jewish boys, Neil is often impatient of her concern and desperately, sometimes bluntly, tries to reassure her so that she will leave him alone. He works at the Newark Public Library in a respectable position that promises early promotion to the kind of industrious, conscientious young man Neil appears to his immediate superiors to be.

But nice Jewish boys also have strong masculine glands, and Neil is no exception. When he first sees Brenda, no wonder his heart jumps. Although this is not an attraction Roth often deals with later (Neil is not enticed by the forbidden fruit a shiksa, or gentile woman, represents to an older generation of Jews), in its way the situation is still typical. Brenda is Jewish; it is at a Jewish country club that Neil meets her. But Jewish American Princess that she is (Neil, as narrator, never uses the phrase himself), Brenda is rich, spoiled, and smart, if somewhat short-sighted (literally and perhaps figuratively). She knows her attractions, and she knows how to use them.

And so when Neil calls her, Brenda does not put him off. Evidently without a current boyfriend (though she has had her share in the past), she allows Neil to meet her at tennis with her girlfriend, Laura Simpson ("Simp") Stolowitch. The game Brenda plays is another good initial indication of her character. Cocky, confident, she wins the set from Simp, but not in the "one more game" she tells Neil it will take when he arrives. Though dusk is falling, and falls, the two battle on into the dark, giving Neil a further chance to size Brenda up. He is struck by her ferocious play, her unwillingness to let the set end in a tie, and her reluctance to rush the net and put herself in physical jeopardy: "Her passion for winning a point seemed outmatched by an even stronger passion for maintaining her beauty as it was" (GC, 20). After the game is over, as they walk off the court together Neil falls a step behind Brenda, giving him another opportunity to "appreciate" her: "Her hands did not twitch at her bottom, but the form revealed itself, covered or not, under the closeness of her khaki Bermudas. There were two wet triangles on the back of her tiny-collared white polo shirt, right where her wings would have been if she'd had a pair. She wore, to complete the picture, a tartan belt, white socks, and white tennis sneakers" (GC, 21).

The suggestion of wings may be deliberately misleading, for Brenda is no angel, no more than Neil is, though to all outward appearances they are a nice Jewish couple.[2] Moreover, in Neil's romantic/erotic gaze the wings image may be justified. Falling under a spell, he ignores warnings against the temptation Brenda represents. Although he registers her eagerness to win, which later will have important consequences for them—or him—and is irritated by her flip reply to where she goes to school, he perseveres in his pursuit of her. Further warnings, such as Brenda's comments on living in Newark or on the nose job she has had ("I was pretty. Now I'm prettier"; GC, 23), are also registered—and ignored.

Neil counters her responses with sarcastic wit, which Brenda either doesn't get or criticizes as being "nasty." Intent on the relationship, which he finds challenging, he tries to recover "civility," more or less successfully. When he asks for a closer look at her nose, Brenda takes the gambit, on which she too seems intent, and says, as he peers at her, "If I let you kiss me would you stop being nasty?" (*GC*, 24). Whether or not this is another tease, or something more, Neil thinks he feels "a faint fluttering, as though something stirred so deep in her breasts, so far back it could make itself felt through her shirt. It was like the fluttering of wings." That the wings were so small, smaller than her breasts, does not bother him: "it would not take an eagle to carry me up those lousy hundred and eighty feet that make summer nights so much cooler in Short Hills [where Brenda lives] than they are in Newark" (*GC*, 24).

That is how it all starts; the few pages that constitute the first chapter of the novella present the basic contours of the story and its theme. About halfway through the book, however, the story takes a different twist, as the burlesque-show joke deepens into something else. As often happens to nice Jewish boys, what starts out as an affair turns into love—with all its attendant complications. As this aspect of the story unfolds, Neil's true character reveals itself, also involving complications, for the writer as well as the narrator. From this earliest stage in his career, Roth shows that he cannot resist the urge to develop the character of a *schlemiel*. That is what Neil Klugman, despite his surname (which means "clever fellow"), turns out to be, though about this aspect of his protagonist's character Roth seems to be somewhat ambivalent or uncertain.[3] On the one hand, he has developed and seems reluctant to surrender the sympathy Neil has earned; on the other hand, he finds all but irresistible the comedy latent in the predicament Neil gets himself into by falling in love with a girl like Brenda. But we are getting ahead of the story. Neil has still to meet Brenda's family, the Patimkins.

Mr. and Mrs. Patimkin are among the nouveau riche Jewish families that years earlier moved out of the city and into the suburbs. The fortune Mr. Patimkin made in the war by supplying sinks to army barracks is partly responsible for that; the rest is the result of his continuing hard work and shrewdness as a businessman who knows how to make a buck— lots of them. The Patimkin household thus comes in for the kind of satire that has since become a rich source for Roth's wit and humor—and his trademark, as viewed by many critics. When Brenda invites Neil to dinner for the first time, we see what lies ahead for him—and the Patimkins. The invitation comes after another day at the country club pool, where

Brenda and Neil have disported themselves in the water and engaged in further erotic play. The invitation is spontaneous and, for Neil, unexpected, as he tries to explain to his naturally worried Aunt Gladys why he will not be home for dinner that night.

Neil has already met Brenda's older brother, Ron, at the pool. He is built on the lines of a Greek god, as Neil describes him: "suddenly, like a crew-cut Proteus rising from the sea, Ron Patimkin emerged from the lower depths we'd just inhabited and his immensity was before us" (GC, 29). Ron is a playful, harmless Proteus, not very bright, but amiable and, like all the Patimkins, athletic. The comic juxtapositions Roth uses to describe Ron he also uses to describe Mr. Patimkin at the dinner table: "He was tall, strong, ungrammatical, and a ferocious eater" (GC, 31). Brenda's kid sister is rather less amiable, not yet a princess but certainly a princess-in-training. Julie is "ten, round-faced, bright, who before dinner, while the other little girls on the street had been playing with jacks and boys and each other, had been on the back lawn putting golf balls with her father." Though she is the handsomest of them all, Mrs. Patimkin appears ominous and arouses an immediate dislike, or fear, in Neil: "She was disastrously polite to me, and with her purple eyes, her dark hair, and large, persuasive frame, she gave me the feeling of some captive beauty, some wild princess, who has been tamed and made the servant of the king's daughter—who was Brenda" (GC, 31).

The comic potential of such a cast is great, and Roth exploits it fully and economically. Instead of transcribing the fragmented or garbled talk interrupting the Patimkins' energetic eating, he consolidates dialogue and description and presents them both in "one fell swoop." The result is just as funny as—perhaps funnier than—the actual talk, which the reader can easily imagine. Eating among these Brobdingnagians seems to reduce their guest, even to diminish him physically (or so he thinks), and gives early indications of the schlemiel that will emerge. The conflict between Mrs. Patimkin and Brenda also emerges, ever so subtly. In the midst of everything the erotic play continues, as Neil feels Brenda's fingers fondling his calf under the table.

After dinner the comedy continues, with somewhat darker overtones. Brenda describes her feelings about her mother and the jealousy between the two women, mother and daughter, which she calls "practically a case study" (GC, 35). An excellent tennis player in her youth, Mrs. Patimkin arouses Brenda's admiration for what she was—then. Now the two constantly battle about money, about clothes, about everything. Brenda's snobbery again shows itself, but Neil chooses to ignore it, afraid to "lift the cover and reveal that hideous emotion I always felt for her, and is the underside of love" (*GC,* 37). If Neil is falling in love with Brenda, he is nevertheless aware of the lust that has drawn him to her and keeps him by her side.

At this moment Julie interrupts, and another indication of Neil the schlemiel emerges, as he lets a basketball thrown at him bounce off his chest. Like Mr. Patimkin, Neil allows the child to win a game of "five and two," though a part of him desperately wants "to run little Julie into the ground" (*GC,* 38). Extremely self-conscious, he feels the gaze of the Patimkins and even Carlota, the black maid who served dinner. Feeling humiliated, Neil is reassured when Brenda says that even Ron, a star basketball player, lets Julie win.

The next morning Neil, at work in the library, has an experience that seems to comment on his involvement with Brenda and her family. As he goes to work he sees a little black boy in front of the library growling and snarling at the cement lions that guard the building. "Man, you's a coward," the boy says to one of them, and then growls again (*GC,* 42). Shortly afterward the boy enters the library and asks Neil where the "heart" section is. He means the *art* section, and Neil later finds him absorbed in a folio of Gauguin reproductions. The boy is struck by the serenity and beauty of the Tahitian women in the paintings: "These people, man, they sure does look cool," he says. "They ain't no yelling or shouting here, you could just see it." Turning the pages, he shows Neil another picture and says, "Man, that's the fuckin life" (*GC,* 47).

The boy's rapture is not quite what Neil feels about Brenda and Short Hills, but it's close. In fact, Neil makes an explicit comparison, as he daydreams about meeting Brenda that evening in Short Hills, "which I could see now, in my mind's eye, at dusk, rose-colored, like a Gauguin stream" (*GC,* 48). His rose-colored expectations are disappointed, however, for when he arrives Brenda and her family drive Ron to the airport, leaving Neil at home to baby-sit Julie. Angered by the imposition, he sends Julie off to watch television alone. His impulse is to leave quietly and return to Newark, where he feels he belongs, among his own humble people. But he doesn't leave. Instead, he explores the house, or rather the basement, where among other things he finds an unused bar with two dozen unopened bottles of Jack Daniels—"the bar of a wealthy man who never entertains drinking people, who himself does not drink, who, in fact, gets a fishy look from his wife when every several months he takes a shot of schnapps before dinner" (*GC,* 52)—further comic commentary on the middle-class Jewish household the Patimkins' represents. Wanting a drink now himself, Neil is afraid to break the seal of one of the unopened bottles. He muses that the bar had not seen a dirty glass since Ron's bar mitzvah and probably wouldn't see another until one of the children was married or engaged. He then finds an old refrigerator full of fruit, to which he helps himself until discovered by Julie, who surprises him in the act of eating a nectarine. The handful of cherries he has also taken he drops into his pocket, afraid of further discovery.

Neil gets his revenge against Julie for the interruption and the game of five and two when he unmercifully beats her at Ping-Pong in the basement recreation room. Actually, Julie quits in hysterics before he is able to score the final point. She is outraged that Neil, no longer under the gaze of the family, will not make concessions and let her win, as he and the others had always done before. He completes his revenge after the family has gone to bed that night, when he makes love to Brenda for the first time: "How can I describe loving Brenda?" he muses. "It was so sweet, as though I'd finally scored that twenty-first point" (GC, 56). The juxtaposition of events is deliberate and reveals what the love affair is truly about: winning. The question is, Who is winning what?

In the episodes that follow Roth reemphasizes that the affair is a game—another aspect of the burlesque-show joke, or tease—and not truly love, despite Neil's longings and self-deceptions. First Neil plays games with an elderly, jowly gentleman who tries to check out the Gauguin book the little boy has been looking at during his daily trips to the library. Neil explains that the book has a "hold" on it and cannot be taken out. Later Neil and Brenda are at the country club; it is late evening, and they are alone. As the lights go out around the pool, Neil thinks they should be going home, but reassuring him it's all right to stay, Brenda starts asking him questions about himself—for the first time since they met. Although initially these are questions her mother wants answered, soon Brenda admits to her own curiosity, and then asks Neil if he loves her. He hesitates, and she says she will sleep with him anyway, whether he loves her or not. When he says he does not, she answers, "I want you to." He refers to his library job, but she seems untroubled by his humble occupation, and continues: "When you love me, there'll be nothing to worry about" (GC, 62). Then they begin playing pool games, hiding from each other for longer and longer intervals, until Neil, anxious, confesses, "I love you . . . I do" (GC, 64).

Gamesome, manipulative Brenda wins that one as she wins others. By now fully aware of what is happening, Neil seems not to care. They see each other every evening, make love whenever possible, and finally

Brenda invites Neil to spend a week of his vacation at her house. Then they make love every night in her room. The day Neil arrives is the day Ron announces his engagement to Harriet, his girlfriend in Milwaukee, and the house plunges into turmoil preparing for a Labor Day wedding. Why the wedding is so rushed is not clear, though there are hints that Harriet may be pregnant. Neither is an explanation offered as to why the wedding is arranged by the groom's parents and not the bride's, following tradition. Perhaps no explanation is needed. Mr. Patimkin, the equivalent of a *nogid* (rich Jew of the shtetl; Gittleman, 168) enjoys showing off what his money can buy, and in any event Roth wants Neil to be a wedding guest.

Roth's introduction of these events, however, is not simply to find yet another opportunity for satiric comedy, which first Harriet's arrival and then the wedding celebration afford. He means to juxtapose Neil's affair with Brenda against Ron's wedding to Harriet so that the issue of marriage between Neil and Brenda can come to the fore, as it does. Rather than proposing marriage to Brenda, which is the way their relationship seems to be heading, Neil instead proposes that she get a diaphragm, thereby forcing quite a different kind of issue.

Brenda rejects Neil's proposal, claiming that they are OK as they are, but Neil presses her. Although the best argument he can offer is that a diaphragm will make sex more pleasurable for him as well as safer for her, he ultimately admits that he wants her to get one simply to please him, to yield to his desire. It is another contest of wills between them, another attempt by Neil to assert his manhood against Brenda's domineering spirit. In many other respects she has successfully led him around by the nose, so that by the time he is living in her house he has actually begun to look like her, not only in dress—sneakers, sweat socks, khaki Bermudas, and all—but in manner and deportment; he has begun to look the way she wants him to (*GC,* 81). He has started to fit into the Patimkin family, much to his Aunt Gladys's disgust but precisely as Brenda wants. It is time for Neil either to assert himself or to lose his manhood altogether.

Why, then, doesn't Neil ask Brenda to marry him? He is sure he loves her, and she him, but somehow things don't seem quite right, as she promised him they would be the night at the pool. Fearing that anything other than a resounding "Hallelujah!" to a marriage proposal would utterly daunt him, he proposes the diaphragm instead, hardly realizing how much more daring the latter would actually be. More evidence of the kind of schlemiel Neil is occurs in a scene at Patimkin Kitchen and Bathroom

Sinks. There Neil watches in amazement as men load sinks onto a truck, tossing them to one another, oblivious of the danger of dropping them. Suddenly Neil imagines himself directing them and hears himself screaming warnings. His reverie continues: "Suppose Mr. Patimkin should come up to me and say, 'Okay, boy, you want to marry my daughter, let's see what you can do.' Well, he would see: in a moment that floor would be a shattered mosaic, a crunchy path of enamel. 'Klugman, what kind of worker are you? You work like you eat!' 'That's right, that's right, I'm a sparrow, let me go.' 'Don't you even know how to load and unload?' 'Mr. Patimkin, even breathing gives me trouble, sleep tires me out, let me go, let me go'" (*GC,* 103). Is this the real Neil Klugman? Where is the sensitive, clever young fellow Roth has been presenting to us? Where is the assertive, masculine chap who orders his lover to get fitted with a diaphragm? Is he capable only of stealing fruit and beating little Julie at Ping-Pong so long as no one is looking? or of telling transparent lies so that the black boy can enjoy his book in the library a little longer?

Obviously Neil is both men, and therein lies Roth's ambivalence toward his character[4] and the source—conscious or otherwise—of both subterranean and surface comedy. While Neil's wit can puncture the pretentiousness of the Patimkins and other social-climbing middle-class Jews, he is also vulnerable within himself. He lacks the *cojones* of a real man. Arguing vehemently with Brenda about the diaphragm, he eventually agrees not to force her to get one. Whereupon she does.

The victory that should have been Neil's therefore becomes Brenda's. She even makes him accompany her to New York to the doctor's office, though she does not force him to go in with her. And when she comes out and Neil does not see her carrying a package, he thinks she may have changed her mind. Actually, he is relieved, but then his emotion turns completely around when Brenda tells him she's wearing the device. "He said shall I wrap it up," she explains, "or will you take it with you?" Whereupon Neil cries, "Oh Brenda, I love you" (*GC,* 112).

Roth's ambivalence toward Neil is matched by Neil's toward Brenda and leads to further indications of his schlemielhood. Even as Brenda apparently yields to Neil's wishes and is fitted with the diaphragm, Neil wanders away to St. Patrick's Cathedral and indulges in a kind of prayer: "God, I said, I am twenty-three years old. I want to make the best of things. Now the doctor is about to wed Brenda to me, and I am not entirely certain this is all for the best. What is it I love, Lord? Why have I chosen? Who is Brenda? The race is to the swift. Should I have stopped to think?" Getting no answers, he perseveres, confessing his carnal and acquisitive nature and identifying it with God: "I am carnal, and I know You approve, I just know it. But how carnal can I get? I am acquisitive. Where do I turn now in my acquisitiveness? Where do we meet? Which prize is You?" Suddenly he feels ashamed and, still without an answer, walks out into the hubbub of Fifth Avenue, and hears, "Which prize do you think, *schmuck*? Gold dinnerware, sporting-goods trees, nectarines, garbage disposals, bumpless noses, Patimkin Sink, Bonwit Teller—" (*GC,* 111–12). The answer, which in his imagination Neil again insistently identifies with God, gets only a celestial belly laugh.

In later novels, preeminently in *Portnoy's Complaint* but also in *My Life as a Man* and in others, Roth develops ambivalence toward his protagonists for comic effect. His attitude can be related to the typical kind of Jewish humor in which Jews make fun of their own inconsistencies and contradictions, while frowning on anyone else's doing so. But Roth has other sources of humor. His excellent eye and ear capture, and his typewriter accurately transcribes, observations that not only are funny in themselves but serve as social commentary and as commentary too on the observer, in this instance Neil Klugman. Aunt Gladys is an excellent case in point, and though a minor character, she is surely a contender for the real heroine of the novella.

As against Neil's false sense of superiority and the Patimkin women's wealth and pretentiousness, Aunt Gladys stands as a model of common sense, hard work, wry humor, and shrewd perception. An early version of the typical Jewish mother in Roth's fiction, she partly eludes the stereotype by knowing how and when to stop nagging Neil, by her reduced role in the fiction (compare Sophie Portnoy later on), and by her innate stature as above all a decent, caring woman. Forever complaining about the work she has to do—for example, the four different meals she has to prepare at four different times for the members of her household, including herself—she simply gives vent to her feelings in a harmless, usually humorous way. Neil does not try to explain her odd dinnertime routine except to say that his aunt is "crazy" (*GC,* 14). From his rationalist viewpoint it certainly seems that way, but underlying the "craziness" is a firm resolve to serve the needs of her loved ones. Neil's flip comment thus boomerangs. Witty as he is, her wit matches his but, more important, Aunt Gladys differs from Neil in the depths and strengths of her commitments. Funny in her remarks and her fractured syntax—"I'll see it I'll believe it" (*GC,* 68)—she is not merely a figure of fun but a standard of humanity against which others in the novella, including Neil, pale.

Roth wisely does not sentimentalize Aunt Gladys; in fact, he strongly opposes sentimentality, as he shows in his satiric portrait of Ron Patimkin. Large and amiable, Ron is devoted to the "light classics" of André Kostelanetz and Mantovani but above all to the album that gives this story its title and theme. Lying on his bed after a basketball game in the evening, Ron enjoys listening to the graduation record narrated by "a Voice, bowel-deep and historic, the kind one associates with documentaries about the rise of Fascism" (*GC*, 114). Nostalgia for the Class of '57 lulls Ron to sleep as he hums along with the band and the Voice intones "goodbye, Ohio State, goodbye, red and white, goodbye, Columbus . . . goodbye, Columbus . . . goodbye" (*GC*, 116). The perfect ending to a perfect day.

At Ron and Harriet's wedding the family portraits Roth draws are not only funny in themselves; like that of Aunt Gladys, they say something about Neil and his priggishness and about the world he lives in. After describing Mrs. Patimkin's side of the family, Neil turns to Mr. Patimkin's half-brother, Leo, a traveling salesman who tells Neil the story of his life. The humor darkens here as, embittered by his lot in life (only two good things ever happened to him, and one he can hardly remember), Leo advises Neil that he has a good thing going with Brenda and should not "louse things up" (*GC*, 129). The good thing Leo remembers is that his mother-in-law found a rent-controlled apartment in Queens for him and his wife. (Later he recalls the other good thing—Hannah Schreiber, whom he met in the army and who believed in "oral love"; *GC*, 127.) The other guests, mostly Ron's friends and Harriet's, come in for their share of caricature—for example, Gloria Feldman, "a nervous, undernourished girl who continually looked down the front of her gown as though there was some sort of construction project going on under her clothes" (*GC*, 121). But for most of the evening Neil dances with Brenda until, having drunk too much champagne, she gets sick in the ladies' room and falls asleep on a sofa in the lobby, while Neil listens to the rest of Leo's tale of woes.

Despite Uncle Leo's advice, Neil does louse things up. He does soon after the wedding, when Brenda leaves to go back to college. The Jewish New Year approaches, and unable to come home for the holidays, Brenda persuades Neil to take off from work and come to Boston, where she has reserved a hotel room for them. Obedient as ever, Neil wangles the days off and travels to Boston. Expecting a joyous reunion, he even contemplates matrimony (*GC*, 137). But he is in for a shock. Confessing only to an "oversight," Brenda tells Neil that she has left her diaphragm at home, where her mother has found it.

The letters Brenda receives from her parents force her into a choice she apparently never thought she'd have to make. Her parents are bitterly disappointed in her and obviously have no use for Neil, but now Brenda must choose where her loyalties lie. It is hardly a difficult choice, given her love of luxury and ease—none of which Neil, as a librarian, could ever afford. The issue turns ludicrous as, prompted by a remark in her father's letter, the discussion focuses on whom Brenda will bring home for Thanksgiving: her roommate Linda from last year or Neil.

For his part Neil tries to make Brenda see that, consciously or not, she left the diaphragm at home because she *wanted* her mother to find it and so end the relationship. Although Brenda rejects this argument as so much "psychoanalytic crap" (*GC,* 144), Neil has a point. But it no longer really matters. Things are over between them. Whether Brenda *can* see or not is irrelevant; myopic as ever, she here *refuses* to see.

Why Brenda acts as she does remains unexplained and is a little curious, since she seemed genuinely to want to be with Neil during the Jewish holidays and urged him to come to Boston. In Bernard Rodgers's analysis Brenda resembles Daisy in *The Great Gatsby*: like Jordan Baker, Daisy, and Tom Buchanan, she is one of those careless people who "smashed up things and creatures and then retreated back into their money or their vast carelessness . . . and let other people clean up the mess they made" (quoted in Rodgers, 44). Not that Neil has a big mess to clean up; Brenda will be welcomed back on more or less the same terms as before by her doting father and jealous mother.

All of this forces Neil—unable once again to "win" with Brenda—to see himself as he is. This he does literally by looking at his reflection in the front window of the Lamont Library. He does not especially like what he sees there any more than he liked the insight his meditation in St. Patrick's Cathedral had given him. Moreover, he seems puzzled by his motives and impulses:

What was it inside me that had turned pursuit and clutching into love, and then turned it inside out again? What was it that had turned winning into losing, and losing—who knows?—into winning? I was sure I had loved Brenda, though standing there, I knew I couldn't any longer. And I knew it would be a long while before I made love to anyone the way I had made love to her. With anyone else, could I summon up such a passion? Whatever spawned my love for her, had that spawned such lust too? If she had only been slightly *not* Brenda . . . but then would I have loved her? (*GC,* 147)

Like many of Roth's later protagonists, Neil is unable to resolve these questions. He ends by simply taking the train back to Newark in plenty of time to get to work on the morning of Rosh Hashanah, the start of the Ten Days of Penitence and one of the holiest days in the Jewish calendar.

None of the five short stories collected along with "Goodbye, Columbus" in Roth's first published volume has quite the same range of wit and humor as the novella. But if "The Conversion of the Jews" is in part a ludicrous melodrama and "Epstein" borders on the tragic, they also reveal not only Roth's own moral earnestness but his witty perception into the contradictions and inconsistencies of human lives—elements that can make men and women simultaneously comic and pathetic, funny and sad. In "The Defender of the Faith" Roth opened himself to accusations of anti-Semitism, or Jewish self-hate, accusations he has rejected, arguing vigorously in defense of the artist's freedom to pursue and present truth as he sees it and of the universal, not peculiarly Jewish, nature of his theme.[5] Yet the story is essentially comic, its humor underlying and occasionally covering over the darker elements of its characters and situations. "You Can't Tell a Man by the Songs He Sings" has nothing particularly Jewish in it, but "Eli the Fanatic" contains much of the dark humor found in "The Defender of the Faith."

## "The Conversion of the Jews"

Little Ozzie Freedman is the kind of boy who, because of his independent spirit and relentlessly inquiring intellect, is constantly getting into trouble with his elders. The framework for "The Conversion of the Jews" is the *heder,* or Hebrew school, Ozzie attends and where he comes into conflict with his teacher, Rabbi Binder. What gets Ozzie into trouble is his insistence on following the logic of scripture even to the point of recognizing the possibility of a Virgin Birth. For a Jewish rabbi teaching a class of would-be bar mitzvah boys, this is surely asking too much. That Jesus was "historical . . . a person that lived like you and me" is as far as Rabbi Binder is willing to go. He insists that Jesus's birth, like anyone else's, had to come through human intercourse, not divine intervention. But Ozzie cannot resist the force of logic: if God could "create heaven and earth in six days, and make all the animals and the fish and the light in six days—the light especially," then he asks Rabbi Binder "why couldn't He let a woman have a baby without intercourse" (*GC*, 152–53). For a third time Ozzie's mother is summoned to school to see the rabbi.

Roth plays Ozzie's stubborn inquisitiveness off against his friend Itzie's more practical, wise-guy attitudes and coarser diction: "Itzie preferred to keep *his* mother in the kitchen"; "'Sure it's impossible. That stuff's all bull. To have a baby you gotta get laid,' Itzie theologized" (*GC*, 151–52). The contrast is comic, underscored by Itzie's amazement, which he expresses in humorous gestures and exclamations of disbelief at his friend's temerity. But worse—or better—is yet to come.

That Friday night Ozzie resolves to tell his widowed mother about the summons to see Rabbi Binder, but not before she lights the Sabbath candles. A "round, tired, gray-haired penguin of a woman," in the act of lighting the candles she is transformed for Ozzie into a radiant being "who knew momentarily that God could do anything" (*GC*, 155). He is therefore all the more astonished when, after he tells her about what has happened at heder, for the first time in their life together she hits him across the face with her hand.

The comic contrast of earlier episodes between Ozzie and Itzie now turns somber. Tension mounts on the following Wednesday at heder when, during "free-discussion" time, Rabbi Binder calls on Ozzie to give the class "the advantage of his thought." Ozzie at first resists but, on repeated provocation from the rabbi, demands, "Why can't He make anything He wants to make!" (*GC*, 158). The question causes a commotion in the class, and Ozzie cries out repeatedly, "You don't know, you don't know," until, probably by accident, Rabbi Binder's hand catches Ozzie squarely on the nose, making it bleed.

In the ensuing uproar Ozzie runs onto the roof and locks the door behind him. He has no thoughts of suicide, but the image of him several stories up on top of the building strikes fear in the hearts of all who behold him. Arriving for her appointment, Ozzie's mother is instead greeted by her son on the roof, a crowd gathered below, fire trucks clanging, and a net spread out to catch the boy if he jumps. What a surprise! All pleas for Ozzie to come down fail, and Rabbi Binder's threats—"I'll give you three to come down"—are ludicrous. Mrs. Freedman's cry that her boy not be a martyr is taken over by Ozzie's classmates, who, led by Itzie and not understanding the term, egg him on with "Be a Martin, be a Martin" (*GC*, 167).

The farcical situation evokes increasing humor but seriousness too, as in the growing darkness of the autumn evening Ozzie makes first Rabbi Binder and then everyone else, including his mother, get on their knees. In this posture of gentile prayer Ozzie makes the rabbi, his mother, and even the poor old sexton, Yakov Blotnik, confess that "God can do Anything"—even make a child without intercourse. By now everyone is kneeling, and Ozzie finally extracts their promise never to "hit anybody about God" (*GC,* 169–70). Only then does he jump "right into the center of the yellow net that glowed in the evening's edge like an overgrown halo" (*GC,* 171).

Some critics, while generally admiring Roth's stories, find them a little too neat, too pat. Alfred Kazin, for example, believes that in "The Conversion of the Jews" Roth is too anxious not only to dramatize the conflict but to make the issue "absolutely clear"; he needs to find the creative writer's delight in "life for its own sake" and become less concerned with the design of his fable.[6] But Kazin seems to miss the point here: in the world of the child, simplicity rules, as it does for Ozzie Freedman. Therein also lies the humor of the story and its import: adult sophistications and their consequences are finally no match for the single-mindedness and courage of a little boy, for whom the logic of God's omnipotence and mercy overwhelms all other considerations. That recognition, literally and figuratively, brings the others to their knees.

## "The Defender of the Faith"

"The Conversion of the Jews," with its beatific ending, brought ample criticism to Roth from many in the Jewish community, who overlooked its comedy[7] and concentrated instead on what they regarded as anti-Semitism in the story. "The Defender of the Faith" contains fewer funny moments but, if anything, a sharper wit and a tough-mindedness that insist, both in the story and its telling, that Jews are in most respects like other human beings. If Malamud's recurrent theme is that "All men are Jews," then Roth's is that "All Jews are men,"[8] as illustrated in the fictional portrayal of Sergeant Nathan Marx and the three Jewish recruits whose basic training he supervises.

Rotated back to the United States shortly after the fighting ends in Europe in 1945, Sergeant Marx is a veteran and a war hero, with ribbons to prove it. He wins the admiration and respect of his commanding officer and others he associates with at Camp Crowder, Missouri, but Sheldon Grossbart is something else. Swiftly ascertaining that Marx, like himself, is Jewish, Grossbart begins requesting special treatment, at first in relatively minor matters but eventually in some of much greater importance. Playing on Marx's sense of guilt more than on any sense of solidarity he might have with his landsmen (that is, fellow Jews), Grossbart finagles special passes and exemptions from onerous duty for himself and two of his friends. When nothing else works, he writes letters—signing his father's name—to his parents' congressman. These prompt the commanding officer and higher authorities to inquire into such matters as the food that men brought up in kosher homes must eat.

Grossbart's cleverness—for example, his wishing Marx a "Good *shabbus, sir!*" as, exempted from a "G.I. party" (Friday-night barracks cleaning), he runs off to "Jewish Mass"—eventually backfires. Too smart by half, he manipulates not only Marx but others to the point of getting his orders changed from being shipped out to the Pacific (where the war is still raging) to being sent to Fort Monmouth, New Jersey, closer to his parents' home and certainly much safer. But this time Grossbart goes too far. Marx, furious, arranges to have someone else sent to New Jersey and Grossbart to the Pacific with the rest of the company.

The comedy in this story derives partly from the competition that develops between Grossbart and Marx, their contest of wit, a game that finally becomes deadly earnest. In this respect it resembles the games Neil and Brenda play in "Goodbye, Columbus." Grossbart is usually smart enough to know when to attack and when to retreat, when to show guts and when to act meekly, as in the Passover seder incident. But Marx is no dummy. Even his sense of guilt (at not being much of a Jew) has its limits. He realizes full well who and what Grossbart is and finally confronts him in a towering rage: "Grossbart, you're a liar! . . . You're a schemer and a crook. You've got no respect for anything. Nothing at all. Not for me, for the truth—not even for poor Halpern! You use us all—" (*GC*, 210). Discovering and then shifting Grossbart's orders are the final victory, however vindictive, that Roth awards Marx, who has certainly earned it.

If "The Conversion of the Jews" appeared too simple or too clear to Alfred Kazin, the "moral complexity" of this story exhilarated him, for in it Roth shows "the Jew as individual, not the individual as Jew." Moreover, Roth "caught perfectly the drama of personal integrity in the face of group pressures that is so typical of American literature" (Kazin, 259). He does indeed. But the issue of Jewish identity, which Grossbart forces Sergeant Marx to face, and the conflicts that develop from it are Roth's own. Though they resemble situations in stories like Malamud's "Last of the Mohicans" and "The Lady of the Lake,"[9] the humor is more

sharply satiric and less fanciful. Furthermore, the ending puts the entire
story in an utterly different perspective, when Marx hears Grossbart weeping behind him after their confrontation. As the private swallows hard,
accepting his fate, Marx resists with all his will the impulse to turn and
ask Grossbart's pardon. Struggling, Marx accepts his fate too. Thus, Roth
deftly mingles comedy, satire, and pathos in an amalgam fully justified
by the "moral complexity" of his tale.

## "Epstein"

Mixed comedy and pathos, melodrama and farce characterize "Epstein"
also, though in different doses and for different purposes. So do moral
earnestness and what appears to be, on the surface anyway, a kind of
poetic justice not unlike that meted out at the end to Private Grossbart.
Old, hardworking Lou Epstein's life is suddenly transformed after his
nephew Michael comes to spend a weekend at his home. Epstein is at an
extremely vulnerable point in a middle-aged man's life. His wife of many
years, Goldie, is no longer as attractive as she once was. His son, Herbie,
dead of polio early in life, is kept alive only in memory, and in the
bedroom where his baseball pictures still hang on the wall. His daughter,
Sheila, once a pretty child, at 23 is coarse and unlovely. Engaged to a
folksinger, she is active politically and socially, her leftist values hardly
reflecting those of her middle-class family.

Into this milieu Epstein's nephew enters, slipping inside the house at
night with his date from across the street. At first Epstein thinks it is
Sheila and her boyfriend, Marvin, and braces himself for the inevitable
zippings and unzippings of their lovemaking in the living room. An
unhandsome couple, they fill him with disgust, not lust. Usually he
ignores their vigorous pantings and carryings on, but this night he goes
downstairs to give them a piece of his mind. He is astonished to find not
Sheila and Marvin but Michael and Linda, the girl from across the street,
who make quite a different sight from the one he expected, one far more
erotic and exciting.

Watching unseen and tingling all the while, Epstein at last tiptoes
back upstairs. Until the couple leaves, however, he is unable to sleep, and
no sooner have they gone than Sheila and her boyfriend arrive and the
zippings begin all over again. Epstein ponders to himself: "The whole
world . . . the whole young world, the ugly ones and the pretty ones,
the fat and the skinny ones, zipping and unzipping!" He grabs his great
shock of gray hair and yanks it until his scalp hurts, while beside him
Goldie shuffles, mumbles, and pulls the blankets over her. "Butter! She's

dreaming about butter," Epstein muses. "Recipes she dreams while the world zips." He finally closes his eyes and pounds himself "down down into an old man's sleep" (*GC,* 222).

Later Epstein wonders whether that evening or some other event was the beginning of his "big trouble." But he decides that it all began when it appeared to begin, when he saw Linda's mother, Ida Kaufman, waiting for a bus and offered her a lift. Only recently a neighbor, Ida was unlikely to remain in her house long, now that her husband had died and she had the house in Barnegat to go to. Epstein drives her there, attracted by her voluptuousness, and they carry on an affair for several weeks—until one night Epstein discovers a rash near his genitals.

The rash precipitates a crisis that nearly wrecks Epstein's family and his life. Trying to pass off the affliction as prickly heat, a sand rash, or something he picked up from a toilet seat in his paper bag factory, Epstein fails to convince Goldie, who is sure he has venereal disease. Turmoil ensues; Epstein is ordered out of the conjugal bedroom and into the spare bed in Herbie's room where, unable to sleep, he talks to Michael, reminiscing about the past. It is all both funny and sad: Epstein's arrival with his parents at Ellis Island; the early years with Goldie; Herbie; his estrangement from his brother, Michael's father, years ago. When the young man becomes judgmental, Epstein makes this apologia: "You're a boy, you don't understand. When they start taking things away from you, you reach out, you *grab*—maybe like a pig even, but you grab. And right, wrong, who knows! With tears in your eyes, who can even see the difference!" (*GC,* 235).

The next morning, Sunday, the family has quieted down, but the weekend routine has changed. Instead of Epstein, Marvin the folksinger goes out for lox and a newspaper. As coffee percolates and family members sit around the table, Lou enters and the turmoil resumes. So Epstein has his breakfast at the corner luncheonette. Afterward, wondering where he should go, he sees Ida in her backyard in shorts and a halter, hanging underwear on a clothesline. She smiles at him, and that determines his decision.

Catastrophe follows. At noon a siren goes off. When Goldie, Sheila, and the others see an ambulance across the street, they suddenly realize its import but do not fully grasp it until a stretcher emerges from Ida Kaufman's house with Epstein on it. Sex and stress have taken their toll: he has had a heart attack.

However melodramatic and contrived, the ending of the story is, again, not without its humor. At the sight of her stricken husband Goldie explodes into grief and concern characteristic of a matronly Jewish housewife. In the ambulance on the way to the hospital, the doctor tries to reassure her. When he comments, "A grown man can't act like a boy," Goldie puts her hands over her eyes and Lou opens his. Everything will be all right, the doctor says. "All he's got to do is live a normal life, normal for sixty" (GC, 243). Now Goldie reassures Lou, who cannot or will not talk; though he opens his mouth, his tongue—an image of enforced impotence—"hung over his teeth like a dead snake." He'll live, but it is the end. As for the rash—not a symptom of venereal disease after all—the doctor reassures Goldie that he can fix that up, too, "So it'll never come back."

Epstein's world, like Mr. Patimkin's in "Goodbye, Columbus," is "one taken up entirely by the economics of *making it* in America, and of demonstrating that you have achieved something to those around you," as Sol Gittleman says (Gittleman, 170). Therein lies the tragedy. The pathetic part is how little Epstein has achieved, really, and the comedy derives from what he tries to grab for himself once he realizes how little the little that he has is. Ironically, even the little that he reaches for turns out to be too much. What happens to Epstein is partly the result of the disintegration of "kinship values," which have been the essence of Jewish survival through the centuries (Gittleman, 171), and Roth knows it. Far from attacking Jewish values, then, Roth through his satire is crying out for their realization and, presumably, their restoration in contemporary American life.

Roth's instrument of attack, here as in "Goodbye, Columbus" and in much of his later fiction, is satire, which after we stop laughing helps us better understand the incongruities that have set us laughing in the first place. On the one hand, it is incongruous that a 60-year-old man, Lou Epstein, should try to behave like his young nephew, for Lou is well past the age of "zippings." On the other hand, he has enough life left in him both to envy the young and to think he can emulate them. But the world knows better, he discovers, not so much to his chagrin as to his sorrow. Being carried out of his paramour's home across the street on a stretcher on a Sunday morning is comical, as Roth presents it. What is not so funny (though it has its humorous side) is the image of the future that Goldie holds out for Lou in the ambulance. Marvin and Sheila will marry and run the business, and he can retire. She'll take care of him and they can go someplace together. "Don't try to talk," she says. "I'll take care. You'll be better soon and we can go someplace. We can go to Saratoga, to the mineral baths, if you want. We'll just go, you and me—" (GC, 244). No wonder that, as she talks, Lou's eyes roll in his head.

## "You Can't Tell a Man by the Songs He Sings"

According to critical consensus, the penultimate story in *Goodbye, Columbus* is the weakest. It is also the earliest of Roth's stories in the collection. Nevertheless, it has its humor too and its moral irony, though here the two are not as tightly interwoven as in the other stories. Jokes abound, as when the ex-con Albie Pelagutti, recently returned to high school, asks the boy sitting next to him for "the answer" while they are filling out an occupations questionnaire. Or when Albie turns up for a baseball game in an outlandish costume. Though he has bragged about his skill as a ballplayer, when a fly ball comes his way he lets it land on his chest instead of in his glove and he doesn't know the first thing about holding a bat at the plate.

The unnamed narrator (the boy who gives Albie "the answer" and the one who is duped into picking him for his ball team) learns a lot from Albie and from another ex-con, "Duke" Scarpa. Streetwise, they know when to assert themselves and when to run—for instance, when the cafeteria window accidentally gets broken while the three are horsing around. The ex-cons never make it through high school, but years later, when the Kefauver Committee investigates crime in the area, neither Pelagutti's nor Scarpa's name turns up in the papers. Instead, the well-meaning, decent occupations teacher, Mr. Russo, is victimized when another Senate committee swoops through the state. Refusing to answer some of the committee's questions, he is fired by the board of education for having been a Marxist during his college years. The point of the story becomes clear at the end, as the narrator contrasts Russo's fate with his own experience in the high school principal's office, where he was sent for breaking the cafeteria window. The principal had warned that the file card on which the disciplinary breach was recorded would follow the boy all through his life. Albie and Duke knew that; that is why they ran when the window was broken. The narrator had not run and was punished. Ironically, poor Russo was just discovering a fact of life that his pupils had learned much earlier, while still boys.

## "Eli, the Fanatic"

Like "The Defender of the Faith," "Eli, the Fanatic" is suffused with dark humor. The comedy derives from the contrasts and juxtapositions of an assimilated Jewish community in predominantly WASPish Woodenton suddenly confronted by an Orthodox Jewish yeshiva in its midst. The yeshiva consists of some 18 refugee children presided over by Leo Tzuref[10] and cared for by a nameless survivor of concentration camps. The affluent Jews who have moved to Woodenton in suburban New York—merchants as well as professionals and their families—are disturbed by the presence of this outlandish settlement and want it removed. Not only does the yeshiva violate the town's zoning ordinances, but, more significantly, it is acutely embarrassing for the town's assimilated Jewish residents. The harmony established between themselves and their Protestant neighbors is, they feel, endangered by the yeshiva and particularly by the strange greenhorn, a Hasid who marches around the town in his fantastic black garb shopping for the children. They therefore call on one of their own, Eli Peck, an attorney, to get the yeshiva to move.

Eli does his best under the most trying circumstances. Tzuref is stubborn and refuses to budge, making Eli feel as though he were persecuting the already-too-much-persecuted refugees from Hitler's Europe. Eli's sense of this oppression is repeatedly exacerbated by knowing that these are mainly children he is trying to remove, children who flee from the very sight of him as he walks over the grounds to negotiate with Tzuref. Nor does Eli's home life provide more than scant consolation for him (though it provides much humor for the reader), as the efforts of his very pregnant wife to "understand" Eli invariably have the opposite effect. Having suffered two nervous breakdowns earlier, Eli is by no means heartless or insensitive. He feels for Tzuref and the children, and he feels for his community, whose members increasingly pressure him to resolve the predicament they see themselves in.

Eli tries to compromise by offering Tzuref conditions: first, that the religious, educational, and social activities of the yeshiva of Woodenton be confined to the yeshiva grounds and, second, that yeshiva personnel who appear in public be attired in clothing usually associated with American life in the twentieth century (*GC*, 276). The reply Eli gets from Tzuref is typically succinct:

Mr. Peck:
    The suit the gentleman wears is all he's got.

                                          Sincerely,
                                          Leo Tzuref, Headmaster

Eli therefore once more visits Tzuref at the yeshiva, again frightening the children, to discuss the situation. As usual, the room is dim, unlit by electricity (Tzuref eventually lights a candle). They argue at cross-purposes. Eli, rational, insists that the greenhorn could get another suit; they—he and his clients—will even pay for it, he suggests, smacking his hand to his billfold. Tzuref, otherwise motivated, also smacks his hand to his breast, at "not what lay under his coat, but deeper, under the ribs" (*GC,* 279). Eli's appeal is to the laws of the community; Tzuref's is to the heart, to God's law, not mortals'. He insists that since everything but the man's black suit has been taken away from him, the least the Woodenton Jews can do is suffer a little too.

At an impasse, the two end their discussion, and Eli, guilt-ridden, sneaks off into the night trying not to frighten the little children once more. He finally breaks the impasse in an unusual manner as his wife gives birth to their son in the hospital. He takes one of his best suits, wraps it up, and delivers it to the yeshiva. But the issue is not yet entirely resolved. Although the "greenie" wears Eli's clothes—good suit, hat, shoes, everything—and parades around the streets of Woodenton in them, to the astonished satisfaction of Eli's friends, that is not the end of the affair. Soon afterward, while Miriam is still in the hospital with the baby, Eli hears a noise outside his back door. There he finds the Bonwit Teller box he had used to pack his things deposited on his doorstep. In the box are the black clothes of the "greenie," complete with broken shoes, black hat, and *tsitsit,* the fringed garment worn by Orthodox Jewish men.

Slowly, as he dons the strange clothing, Eli begins to realize why it has been left there. This time when he leaves his house to go to the yeshiva, he scares not the children, who scarcely notice him, but his next-door neighbor, Harriet Knudson, who is busy painting the stones on her lawn pink. At the yeshiva he confronts the greenie, busy painting the porch columns white. Until Eli says "Shalom" he does not turn around, and when he does, recognition takes some time. As they gaze at each other, Eli has "the strange notion that he [Eli] was two people. Or that he was one person wearing two suits. The greenie looked to be suffering from a similar confusion" (*GC,* 304).[11]

In his "mixed-up condition" Eli reaches out to the greenie to fasten the button-down collar of his shirt, but the gesture frightens the poor man, who backs away in terror. Chasing after him, Eli finally corners him and yanks the man's hands away from his face, pleading with him to tell him what else it is he must do. The greenie, raising one hand to his chest and jamming it there, then points off to the horizon, toward the center of Woodenton. Not until the greenie repeats the gesture does Eli understand its significance, and he heads toward the town.

What happens then is both funny and poignant. Roth adeptly portrays the town in its everyday activity and dress, into which the figure of Eli Peck, now dressed as a Hasid, strides. The impact is stunning: "Horns blew, traffic jerked, as Eli made his way up Coach House Road" (*GC*, 307). But Eli perseveres, knowing that everyone thinks he is having another nervous breakdown. He knows he is not insane. If you *chose* to act crazy, he thinks, then you weren't crazy. "It's when you didn't choose. No, he wasn't flipping" (*GC*, 309). Soon afterward he remembers his wife in the hospital and, rejecting the idea of changing back into his own clothes, makes his way to her bedside.

Seeing him, Miriam is nearly beside herself:

"Eli, why are you doing this to me! . . . *He's* not your fault," she explained. "Oh, Eli, sweetheart, why do you feel guilty about everything. Eli, change your clothes. I forgive you."
"Stop forgiving me. Stop understanding me."
"But I love you."
"That's something else." (*GC*, 310)

Love *is* something else, Eli has learned, and it passes understanding. He insists on seeing his newborn son, and as he contemplates the "reddened ball—*his* reddened ball" the interns come and tear off his coat, injecting him with a sedative. "The drug calmed his soul," the story ends, "but did not touch it down where the blackness had reached" (*GC*, 313).

"Eli, the Fanatic," the most powerful story in the collection, brings the volume full circle. Whereas "Goodbye, Columbus" ended with Neil Klugman rejecting love, rejecting religion, ready to start work on Rosh Hashanah, Eli Peck ends with a resolve not to let his wife, his neighbors, or his psychiatrist persuade him to renounce his actions. Through Tzuref and the greenie and the children at the yeshiva, he has learned what none of the others appreciate: the meaning of sacrifice, sacrifice through love, which for Philip Roth appears to be the essence of Judaism. It has cost the greenie everything to end up in Woodenton dressed in a nice tweed suit and decent hat. It has cost Eli just as much to recognize the sacrifice, reciprocate it, and allow comedy to triumph.

Some commentators have criticized Roth for this story as they have done for the others, claiming his ignorance of Jewish tradition or, worse, his innate anti-Semitism and self-hatred. Sol Liptzin, for example, argues that no Hasid would surrender his traditional garb to appease the residents of a New York suburb: Rather, he would devoutly pray for them.

This aspect, Liptzin maintains, shows Roth's "ignorance of the inner motivation and behavior of Jews."[12] Although perhaps technically correct, Liptzin's argument may be beside the point, which is partly to show the chasm between traditional and assimilationist Jews and the difficulty of any rapprochement. Whereas Liptzin claims that Roth is being "theatrical and not genuine," "genuine" seems to signify merely the literal, and, of course, Roth in writing imaginative literature is not being literal-minded. If he is "theatrical," then that is partly what makes the story succeed. It *is* good theater, make-believe, although make-believe dressed up in the trappings of reality.

The Jews of Woodenton, for example, are real enough. Though they speak English, they talk like Jews; Saul Bellow, for one, picked up the Yiddish rhythms that characterize their speech (Bellow, 79).[13] The streets of Woodenton look like real streets too; as Gittleman remarks, Coach House Road is "the ultimate suburban street, with a Colonial-styled supermarket" where the president of the Lions Club, "the epitome of proper, Gentile Woodenton," encounters Eli in his Hasidic dress (Gittleman, 155). The theatrics undoubtedly constitute much of the comedy; in fact, the story opens like the first scene of a play or film, as Eli approaches the yeshiva for his first meeting with Tzuref. Much of the story is in dialogue too, emphasizing the theatrics but also dramatizing the issues. In addition, it lets Roth display the kinds of wit that characterize both Tzuref and Eli, as they talk at cross-purposes during their initial conference and thereafter:

> "The law is the law," Tzuref said.
> "Exactly!" Eli had the urge to rise and walk about the room.
> "And then of course"—Tzuref made a pair of scales in the air with his hands—"The law is not the law. When is the law that is the law not the law?" He jiggled the scales. "And vice versa." (*GC,* 265)

Roth's resolution of the conflict in "Eli, the Fanatic" may be factually or theologically inauthentic, but Eli's insight as well as his courage cannot be dismissed on those grounds. However unlikely, if not impossible, it might be for a Hasid to exchange clothes with a modern Jew in suburban New York, the exchange does provoke comedy on all sides. And underlying the comedy is the essential truth concerning the loss of values, of tradition and identity, that Eli Peck finally comes to recognize and, in his bizarre but necessary way, tries to restore.

Eli is without question a modern assimilationist Jew. But he is also a

sensitive, caring person who knows only too well that an argument has
two sides, that while defending one side you often wish you were on the
other (GC, 268). In this story Roth shows both sides vividly and powerfully. If Eli changes sides at the end, he does so in full knowledge of what
he is doing and why. If he is carried off finally with a hypodermic needle
in his arm, Roth shows that changing sides may not be so easy after all;
that the mores of a community cannot be violated with impunity; that
society will have its revenges. "Okay, rabbi," one of the men in white
coats calls out to Eli in the hospital. "Okay okay okay okay okay
okay. . . . Okay okay everything's going to be okay" (GC, 313). But
everything is not "okay"; the drug soothes Eli's soul, but insofar as it does
not touch it "down where the blackness had reached," nothing is ultimately resolved. In this way Roth's comedy reveals both its depths and
its complexity and shows him at the very beginning of his career, despite
his years, to be a surprisingly mature writer.

# Chapter Three

# *Letting Go*:

## Varieties of Deadly Farce

In several important respects *Letting Go* was a mistake. Overwritten and at times tedious, it is (except for *When She Was Good* and *The Great American Novel*) Roth's least typical novel. Whatever prompted him to write it—the desire for a full-length novel after the success of *Goodbye, Columbus,* which won the National Book Award; the need for personal catharsis following his experiences at Iowa and Chicago; or the urge simply to indulge his indisputable talent for character creation and dialogue—his error was in taking Henry James for his model and inspiration. Philip Roth is not Henry James; nor was he meant to be.[1]

Philip Roth is, well, Philip Roth. Much of his comic genius comes through in *Letting Go,* though often in curiously distorted form. I suspect that the distortions stem not only from James's influence but from Roth's self-confessed "preoccupation with conscience, responsibility, and rectitude" at the time (*RMAO,* 77).[2] When combined with his natural tendency to comedy, these influences and preoccupations result in what might best be called "deadly farce." If the phrase is a neologism, unknown in literary criticism, it may be useful here nonetheless.

Roth's talent for farce—typically a frenzied whirl of mistaken intentions, crossed purposes, or conflicting demands—appears throughout his work. What makes farce deadly in *Letting Go* is the morbidity that grips it, the grim humor[3] that links him finally not with Henry James but, as Roth acknowledges in his later writing, Franz Kafka.[4] Regardless of how conscious Roth was of Kafka's influence at this early stage of his career, the affinity between the two writers is evident. Both writers seem to take delight in placing their characters in uncommon predicaments, most notoriously and obviously in "The Metamorphosis" and *The Breast,* respectively. But both writers can also be much more subtle—so subtle, in fact, that readers are usually astonished to learn that Kafka laughed "immoderately" when reading the first chapter of *The Trial* aloud.[5] I have no idea what Roth's reactions are or were to reading portions of *Letting Go* aloud or to himself, but if the comparison with Kafka holds in this respect as in others, he must have doubled up completely when rereading the episodes of Levy and Korngold in the Herzes' room after Libby's abortion, during Gabe Wallach's efforts to get Harry Bigoness to come to Chicago and sign the adoption papers, and on many other occasions.[6]

The book's opening paragraphs, which set the tone for much of what follows, consist of a letter that Gabriel Wallach's mother has written to her son while on her deathbed. The letter is a confession of guilt, of having taken charge of her husband's life and made him live it not as he chose but as she demanded. Her excuse is that ever since she was a little girl she "always wanted to be Very Decent to People,"[7] always wanted to do things for another's good. She feels that in so doing she has ruined her husband's life but has at last learned the need to let go. And so she ends by saying she doesn't want to say anything; she leaves no instructions.

Mrs. Wallach's noble gesture is fruitless. Worse, when Gabe leaves her letter in the copy of *Portrait of a Lady* he lends to a classmate at the University of Iowa, the man's wife reads it. It later proves an enduring link between him and her, nullifying Gabe's resolve to follow his mother's wish "to do no violence to human life, not to another's, and not to my own" (*LG,* 3). Hence, at the end Gabe's valedictory letter expresses a similar sense of frustration and despair. Traveling abroad after a long period of emotional entanglements, Gabe is not dying in a literal sense, but by his own admission he seems not to have learned much from his experiences. These have brought the young couple, Paul and Libby Herz, to the brink of disaster on at least one occasion—all out of Gabe's misguided attempts to "do things for another's good." Experiences with others, preeminently his erstwhile lover, Martha Reganhart, have also had little salutary effect. Gabe Wallach is not dead, but the question lingers, as it does for some of Henry James's celebrated heroes, whether he is now or ever has been fully alive.

Mrs. Wallach's legacy therefore proves futile, though ironically in a way she could not have anticipated. It is Gabe's failure of commitment that has led him deeper and deeper into his lonely, sterile life. Like Neil Klugman and many of Roth's later protagonists, he remains puzzled over the distinction between loving and clutching and, further, between altruism and self-interest. His counterpart in the novel, Paul Herz, suffers similar confusions, although his reactions are exactly opposite: he marries the girl he thinks he loves and, while the marriage is hardly a success, sticks with her despite every difficulty and one genuine opportunity to separate. Roth thus presents in contemporary terms an almost classic comedy of the *schlemiel* and the *schlemazel*: the poor, bumbling human being who can't do anything right and the poor unfortunate to whom nothing right happens regardless of his efforts.[8] Within this structure Roth also tries to write a serious, Jamesian novel. That it becomes repeatedly punctuated by episodes of decidedly un-Jamesian farce and is peopled by characters of decidedly un-Jamesian bent testifies more than anything else to Roth's individual talent and to the irrepressible energy of his comic spirit.

The elements of farce appear early, almost immediately after Mrs. Wallach's letter, as Gabe describes his first encounters with Paul Herz. It is fall 1953; he and Paul are both graduate students at the University of Iowa: "Paul's costume at that time was the same day in and day out: khaki trousers threadbare around the back pocket, a white T-shirt shapeless around the arms, tennis sneakers and, occasionally, socks. He was forever running—it was this that brought him to my attention—and forever barely making it" (*LG,* 4). Constantly running, as if to hold together the pieces of his life, Paul narrowly escapes one disaster only to fall into another. Such a man, to Gabe Wallach (however he appears to others, including Roth and his readers), evoked sympathy even if he did not or *would* not come right out and ask for it. Attempting to befriend Paul, Gabe invites him for coffee, tries to interest him in his work, and lends him James's *Portrait.* When he recalls his mother's letter stuck within the pages of the novel, Gabe telephones but gets Libby instead of Paul. Deciding not to mention the letter, he allows the call to end abruptly, for Libby too is in a hurry. He is surprised some hours later when Libby calls back to ask for help: Paul's old Dodge has broken down en route from Cedar Rapids, and he needs a lift back to Iowa City. Gabe is further surprised when Libby quietly insists on accompanying him to rescue her husband.

Gabe's description of Libby Herz is as accurate and perceptive as his description of Paul: "My first impression of her had been clear and sharp: profession—student; inclinations—neurotic. She moved jerkily and had the high black stockings and the underfed look. She was thin, dark, intense, and I could not imagine that she had ever gotten anything but pain from entering a room full of people. Still, in an eager hawky way she was not bad looking" (*LG,* 6). The description continues, mingling Libby's peculiar attractions with her annoying anxieties. Although Gabe's initial feeling toward her is one of suspicion (*LG,* 7) and although conversation between them on the drive to get Paul is anything but easy—it is mostly about James's *Portrait* and Libby's admission that she read Gabe's mother's letter—their meeting is momentous in ways neither of them imagines.

After they find Paul beside his disabled car, the Jamesian conversation ends and the farce begins in earnest. The wrecker arrives, and the driver offers Paul $10 for his car. Libby is aghast; she keeps querying her husband about what went wrong with the car and why. Embarrassed by her behavior, Paul tries to resign himself to their hard luck and get Libby to accept it as well. On the way home with Gabe, however, Libby keeps harping on the car, despite Paul's every attempt to reassure her that selling it was their only alternative. Their problem is acute because Paul needs to get back and forth from Coe College, where he is teaching two courses in addition to the one at the university. (Libby is also working toward a degree—the one she never finished at Cornell, where she and Paul were undergraduates together.) Distraught, Libby keeps trying to understand what happened, exasperating her husband until Paul finally shouts at her to shut up, and the rest of the ride proceeds in silence.

When they arrive at the barracks where the Herzes live, Libby poignantly asks Gabe to join them for dinner. It is obviously the least she can do to repay Gabe for his kindness, and he can find no graceful way to refuse. Over a spaghetti dinner served with tomato-juice cocktails, he learns more of the Herzes and their background: a mixed marriage, outraged parents on both sides, an unsuccessful attempt in Ann Arbor to resume their studies, Libby's conversion to Judaism. Everything they did to improve matters had ended in fiasco. And so here they were, poor, struggling, unhappy, still fiercely determined to succeed, yet as badly equipped as ever. They cannot even entertain a guest without embarrassing or discomforting one or the other of themselves *and* their guest.

Sandwiched between Gabe's narration of his evening with the Herzes is his account of a telephone call from his father. Alone in New York, Dr. Wallach, a dentist, misses his son terribly and makes demands on his loyalty and affection that Gabe feels unable to meet. The juxtaposition of incidents, of course, highlights the vast difference between Gabe's lot in life and the Herzes' and emphasizes for Gabe the irony inherent in his suffering as compared with theirs.[9] If the Herzes' parents refuse to acknowledge their children, the exact opposite is true of Gabe's father, who calls many times a week and pleads with his son to come home for the Thanksgiving holiday. Another version of deadly farce in the novel, the telephone conversations resolve nothing to either's satisfaction. Speaking at cross-purposes, father and son end precisely where they began, with wishful thinking on one side and sullen resentment on the other (*LG*, 17–21).

During his sojourn in Iowa Gabe Wallach also meets and briefly lives with Marjorie Howells, a young graduate student from Wisconsin. Their affair—another gentile-Jew relationship—provides a hilarious contrast to the pathos and deadly farce that characterize the Herzes; in fact, it is immediately after Paul has rejected Gabe's offer to lend him his car that Gabe invites Marjorie for a beer: "I did not know, when I asked her to have a beer with me that night, that she was in revolt against Kenosha, Wisconsin; I only believed that few complications could thrive behind such a perfect set of teeth. We had many beers, it turned out, and after a while she was looking across at me with flames flashing in her eyes, and asking me how it felt to be a Jew in America. I asked her how it felt to be a Protestant in America—and she told me" (*LG*, 27). Marjorie Howells is the prototype for many of Roth's gentile young women attracted to Jewish young men (for example, the Pumpkin in *Portnoy's Complaint*) and the source for much wit and humor at their expense. The evening ends predictably in Gabe's apartment: "Halvah and Harvard and Henry Wallace—I suppose I cut an exotic figure." With no lights on and his "sense of reality—as happens in the dark—out the window," the two of them are soon enough both revolting against Kenosha "as though Caligula himself were city manager" (*LG*, 27).

Marjorie moves in, at her own suggestion—insistence, really—and for a while she and Gabe enjoy a typical graduate student affair—doomed, as such, to an existence shorter than a term paper. Gabe contemplates their relationship: shopping together, sipping cocoa in bed, watching Marjorie let down her "whirly blond hair" every few nights to be washed. As she lathered her hair at the sink, he would sit on the edge of the tub translating *Beowulf* to her. "There were nights when it was charming," he thinks, "but there were other nights too, and then the girl at the sink and I on the tub seemed no more facts of this life than those impossibilities, Hrothgar and Grendel, whose words and deeds I had just been trying to comprehend" (*LG*, 29).

When Marjorie falls ill with the grippe, Gabe recognizes how exploitative the relationship is on both sides and resolves to end it. End it he does, but not without fierce resistance from Marjorie, who cannot understand why he throws her out. (Typically, he delivers his ultimatum—that she must leave the apartment—while he is visiting his father in New York during the Christmas break.) Meanwhile, he has had another encounter with Libby Herz, whom he meets one day while out shopping.

During their conversation he realizes that "It was beginning to seem that toward those for whom I felt no strong sentiment, I gravitated; where sentiment existed, I ran" (*LG,* 30). The perception is accurate, an image of himself that Gabe struggles with frequently throughout the novel and never overcomes.

Getting rid of Marjorie Howells, Gabe unwittingly sets up a situation that has important consequences for himself and the Herzes. While Gabe is away and the campus is deserted, Marjorie runs into Paul Herz and has coffee with him. When she moves, he helps her load her things into a cab from Gabe's apartment and winds up having sex with her in her room. Returning from New York and worried about Marjorie, who has left an ominous note and is nowhere to be found, Gabe calls Paul. Libby answers and invites him over, but when he arrives Paul hurries out, explaining that he has work to do at the office. He deliberately leaves Gabe and Libby alone in the bedroom, where she is recuperating from another illness, hoping that Gabe will seduce Libby and release him from the guilt— or, anyway, even up the score—that sex with Marjorie has burdened him with.

It does not work as Paul hopes: Gabe and Libby get no further than a kiss (which Libby agonizingly "confesses" later to her husband). But it is enough to verify the attraction each has felt for the other and to confirm what becomes a rather bizarre relationship. Although on another occasion Libby calls Gabe a "tease" (*LG,* 247), he is more than that for her, as she is for him. Whether it is Libby's vulnerability, the sympathy she evokes, or her unusual physical allure—or all these things—Gabe finds himself repeatedly entering the orbit of her life and unable to break away. For her, as Gabe later realizes, he represents a knight in shining armor who is to rescue her from the miserable life she has with Paul—a rescue Paul himself wishes would take place but (except for the bedroom visit he has permitted to occur) is unable to expedite.

The sad story of Paul Herz and Libby DeWitt occupies the second section of the novel, "Paul Loves Libby." It begins with their undergraduate days at Cornell, where Paul, a senior, meets 19-year-old Libby on the steps of her sorority house. As their romance proceeds Paul "educates" Libby, deflowers her, and feels obliged to marry her. He deceives himself that he really loves her, as she loves him, and that it is love, not obligation, that makes him want to marry her. Parental opposition only intensifies their passion. In despair, his parents urge Paul to seek advice from his uncles, Asher Buckner and Jerry Herz. Asher, an artist, leads a bohemian life but has sense enough to urge Paul to wait a year before rushing into marriage (he himself lives alone but has a young married mistress). Jerry, despite two failed marriages, is a true bourgeois who still believes in married love; he advises Paul to listen to his heart, because the heart, the "unencumbered heart," *knows* (*LG,* 91).

The scenes with Asher and Jerry, with Asher's mistress, and at dinner with Jerry and his youngest daughter, Claire, and her husband—all provide varieties of farce. Not deadly in themselves, they invariably contain deadly elements, as the dinner party with Uncle Jerry shows. At first Paul is pleased with the way Libby has dolled herself up for the occasion, but gradually his "definite burst of pleasure" (*LG,* 93) subsides and gives way to irritation at the way she has decked herself out. Gone were the straight, shoulder-length hair; the overused eyes; "the winterized, libraryized, studentized Libby." In their place is an aspect Paul can only think of as "aspiration" (*LG,* 93–94).

The dinner itself at the Plaza is comic enough, in true Rothian style: the two young women chat about hairdressers; Claire's husband ("an average crew-cut sort of I.B.M. machine") comments unintelligibly about business; Jerry exudes satisfaction with his daughter and her family. Yet through it all drives Paul's growing concern over Libby's transformation, a concern that accelerates to outrage when he learns that she spent $8 to have her hair done. Nearly overcome with doubts at this late stage of their relationship, he warns her solemnly: "I can't afford stuff like that, Libby. We're going to have to live a frugal life. A sensible life. I'm beginning to wonder if we're in agreement. I begin to wonder if you understand—" (*LG,* 98). Libby, of course, does not understand; she merely capitulates, taking the pins out of her hair and letting it tumble down so that she is once again "the old Libby, hair to her shoulders."

Their efforts to arrange a wedding are similarly farcical with deadly components, though here the deadliness is more pronounced. Libby rejects a ceremony at city hall as demeaning, suggesting immorality. She has nothing to be ashamed about, she argues; she's not pregnant or anything. Why should they have to go to city hall? Since Paul balks at the idea of a priest, she suggests a rabbi. But Rabbi Lichtman, like most rabbis, will only marry Jew with Jew, and Paul ends his appeal by cursing the man for his righteousness. The couple finally go to a Yonkers justice of the peace, whose wife in a print dress and nurse's white oxfords fusses over him and the couple, touching the bride "ten times at least" and placing artificial flowers in a vase behind her husband. He, poor man, suffering from gout, has to remain sitting during the ceremony, with his bandaged leg propped on a chair, "staring" at Paul and Libby throughout the proceedings (*LG,* 103).

The deadliest farce involving Paul and Libby occurs sometime later when, having given up their studies at Ann Arbor to try to save money while working, they move to Detroit. Libby becomes unexpectedly pregnant, precipitating a crisis. After much agonizing, Paul urges Libby to have an abortion, about which she is, to say the least, ambivalent. They have been living in a seedy rooming house, and among their fellow tenants is elderly Mr. Levy and, in the house next door, his friend Max Korngold. A onetime big-shot lawyer—or so he lets others believe—Levy is trying to help old Korngold get some assistance from his affluent son. He also has his eye on the stock of men's underwear Korngold has stored in his room after a failed business venture. Levy wants Paul to correct and type up a letter to Korngold's son, extorting from him support for his father. The humorous aspects of the situation, enhanced by the fractured English both Levy and Korngold speak, are undercut not only by the sinister intent but, more seriously, by the marital and moral dilemma Paul is simultaneously struggling with. Somehow Levy catches on to the nature of the dilemma and uses his knowledge to blackmail Paul into cooperating. Meanwhile, Korngold has second thoughts about Levy, suspects his ulterior motives, and appeals privately to Paul for help. All this goes on as Paul injures his hand on an assembly line, Libby is frightened by the prospects of an illegal abortion, and both of them are anxiety-ridden over the cost of the abortion, which will wipe out almost everything they have managed to scrape together.

The climax comes when Paul brings Libby home from the osteopath who performs the abortion. (The incidents involving "Doctor Tom" and his nurse, Mrs. Kuzmyak, also provide a good measure of satire as well as deadly farce.) A half-hour after Paul gets Libby to sleep, a scuffling begins in the corridor outside their room. Levy and Korngold are having a fight and eventually force their way into the Herzes' room. While Libby looks on with drawn cheeks and eyes that are "clouds of black," the men engage in a furious quarrel. Korngold accuses Levy of stealing the stock of men's underwear he has hoarded for years, waiting for a better market in which to sell it. Levy protests that he got a good deal on the lot and has split the proceeds with Korngold. Paul tries to quiet the two of them down and get them to leave the room, where his wife is "very sick." "Recovering," Levy suggests, correcting Paul and insinuating that he knows what has happened (*LG*, 150). After repeated pleas, his patience exhausted, all the "rules" of his life deserting him, Paul finally lunges at Levy. To everyone's horror he grabs the old man by the throat as if to strangle him, screaming, "How much? How much was it? . . . *Give him the money!*" until Levy gives up and Paul feels Libby's arms pulling him back (*LG,* 151). But the incident is not over. Levy leaves, "slicing the air with his cane" and shouting threats against Paul regarding the abortion. Korngold lingers, sheltering for a moment behind Libby, who has gone back to bed; however, he flees as Paul turns first on him and then on Libby. It is a moment of the most intense deadliness, all humor gone, while throughout the scene the contours of farce remain.

After their year in Iowa the Herzes and Gabe Wallach lose track of each other for a time. Gabe goes to the University of Chicago to teach in a humanities program. Here the department and its members are wonderfully satirized. The particular object of ridicule is the new department head, John Spigliano, and his wife, Pat—an ambitious, social-climbing pair. Through the Spiglianos, Gabe meets Martha Reganhart, a young divorcée with two small children who has taken a course from John and works nights as a waitress. Gabe is somewhat taken with Martha, but it is not until he is back in New York, having Thanksgiving with his father and his new friend, Fay Silberman, that he thinks at all seriously about her.

The Thanksgiving celebration at his father's apartment overlooking Central Park West is another occasion for farce, more or less deadly, as Dr. Wallach entertains friends and colleagues preparatory to announcing his engagement to Fay Silberman, whom he has met on a recent trip to Europe. Thanks to Fay—a jolly woman whose gaiety is heavily supported by alcohol—Dr. Wallach's life has since become more joyful. At the Thanksgiving party Fay's drinking disquiets Gabe, who is too discreet to say anything. He is mainly interested in seeing his father happy and off his hands, if not off his conscience. Gabe does not especially like Fay, who tries to win his approval by taking a moment to talk with him during a lull in the party. The mixture of ridicule and pathos in Gabe's description of her (*LG,* 170) epitomizes the party, which culminates in a toast to the engaged couple and concludes with a final glance at the bride-to-be: "Mrs. Silberman's champagne ran down her chin, cutting a trail through her powder" (*LG,* 171).

Just before his talk with Mrs. Silberman, Gabe calls Chicago to speak with Martha Reganhart, who had invited him to her Thanksgiving dinner. The call marks the beginning of a relationship between them that provides some of the cheerier moments in the novel, for Martha Reganhart is a woman of great energy and warmth, one who does everything with considerable gusto and is perhaps more woman than Gabe can handle. She is also a very handsome and sexy lady who, because she is also the mother of two small children, has maintained a firm chastity since her divorce. Gabe does not know all this, though he imagines her "as a green, watery spot in a dry land" and feels in her "something solid to which I could anchor my wandering and strained affections" (*LG,* 169). And for a time he does.

But before Gabe returns to Chicago and takes up with Martha, he has a duty to perform. Having lost track of the Herzes, he received a letter from Libby about a year after the move from Iowa. She and Paul were then living in Reading, Pennsylvania, where Paul was teaching in a small college while trying to finish his novel, required for his doctorate, and where Libby, again recuperating from a serious illness, accordingly had time to read more Henry James and to write letters. Gabe has not answered her letter; however, when a vacancy falls open in his department he recommends Paul to John Spigliano, who hires him. Thus the Herzes and Gabe Wallach resume their acquaintance.

Gabe has had mixed feelings about recommending Paul for the job, which will once more bring him and his wife into close proximity. Believing that the move to Chicago will improve Paul's life in every way, Gabe feels honor-bound to help. On the other hand, he is aware that he might have fallen in love with Libby and she with him, and so he wonders "for whom, and for what end, was he doing favors?" (*LG,* 71). Resolving to maintain "an active life of his own, independent of theirs" (*LG,* 70), Gabe goes ahead and helps Paul get the job.

At first nothing much happens. Silent and self-absorbed as ever, Paul goes his own way, while Libby and Gabe do nothing to further the feelings they still share for each other. Then just before leaving for New York and the Thanksgiving party, Gabe runs into Libby outside of Brooks Brothers department store and they spend an hour together shopping for Gabe's wardrobe. Before parting from Gabe during their amusing, if not altogether innocent, outing, Libby urgently asks him to visit Paul's parents while he is in New York. He agrees but later is puzzled, wondering what good a visit from him could do or why he should feel obliged to make it. Nevertheless, as his father's Thanksgiving celebration winds down, Gabe makes his way to Brooklyn, where the elder Herzes live.

The scene is another occasion for deadly farce, but quite different from the one in Manhattan in Dr. Wallach's apartment. Whereas Dr. Wallach and his friends forced hilarity on one another to disguise their deeper feelings of misery and loneliness, the Herzes refuse any semblance of cheer. "Not everyone can afford a mask, or wants one," Gabe realizes on entering their dim, gloom-ridden apartment (*LG,* 175). He is met by the

Horvitzes, young neighbors who try hard to buck the Herzes up (Maury was Paul's best friend during their boyhood days). But Maury and Doris soon leave Gabe alone with Leonard Herz and his wife, warning him to be careful. Mr. Herz has a bad heart and suffers from constipation and other assorted ills, and Mrs. Herz, a self-appointed martyr, waits attendance on his every need. The spectacle is depressing, not at all helped when Gabe announces who he is and why he has come. When shortly afterward Mr. Herz gets up from his BarcaLounger to go to the bathroom, his wife admonishes him to leave the door open a little and not to strain too much. Her conversation with Gabe is henceforward punctuated by concern for her husband sitting in the toilet: "Leonard, is everything all right in there?" she calls to him. "Don't strain. If nothing happens, nothing happens. You're not engaged in some contest, Leonard" (*LG,* 177).

Gabe's visit is not a success. The elder Herzes are as bitter and resentful over their son's actions as ever. They are superb grudge-holders, against Libby as well. Their wit is sardonic, cruel, against her (whose name they will not even pronounce), against their son, against almost everyone. Here is deadliness at its deadliest—literally, for Leonard Herz is not long for this world. The Horvitzes have tried to explain that to Gabe and surreptitiously ask him to stop by their apartment before he goes. When he does, he is greeted by a scene of comic extravagance and petit bourgeois taste that is subdued only by the occasion of the visit. The ubiquitous pale blue carpeting, low furniture, and "Scandanavian jungle of coffee tables, throw cushions, and potted avocados" aptly set off the Horvitzes' sentimentality and Doris's pure Brooklynese (*LG,* 179–80). Over espresso served in demitasse cups acquired on a cruise to St. Thomas, Maury and Doris tell Gabe something of the Paul they once knew and, coming to the point of their invitation, ask Gabe to urge Paul to "get to work," that is, to become a father, to bring into the world "a child for his mother and father to cherish as once they had cherished him" (*LG,* 184). They do not know, and neither does Gabe at this moment, that Libby's poor kidneys make it extremely dangerous for her to think of conceiving a child again.

Amid this gloom and doom, Gabe wanders, then pushes himself into the contrasting milieu of Martha Reganhart and her family. He had met Martha at the university faculty club one evening, when she was having dinner with John and Pat Spigliano. The occasion, as she tells Gabe, was rather ludicrous: when she was a student in John's summer school class, he had made a pass at her and then, conscience-stricken, wanted to introduce her to his wife—hence, the faculty club dinner. Martha is open, frank, and brave and has a fine sense of humor, besides being tall, buxom, and blond: no wonder John made a pass at her and Gabe finds her attractive. Her failed marriage was not so much her fault as that of her husband, an artist whose being temperamental to the point of violence precipitated the rupture. Alone now in Chicago, Martha is trying to support her two small children while working as a waitress, taking in a roomer, and fending off suitors, including her devoted attorney, Sid Jaffe—until Gabe Wallach comes along.

The telephone call Gabe makes from New York during Thanksgiving offers the first real glimpse of Martha's ménage. In contrast to the deadly farce at his father's apartment and later at the elder Herzes' in Brooklyn, Martha is having a healthier, more typical American Thanksgiving at home with her children and Sid Jaffe. Gabe's call evokes a bit of turmoil fairly characteristic of her family situation. What mainly comes through, however, are Martha's energy and essential soundness, which her humor above all brings out. For example, she teases Gabe by asking, "Is there really a father and a party or is some tootsie nestled beside you in her underwear?" (LG, 165). As the conversation continues, Gabe feels that Martha is well worth pursuing. And that is precisely what he does when he returns to Chicago.

Martha's household provides some of the most touching, funny, and natural scenes in the novel, scenes plainly designed to contrast with other episodes, especially those involving Paul and Libby Herz. Like Paul, Martha must struggle to exist. Like Paul, she too has obligations and responsibilities, profound ones, that affect her very being and her outlook on the world. But unlike Paul, she has a more robust attitude, unafflicted with guilt or remorse, and a healthier sense of herself. Not that she is totally sure of who and what she is or where she is going. Like most mortals, she has her confusions and ambivalences. Some of these are revealed through her contacts with Sissy, the young hospital technician she has taken in as a boarder to help pay the rent. Sissy is uninhibited, sloppy, brash, and addicted to playing phonograph records at any hour of the morning or night. Hence, whatever help she affords Martha in running her household is offset by her behavior.

Martha's interior monologue one morning characterizes her conflicting attitudes toward Sissy while also revealing a good deal about her own character. Annoyed by Sissy's habits, Martha is also glad for the company Sissy provides when, for example, she gets home late at night after work. Nevertheless, she upbraids herself for always "latching onto people just as they were going through some treacherous maturing period in their lives." Her next roomer, she promises herself, will be at least 80—"better they should die in her spare room than grow up in it" (*LG,* 196). Martha's next roomer, however, is not 80, and it is uncertain how much "growing up" Gabe accomplishes while living with her.

Gabe finds himself staying with Martha by catching the flu, the result of always having to get up and leave in the middle of the night while their affair is in its early stages. Meeting her late one evening after work, he wants to go back to his own apartment without, as usual, first spending time in hers making love. He is ill, he says, but she insists, and once in her bed he finds he cannot get out of it. Martha is just as happy to let him stay there; in fact, she encourages him, delighted that he is willing for a while to indulge in "pig heaven," as she calls it—lounging in bed, being waited on by her and her children, not going to work. And Gabe's advent spells Sissy's exit.

While Sissy moves out, helped by her boyfriend, Blair, and amid the tears and expostulations of Martha's daughter, Cynthia, Gabe contemplates the situation he now finds himself in. Recognizing that he may have fallen in love with Martha, he is nevertheless sure that he is "not falling in love with Martha's predicament." He ponders the complications posed by her two children—must he love them as well as Martha? Is that what he wanted? (*LG,* 277). When, honestly and plaintively, Martha shortly afterward asks him to stay and live with her, Gabe closes his eyes for a moment. He hopes "that what I ought to do and what I wanted to do would be one." When he opens his eyes again and looks down at Martha's face, he "believed they were" (*LG,* 279).

Belief in this context is not quite conviction, let alone commitment; for Gabe, reality and illusion may again be in conflict. He may be deceiving himself, but Martha does not press him for more than he can give, at least not now. In bed she says, "It isn't marriage, you know . . . nobody has to marry me. . . . I don't need a husband, sweetheart—just a lover, Gabe, just someone to plain and simple love me" (*LG,* 279). Affairs, however, if they go on for any length of time, have a way of turning into something else, as Neil Klugman discovered in "Goodbye, Columbus." Thus, Gabe's uncertainty about Martha and her children, his inability to make a commitment to her and/or to them, seriously undercuts the relationship. As with so many of Roth's protagonists, moral conscience conflicts with hedonistic inclination, failing any satisfactory resolution. In *Portnoy's Complaint* the conflict extends to its absurd and comic extreme, but it has already become apparent in the novella and stories of *Goodbye, Columbus,* and it recurs here. In the immediate aftermath of Martha's plea, it appears, for example, in an ironic and farcical turn of events.

When Gabe awakens the morning after he and Martha have apparently come to agreement about living together, he is feeling much recovered from his flu attack. More than that, he experiences "the cheery disposition not only of a physical convalescent, but a moral one as well" (LG, 279). He therefore determines to relieve Martha of the burden of caring for him and gets out of bed to groom himself. But as he looks around the bathroom, searching in vain for a clean, sharp razor to shave with, he is first astonished, then dismayed, and finally enraged. The cheery travel posters initially please him; the long blond strands of hair on Martha's brush do not disconcert him. Opening the medicine chest, however, utterly destroys his complacency: the mess he sees in that "square foot of chaos" was, he feels, "a knife sunk right down into the apple of my well-being" (LG, 280).

Total disaster follows. Still eager to find a razor blade, Gabe clutches Martha's old misshapen bathrobe around himself and charges into the kitchen, where Mark and Cynthia are eating Wheatena and Martha is talking with a man. It is only the janitor, it turns out, but Gabe is horrified to be found this way and flees back to the bathroom. The crisis he precipitates is, visually, funny enough, though its implications and its consequences are not. As Gabe sits fuming in the bathroom, Martha knocks and enters. An argument ensues in which Gabe registers his moral outrage at Martha's disorderliness. If he once took disarray in her apartment as "the sign of a relaxed life" and "evidence of a deep humanitarianism" (LG, 281), he does not now. Her closets have presented a different story, and his feelings are exacerbated by chagrin over the kitchen episode. On her part, Martha is angry at his thoughtlessness (her children play with the janitor's kids), his accusations, and his apparent need, as she sees it, to start a fight in order to end their relationship. Characteristically, she confronts him directly: "If you want to leave, Gabriel, just leave, all right?" (LG, 283).

Gabe does leave, but not for long. Out of loneliness and despair he attends the Spiglianos' Christmas party (another occasion for amusing and apt academic satire). There he drinks too much, behaves badly with one of his female colleagues, watches Paul Herz get into an unfortunate argument, and generally has a rotten time. When he finally gets home to his own apartment he waits as long as he can and then telephones Martha, apologizing abjectly for his behavior (LG, 300). As testimony to her basic humanity and generosity, she forgives him, knowing full well how drunk and miserable he must be to call her like that.

As Gabe and Martha settle down with her children to not-quite-do-mestic-bliss, they decide to give a dinner party. They feel a need for some form of public approval to be granted, if only through one couple, "one pair of outsiders to whom we could display our fundamental decency and good intentions, to whose judgment we could submit evidence of an ordered carnality and a restrained domestic life" (*LG,* 308). So whom do they invite? Paul and Libby Herz.

With intentions like those and guests like these, the inevitable follows, like a hangover after too much carousing. The evening begins in strain and ends in disaster. Underlying Gabe's intentions is also the desire to impress upon Paul and Libby the seriousness of his relationship with Martha and to bring "to an unbloody conclusion" a painful chapter in his life (*LG,* 308). But if he really thinks he can end his involvement with the Herzes, he has seriously miscalculated his continuing concern for their hard-luck life, his emotional ties to Libby, and hers to him.

The tension mounts even before the Herzes arrive, with a quarrel be-tween Gabe and Martha over their domestic arrangements, specifically money matters. Leaving the argument unresolved, they prepare for their guests, who are greeted at the door by Martha in a bizarre outfit of orange skirt, off-the-shoulder blouse, strands of colored beads, and her "Hu-manities II" sandals (*LG,* 308). To emphasize the hippie look, she has combed her hair straight out—hardly the sedate look Gabe was expecting or hoping for. By contrast, "to make my Martha brassier," Gabe muses, "Libby that day was the child saint about to be lifted onto the cross. There was even in her very flat-chestedness something that lent her an ethereal and martyred air" (*LG,* 309).

The cross-purposes that turn the evening into a deadly farce accelerate through the sumptuous dinner, two expensive bottles of French wine, and the appearance of Cynthia and Mark in fresh pajamas, ready for bed. Paul is uncommonly solicitous of his wife, serving her food and urging her to eat, but otherwise is his usual uncommunicative self. Demure Libby sits as if in silent disapproval throughout the meal and is especially irritated, it seems, by the children's appearance. Offended by everyone's behavior, Martha smoulders in disgust and outrage. Gabe tries his best to enliven the party with anecdotes and chatter, but his efforts only make matters worse. He truly puts his foot in his mouth when, in absolute innocence, he inquires about the adoption proceedings Paul has told him he and Libby have begun.

Libby is unaware that Gabe knows about their plans, and her response makes an awkward situation even more so. As Gabe tries to reassure Libby that adoption is a good idea, Martha comes in from the kitchen and asks,

"What is?" For some little while she has absented herself from the others
to gain a measure of composure. When she reenters and makes an effort
to be gracious, it backfires terribly. Robust Martha, Gabe's bedmate and
the mother of two fine young children, is the antithesis to Libby in every
respect; moreover, Libby's discomfiture is complicated by waves of jealousy. To put the final touches on their dismal evening, Libby tells Gabe
that Paul was called in to see the dean that day. Apparently Spigliano is
out to get him fired, and the conversation eventuates in comparisons
between Reading and Chicago, mostly in Reading's favor. By this time
Martha has again absented herself, Gabe is furious at Libby's insinuations
concerning his motives, voices are raised, and the Herzes leave.

Gabe's relationship with the Herzes does not end there, although it
brings his relationship with Martha to the brink—not of separation but
of marriage. The quarrel before dinner resumes after the Herzes leave and
Gabe returns from a long solitary walk. He enters the bedroom, where
Martha lies awake staring at the smoke rings from her cigarette. After a
few minutes Gabe starts apologizing for inviting the Herzes, but Martha
tries to turn the conversation back to money matters. Instead, they argue
about both—Libby Herz and Gabe's involvement with her, and Martha,
her children, and her financial problems. The conversation concludes with
Martha's desperate declaration, "Oh Gabe. . . . The hell with all
that. . . . I want you to marry me or give me up. I'm too old to screw
around like this" (*LG,* 321).

Roth ends the chapter with Martha's words and juxtaposes against
them Libby's plight as an unhappily married, frail woman, trying to fill
her days with meaningful activity and hoping for a child on whom to
expend love and devotion. The scene that follows between Libby and her
unexpected visitor, a man from a Jewish adoption agency, is yet another
variety of deadly farce. So is Gabe's meeting with Theresa Haug, the
young hillbilly who works with Martha as a waitress and has become
pregnant. Through Theresa, in whom sympathetic Martha has taken an
interest and to whom she has already lent a sizable sum of money, Gabe
sees an opportunity to help the Herzes and Theresa too—for her child will
be illegitimate, it appears, and the Herzes, a mixed couple (her conversion
hardly counts, Libby says), have little chance of getting a Jewish baby
through an agency. Hence, with Martha and her attorney, Sid Jaffe, Gabe
begins the long process of preparing Theresa to let the Herzes adopt
her baby.

Gabe's efforts culminate in the deadliest farce of all. First, though,

Martha's ex-husband, now a successful artist, returns to Chicago briefly to claim the children. So as to live a little more freely, and with Gabe, Martha reluctantly agrees to let them go. But despite the children's absence and all the domesticity a family involves, the new arrangement between them does not work out. Gabe remains ambivalent and unable fully to commit himself; Martha remains restless and anxious about her future. Putting space between them, Gabe goes back to New York for a visit with his father and his bride-to-be, during which interval Mark Reganhart dies in an accident while staying with his father and stepmother, Dick Reganhart's second wife. Gabe and Martha never resume their relationship; Martha agrees to marry Sid Jaffe.

Meanwhile, Paul has also gone to New York, called away by his father's heart attack. En route he contemplates leaving Libby. He reviews their unhappy life together, particularly their sex life, which has deteriorated into deadly farce of still another variety (*LG,* 431–33). Confused and unsure how to act, he stays with his Uncle Asher for a few days, refuses to visit his father in the hospital, and later balks at attending the funeral. But he soon succumbs to the moral imperatives that dominate his life. After the funeral Paul returns to his wife and the new child Theresa Haug has brought into the world, it seems, for them. They name the little girl Rachel, and their life starts heading in a new direction. They are not exactly happy: Paul still has his demons, but Libby finds a measure of fulfillment. They are completely unaware of further complications threatening their newfound contentment, complications that again propel Gabe into action.

The complications arise from the fact that Theresa is not unmarried after all. The name Haug was an alias she adopted while separated from her husband, Harry Bigoness. Now, reunited with Harry, she rejects anything further to do with the adoption of her child, including the final step that the proceedings require. When she and her husband are summoned to Chicago from Gary, where they live, to sign papers in the presence of the court, Harry refuses to let either of them do so. Ignorant and unemployed, he is stubborn and intransigent. But like many of his type, he is also shrewd, with an eye to the main chance. All these qualities reveal themselves in deadly farce when Gabe drives out to persuade the Bigonesses to cooperate.

Gabe finds not Theresa but Harry at home doing the housework when he arrives. The father of three small children from a previous marriage, Harry avoids answering the door, but Gabe enters anyway. Amid crawling and crying children, dishes crashing, Harry's repeated demands that he leave, and a little girl's insistent pleas for a peanut-butter sandwich, Gabe tries to explain why he has come. Bigoness will have none of it, and he adamantly refuses to have anything to do with "paper-signing" (*LG,* 555). Appealing to reason, Gabe says that the papers he needs to sign will not involve him in responsibilities but do just the reverse—for him and for Theresa too. Bigoness, however, stonewalls. He has had enough of signing papers, he says, insisting that "the only way you don't get stuck is you don't sign" (*LG,* 556).

The crossed purposes continue almost endlessly, abetted by the different languages the two men speak. Bigoness believes Gabe represents a black market enterprise; Gabe cannot disabuse him of the notion. Gabe's cultured, rational language moreover is directly at odds with Harry's homely dialect. When the latter mentions being out of work for five months with bills piling up, Gabe finally catches on. Since it's a question of money, he bargains with Bigoness over the costs of the trip to Chicago. Believing he has concluded a deal, that Bigoness and Theresa will go to Chicago to sign the necessary papers, Gabe leaves, feeling satisfied with himself that he has held firm and in so doing has accomplished a great deal.

In fact, he has accomplished nothing. Bigoness telephones a day later to say he and Theresa can't afford to come to Chicago after all. In a fury, Gabe drives back to Gary, and the farce continues, its deadliness intensified by the illness of one of the infants, who has an intestinal disorder. The farce is also heightened by Gabe's preoccupation with a penicillin shot he has to get that afternoon and his date with a new girlfriend afterward: he is operating on a tight schedule. Bigoness could not care less, and Gabe, of course, tells him nothing about his plans, which torment his consciousness as their argument resumes.

They quarrel more vigorously than ever and apparently get nowhere. Just as Gabe is about to lose his temper completely, Bigoness is summoned downstairs for a telephone call. During his absence Gabe explores the apartment and comes upon a squalling child strapped on the toilet seat. Nearly overcome by rage, the child's screaming, and the powerful odor of feces, Gabe struggles to undo the straps around the little boy and at the same time retain his sanity and self-control. Releasing the child after two attempts, he picks him up to carry him out and clean him, whereupon Bigoness enters and yells at Gabe to put the boy down. Their argument resumes once again, once again furiously, as Bigoness, now a worried parent, tries to comfort his howling infant.

Finally Gabe confronts the issue directly: "Why don't we make some kind of deal. . . . I want a favor and you need money," he says (*LG,* 587). Bigoness plays it smart, and after much bickering, as farce evolves into a game of chicken, he agrees to a cash settlement. Gabe leaves, late for his doctor's appointment and too late for his date and the wedding gift he had meant to buy for his father and Fay. When he gets home Libby calls, asking him to baby-sit the next evening, Christmas Eve, while she and Paul go to dinner and a movie before meeting Paul's mother, who is coming for a visit—to see the new baby and at long last become reconciled with her son and daughter-in-law.

While Gabe baby-sits and Paul and Libby are having their night out, unaware of all their friend has been through in their behalf, Gabe calls the Bigonesses to make sure everything is all right. He is still a little shaken and anxious, and with good reason: for a second time Bigoness threatens to renege. Despite all Gabe's efforts to end it, their deadly farce continues, moving to new heights (or depths) as the concluding episode of the novel.

Getting nowhere by telephone, Gabe feels compelled to take Rachel with him and drive to Gary, to demonstrate the reality of the situation to Bigoness. It had all become too abstract, he believes; he must put Harry "in touch with the simplest human facts. He was stupid, but he had feelings. If he could meet Paul, see Libby—see Rachel. . . . In one way it was all so simple" (*LG,* 598). But it is not that simple, he discovers when he arrives, and a three-cornered argument begins including Bigoness's friend Vic. Here, however, Roth changes his strategy. Instead of presenting a third face-to-face encounter between the male antagonists, he focuses on the situation through Theresa's consciousness.

Bigoness has ordered his wife into the bedroom while he deals with Gabe. As the argument among the men rages, she thinks of herself and her own situation—how young and how deprived she is, and how she is made to work for her husband like a slave. She especially turns her hostility against little Walter, the sick child Gabe rescued from the toilet seat. When she goes into the children's room to try to hear better, she thinks Walter is only pretending to sleep and begins first scolding and then hitting him. His howls bring his father into the bedroom, followed by Gabe and Vic. The argument, continuing violently, now pulls Theresa in, whereupon she rushes into the living room, where Rachel lies in her basket.

Theresa picks up the child and for a few moments indulges her natural maternal feelings. But immediately Bigoness and Gabe interfere, and the quarrel roars on, becoming more and more violent. As Vic grabs Gabe's shoulder, Bigoness lunges toward Theresa, who breaks for the bedroom with the baby. While she and Bigoness argue, something happens in the living room. Although Vic insists he did not strike him, Gabe is on the floor on his knees, his forehead touching the rug, his arms over his ears. Whereas before everyone was screaming at one another, fear now silences them. At last Gabe mumbles something about a phone call, and Theresa takes him downstairs, where he manages to dial the Herzes' number. But he is unable to speak, and Theresa must. After giving her address and wondering if Gabe had rung the police, she whispers, "Are you the man who's got a little baby? . . . Come get it then! . . . We don't want it!" (*LG,* 628).

The farce is finally over, and the novel ends, as it began, with a letter. This one is from Gabe to Libby, a long-delayed reply to an invitation to Rachel's first-birthday party. The card has been forwarded many times, since Gabe has moved around a lot and indeed is still moving. Like his mother's letter, Gabe's is an apologia, detailing his perceptions of what has happened, particularly on the previous Christmas Eve, when he had come so close to wrecking everything for Paul and Libby. Although Libby has sent only the printed card with no word or remark written on it, Gabe assumes it is intended as "an invitation to be forgiven—for me to feel free to accept your forgiveness" (*LG,* 630). But he cannot accept it, as he believes he is not properly penitent. Having lived indecisively for so long, he is unwilling to forget or obliterate his "one decisive moment," at least for the present.

Gabe's letter is also a valediction—to Libby and their friendship. Thanking Libby for letting him know he is off the hook, he ends, "But I'm not, I can't be, I don't even want to be—not until I make some sense of the larger hook I'm on." Making sense of that "larger hook" concerns much of Roth's subsequent fiction and propels the comedy of crossed purposes, farcical conflicts, ironic juxtapositions, and hopeless entanglements.

## Chapter Four

# Floating, Submerged, and Drowned Comedy in *When She Was Good*

Like an actor refusing to be typecast, Roth wrote *When She Was Good* with nary a Jew in it. Or, as Jonathan Baumbach has said, "*When She Was Good* is a surprising tour de force, an accomplishment comparable, say, to Zero Mostel doing an extended imitation of Jimmy Stewart."[1] If thus far Jewish life had provided a major source of Roth's comedy, it was not the sole source, as his third book showed. Still under the influence of James, Flaubert, Tolstoy, and such American writers as Sherwood Anderson, Theodore Dreiser, and Sinclair Lewis, Roth wrote a novel that above all focuses on moral earnestness. As in *Letting Go,* moral earnestness sometimes develops into deadly farce, although the last episodes in the book eschew farce for high melodrama that drowns any vestige of humor. The absurdity of many of the characters' actions, deriving from absurdly held convictions, fuels much of Roth's wit, whereas in the book's lighter moments—and there are a few, despite the novel's somber opening scenes—Roth's other kinds of humor float easily.

The effort to make this novel as American as apple pie involved introducing a bevy of all-American characters—and a good serving of pie too. All of the characters live in the heartland of America, not far from Chicago, in a mythical town called Liberty Center in an unnamed state. There is Willard Carroll, whose boyhood experiences have inspired the dream of his life: "Not to be rich, not to be famous, not to be mighty, not even to be happy, but to be civilized."[2] There is his daughter, Myra, a sensitive, fragile young woman who marries a well-meaning but hopeless weakling, Duane "Whitey" Nelson. And there is their daughter, Lucy, the novel's protagonist—and everyone else's antagonist—a woman fiercely determined not only to do right but to get everyone around her to follow her own stern morality. Other important characters are Roy Bassart, whom Lucy marries, and his family: Lloyd Bassart and his wife,

Alice; and Uncle Julian Sowerby, his wife, Irene, and their daughter, Eleanor, a school friend of Lucy's. In addition, there are other school friends of Lucy's and Roy's and the usual small-town folks in Liberty Center and Fort Kean, where Lucy goes to college and Roy attends a proprietary photography school.

Not the usual ingredients of a Roth novel—deliberately not. Already under attack by some members of the Jewish community for *Goodbye, Columbus*—but nothing compared with what came after *Portnoy's Complaint*—Roth focused on aspects of his experience far removed from Newark and the life he knew intimately as a boy growing up there in the 1930s and 1940s. Of course, he had had some experience of the Midwest too, having attended the University of Chicago and the University of Iowa, settings for extended episodes in *Letting Go*. In fact, throughout much of his fiction Roth seems preoccupied with the white Anglo-Saxon Protestant culture foreign to his upbringing but prominent in his later life. Collisions between the two cultures—heartland WASP and eastern first- or second-generation Jewish—often explode in hilarity in his later fiction and are signaled, for example, in the Marjorie Howells–Gabe Wallach episode in *Letting Go*. Absent such collisions, absent any Jewishness at all, where is the comedy in *When She Was Good*, Roth's implacably WASP novel?

Much of it is submerged or heavily camouflaged by the bleak, meager existence, spiritual as well as material, of the major characters. For example, though she is hardly a vivid presence in the book, Willard's wife, Berta, repeatedly undercuts her husband's pretention to what he calls "civilized" behavior, which she sees as just plain foolishness, if not worse. Forever forgiving, forever appealing to reason, forever trying to help the members of his family, but invariably frustrated in his efforts, Willard is an angel, perhaps, but an ineffectual one. For years he has supported his daughter and her shiftless, frequently drunken husband, much to Berta's disgust. At one point he almost rebels when he witnesses his son-in-law stretched out in the living room about to munch an apple—"in Willard's parlor, eating Willard's food!" (*WSWG*, 13). Instead, he decides to spend the time looking through his mementos. So much for Willard's moral indignation! Moments later, when he discovers that from among his mementos his medals are missing, he immediately—and rightly—suspects Whitey; when he returns to confront him, however, Whitey is fast asleep, and so Willard puts the matter off to the following day. Confirming his suspicions by a visit to the local pawnshop, he then only lectures Whitey privately on the enormity of his crime, accepts his apologies, gives him another chance, and passively listens to a stream of extenuations and prevarications.

From his first appearance in the novel Roy Bassart is the subject of more directly overt humor. A young man of 20, recently discharged from the army, he is the epitome of many American men of that age and time—that is, summer 1948. Uncertain what to do with his future, "he sat around for six months listening to people talk about it" (*WSWG*, 43). Vague, unhurried, dressed in army fatigues, he lounges around, visits his Uncle Julian, and literally watches the world go by, looking at whoever it is advising or questioning him "through a frame that he made with his fingers" (*WSWG*, 43). Later, with some prompting from his girlfriend, Lucy, Roy decides to become a photographer.

Well before then, however, he becomes entangled in a number of broadly comic situations that to him appear to be serious predicaments but to the reader can only be regarded as funny. Like any normal young man in the era before the pill, Roy encounters his share of difficulties with girls whom he finds attractive but who refuse to let him go as far as he wants with them. In high school he was tantalized almost unmercifully (and unwittingly) by Ginger Donnelly, the head cheerleader, who did cartwheels the length of the football field after a touchdown: while everyone else was standing and cheering, Roy was forced to sit still with his erection (*WSWG*, 57). His sweetheart during his senior year, Bev Collison, would let him kiss her at first only while they kept their coats on, even if the kissing went on for an hour at a stretch. Many weeks later she allowed him to remove his overcoat, and finally to touch her "wherever he wanted anywhere above the belt so long as it was outside her clothes" (*WSWG*, 59). After further struggling and persuading, with minimal progress in their petting, on the Saturday before graduation "it happened; in the pitch-black living room he got two fingers down onto her nipple. Bare. And the next thing he knew she was off visiting her married sister in Superior, and he was in the Army" (*WSWG*, 59).

Such sexual olympics and their anticlimactic consequences are, of course, one of Roth's fortes, as he demonstrates par excellence in *Portnoy's Complaint*. Roy's predicament deepens after he returns from the army— still a virgin and still trying to find a girl who will "go all the way." Part of his problem is that he feels it must be a girl whom he can respect, not just an "easy lay," let alone a professional. Enter Lucy Nelson—and, eventually, problems of much larger magnitude than Roy could ever imagine.

Impossible as it may be to regard Lucy Nelson as a humorous character, one finds something profoundly comic—in an existential sense—in her ferocious claims to moral superiority and to a code of behavior that in actuality even she cannot maintain absolutely. Traumatized early by her father's behavior, particularly toward her mother, she develops a mistrust of men that turns into hate. Like her grandmother Berta, she sees quite through her grandfather Willard's futilities as they involve her father and mother and their life together. At one point in her loneliness as a school-girl, Lucy becomes friendly with a Catholic girl, Kitty Egan; takes instruction from Father Damrosch; goes on a retreat; and prays hard that her life and the life of her family will change. During this period of strenuous religious devotion, however, an event occurs that terminates her faith in divinity and reveals her true nature in all its vindictiveness and misanthropy. Dedicating herself to a life of "submission, humility, silence and suffering," Lucy abruptly changes tactics one night when her father pulls down the shade and upends the pan of water in which her mother was soaking her feet. Then, "after calling upon Saint Teresa of Lisieux and Our Lord—and getting no reply—she called the police" (*WSWG*, 80).

Typically, Roth presents the incident in the form of humorous anticlimax,[3] but its consequences afterward for Lucy and her father are little short of catastrophic. Whitey Nelson believes his daughter's action is symbolic of her inmost desire—to see him jailed forever, or worse—and subsequent events confirm his belief. Lucy is utterly unrepentant, convinced not only of her moral rectitude but of nothing in an afterlife to look forward to. Abandoning the church and reaffirming her moral stance, she imagines a conversation with Father Damrosch in which she argues that "they" are not going to ruin her life—her only life. "I am their superior in every single way!" she cries. "People can call me all the names they want—I don't care! I have nothing to confess, because I am right and they are wrong and I will not be destroyed!" (*WSWG*, 83). This is Lucy's credo, and she lives it to the end of her short unhappy life.

Given these attitudes and convictions, Lucy as Roy's lover and later as his wife and the mother of their child, may seem startling. Her meeting with him at her friend Ellie Sowerby's home is the beginning of an unfortunate but sometimes comical union between an ordinary, easygoing young man and a woman extraordinarily convinced of her essential superiority to everyone around her. The union occurs because through a variety of circumstances both parties have been set up for it: Roy by his particular quest, Lucy by her loneliness and gradual sexual awakening

(*WSWG,* 95–96). Other incidents, such as Lucy's brief acquaintance with an admirer, Mr. Valerio, the school band director, also contribute to the match, or mismatch, that begins casually enough.

Roy has bought some camera equipment and begins taking pictures of his cousin Ellie and then of Lucy. A trivial misunderstanding occurs between Roy and Lucy, which Roy tries to resolve, first at Ellie's house and then at the dairy bar where Lucy works nights and weekends to earn money for college. When he offers her a lift home in his secondhand Hudson, she rebuffs him repeatedly. Finally she turns on him, insisting that he leave her alone. But as the narrator comments, "from then on, he was unable to" (*WSWG,* 99).

Their relationship develops through countless picture-taking expeditions after school and during evening rendezvous, when Roy drives Lucy home after work, stopping first at the local lovers' lane: "There Roy would turn off the lights, flip on the radio, and try with all his might to get her to go all the way" (*WSWG,* 100). The humor of their encounters in "Passion Paradise" centers on the banality of the situation—Lucy's resistance, Roy's persistence—and the dialogue Roth accurately records. All the usual accoutrements are there: the love songs on the radio ("It's Magic," "Nature Boy"), the young man singing along with Vaughan Monroe or Dick Haymes, the debate about getting into the backseat, the "trust me's" and the "No's!" Eventually Roy does manage to go all the way, explaining why he did not have a condom but reassuring Lucy that "interruption" was protection enough. The comedy becomes still more ludicrous, for as events unwind, Lucy finds she does not like Roy Bassart very much. But caught between her sexual appetite and her intellectual and moral appraisal of Roy's character, she continues to yield to sex, while repeatedly resolving to end the affair.

Her revised resolutions or, rather, her revised dates for notifying Roy are a form of submerged or low-key humor Roth enjoys using in this novel. Again, the banality of language and situation both camouflage the comedy and contribute to it: "It looked as though the bad news could not be broken to Roy until Sunday: the following night there were already plans to drive up to the Selkirk Fair with Ellie and Joe, with whom they doubled at least once a week now that Lucy was working only during the day; and on Friday evening Roy expected her to go over to Winnisaw with him to see *A Date with Judy*; then on Saturday there was the barbecue at the Sowerbys'" (*WSWG,* 116–17). Thus the banal, all-too-human comedy progresses. When Lucy enters Fort Kean College for Women, Roy enrolls in a school of photography and design. She lives in a dormitory; he takes a room with a large bed in a private house, but with no private entrance. Nevertheless, using the window for entrance, they go on as before. Still Lucy tries to end the affair, and still Roy persuades her to continue, until at last she becomes pregnant—precisely at the moment of her strongest resolve to call it quits.

Lucy's meeting with the school doctor who diagnoses her condition becomes a deadly farce much in the manner of *Letting Go,* combining melodrama, moral earnestness, pathos, and comedy. The doctor is a kindly, understanding man whom Lucy at first typically misjudges but then appeals to as strongly as possible for help. He tries to get her to recognize not only her lover's responsibility but her responsibility to him. Lucy, however, seems unable to follow the argument, self-absorbed as she is, now as always. Proclaiming that she is not "bad," like other girls who do what she did "with all different people," she cries with utter sincerity, "I'm good!" (*WSWG,* 141).

Lucy's proclamation is as sincere as it is misguided, and it lies at the root of her continuing predicament. Because of her conviction she is unable to understand properly either her actions or anyone else's. She is totally unaware of any contingency that impinges on human beings and their behavior, least of all her own, and that is what makes her comic, if darkly so. To the very end of her life she clings fiercely to her conviction, which finally undoes her, as it does in the doctor's office. Unable to get the help she had come for, she leaves in a huff, asserting her self-reliance as well as her self-righteousness, and spurning the doctor's gestures of concern.

Finding no other recourse, Lucy decides to marry Roy after all, but that is just the start of a long deadly farce, or series of farces, beginning with their individual attempts to break the news to their families during the Thanksgiving break. Lucy's family reacts with stunned surprise when she makes her announcement during the holiday meal; within five minutes only Berta is left at the table. While Lucy remains locked in her room, rejecting everyone's appeals to come out, her grandmother stays put: refusing to allow the occasion to be ruined as it so often had been in the past, "She alone ate right through to the mince pie" (*WSWG,* 145). Meanwhile Roy has his own problems, first with his family and then with Lucy, when he hesitates to reveal the couple's plans and tentatively agrees to think over his parents' suggestion that they wait until June.

Waiting until June is, of course, not possible. Another deadly farce develops in Roy's room in Fort Kean when his landlady enters during his argument with Lucy about what to do and how to do it. Since Lucy is not supposed to be there, Roy introduces her as his fiancée and announces that they will be married at Christmas. Her doubts assuaged, at least for the moment, and the landlady mollified, if just barely, Lucy leaves as she came in, by the window. But in the succeeding days she has second thoughts, realizes that she does not really want to marry Roy, and decides to go home and tell her family exactly what the situation is. More deadly farce ensues. When Lucy's mother tells Berta that her daughter is home because of the grippe, Lucy gets a hot mustard plaster applied to her chest. Lying in bed, she finds both her mother and her father unexpectedly understanding. Despite the snide remarks with which she punctuates his discourse, her father proposes first one alternative and then another. Apparently he knows where and how an abortion can be obtained. But this solution explodes in his face when he reveals that Myra also underwent an abortion after Lucy was born and they felt they could not afford another child. Again, Lucy's moral outrage ruins whatever help her parents might have given her.

Roy and Lucy get married at Christmas, after Roy, in a weak moment, reveals to his parents why the couple must get married soon. On one of many weekend visits to Liberty Center during the following months, Lucy learns that her father has blackened her mother's eye during a quarrel. When Lucy sees her mother to confirm the fact, Whitey lucklessly chooses that moment to return from a penitential absence of several days, but Lucy bars him from the house. He disappears—for good, it appears—and several days later Lucy's son is born.

Roy decides to quit school, which he regards (with some justice) as a waste of time, and find work. After several months of fruitless searching, he lands a job as a photographer's assistant in Fort Kean but is soon dissatisfied with the work, as well as with Lucy's frequent criticisms and complaints. At one point he suggests a trial separation; Lucy, however, will not hear of it. Though she does not love him and never has, she expects Roy to remain as her husband and do his duty by his family, as a man should. And so he does, however grudgingly, trying his best to make the most of everything, putting aside his hopes for a photography studio of his own and slaving away for Wendell Hopkins, his boss.

At one point after staying away from home for two days following an argument, Roy returns and proclaims he is a new man. Although his behavior does indeed change, Lucy remains skeptical, regarding most of the change as merely pretense, its persistence notwithstanding. Meanwhile, during her father's long disappearance Lucy's mother has begun seeing other men, one in particular: Blanshard Muller, a solid citizen who has a good business and who has recently become a widower. When Muller eventually asks Myra to marry him, the prospect of her mother's marital happiness has an odd effect on Lucy, who discovers to her surprise that she does not really care whether her mother marries Muller or not: "And yet it was what she had prayed for all her life—that a man stern, serious, strong and prudent would be the husband of her mother, and the father to herself" (*WSWG,* 225). On the drive home after a visit to Liberty Center, where she and Roy had heard the news of Muller's proposal, Lucy further contemplates everything that has happened: her mother's pending remarriage, her husband's dedication, her child's welfare assured. Yet somehow she feels miserable in a way she previously had not. Though she has won all her battles and everything is turning out the way she wants, she has the illusion that "she was never going to die—she was going to live forever in this new world she had made, and never die, and never have the chance not just to be right, but to be happy" (*WSWG,* 226). This is the crux of Lucy's predicament, and Roth's wit conveys the deep irony of her illusion, that she will be condemned to live forever in the world *she had made* and never have the chance "not just to be right, but to be happy."

Lucy's chance for happiness comes a little while later when, persuaded that Roy has truly changed, that he has become a mature individual, she lies in bed with him on Valentine's Day night. Roy talks about the possibility of having another child, the little girl he has always wanted. He has even thought of a name, Linda Sue. Overcoming her habitual skepticism, Lucy brings herself to accept Roy's sincerity. She stops using her contraceptive device and begins to imagine a happier life for herself and her family. The image of an endlessly unhappy life disappears, she sings songs with her little son, and she finds herself happier than she has ever been: "The sensation she began to have was that the awful past had finally fallen away, and that she was living suddenly in her own future" (*WSWG,* 233).

The sensation does not last long. The past returns in the form of a letter from her father, one of a long series going back to his disappearance from Liberty Center. Myra, it seems, has kept in touch with Whitey over the years, using a private post office box to receive mail from him. Feeling she has to confide in him about her plans, Myra has written him that she has decided on a divorce so that she can marry Blanshard Muller. The news has a disastrous effect on Whitey, who has been living and working in Florida, where he has done pretty well, almost getting married again himself. But Myra's letter causes him to act foolishly, and he winds up in jail, this time for theft, with a sentence of 18 months.

Lucy learns all this on another trip to Liberty Center when, filled with her feelings of a new life about to begin, she enters her grandfather's house just as Muller is leaving. Myra has told him she cannot marry him after all. Everyone is upset, and Lucy becomes incensed when she hears why. She instantly reverts to character and tells everyone off, including her husband after they return home. It is a fatal mistake. Her actions so thoroughly frighten and antagonize her husband and her son that they abandon her during the night. Lucy follows them by bus to Liberty Center, causes a furor, and, when the police are called, runs off. Her frozen body is discovered the next day in the snow that covers Passion Paradise.

The scenes in Liberty Center as Lucy confronts first her husband and his relatives and then hers transcend deadly farce. For Lucy in her mental agony has become insane, and unlike Gabe Wallach's temporary insanity among the Bigonesses in *Letting Go,* her madness or the situation that precipitates and later surrounds it is not at all funny. Whatever humor is in these scenes is more than submerged; it is drowned. Roth's prose conveys the driving power of Lucy's paranoia and her mad determination to see justice done—justice as she conceives it. What has driven Lucy to this state is her mother's accusation during Lucy's confrontation with her earlier about the reason for declining Blanshard Muller's proposal. Juxtaposed against Lucy's new and hard-won hopes for happiness, Myra's shriek—that Lucy's father was now where Lucy "always wanted him to be" (*WSWG,* 259)—shatters her daughter's precarious mental balance. It propels Lucy first into shocked recognition, then into denial, and finally into the reversal of everything she had begun to hope for and depend on. Significantly, Myra's accusation provides the peripety of the drama, followed by Lucy's recognition—a recognition Lucy instantly rejects, diminishing her potential as a tragic figure and maintaining her as a grimly comic one.

The relationship between Lucy and her great-aunt Ginnie, who appears briefly at the beginning of the novel, may help clarify an essential point Roth makes. Having suffered severe brain damage during an early illness, Willard's sister cannot understand "the most basic fact of human life, the fact that I am me and you are you" (*WSWG,* 11). In a sense this is Lucy's difficulty too. She cannot adequately distinguish between identities—essential for all normal human relationships—but instead insists, however narcissistically, that others follow in the image she has created for them.[4] Roth thus extends and develops a major theme in *Letting Go.* Lucy's illusion of a life endlessly miserable is directly related to a will-to-good that becomes confounded in an overriding will-to-power.[5] Her transient dream of happiness is shattered when she must face the justice of her mother's accusation, and the will-to-power resumes control of her life. But the time comes when Lucy is finally powerless against the combined wills of those whom she would control and who see in her will all the naked fury of which it is capable.

# Chapter Five

# The Comedy of Excess:

## Portnoy's Complaint

With *Portnoy's Complaint* Philip Roth came into his own.[1] As a humorist, novelist, and wordsmith, he demonstrated beyond any doubt that he was a force to be reckoned with in contemporary fiction. Sheldon Grebstein and others[2] have analyzed several kinds of comedy, wit and humor that abound in this, Roth's third full-length novel, but the categories are far from exhausted. Despite Irving Howe's disclaimer,[3] the book rewards rereading, just as a good routine by a stand-up comic (one of the models for Roth's stream-of-humor novel) gets funnier on rehearing—a fact that explains why our best comedians also make records.

Humor depends upon conflict and surprise, and *Portnoy's Complaint* is full of both. Its very form is a tour de force: Roth takes the analysand's monologue as the basic structural principle for the novel—Alexander Portnoy, Assistant Commissioner for Human Opportunity in New York City, is Dr. Spielvogel's patient, hoping to find a cure for what ails him. What ails him is—everything. He feels that from his earliest years he has been a victim of the conflict generated in him between the desire to be and do good and the strong tendency to indulge himself in pleasure, particularly forbidden pleasure. How to resolve the conflict becomes his chief concern. But first he must try to understand the nature of the conflict: its genesis and its consequences. Therein lies much of the surprise and the humor, although to Alexander Portnoy his predicament is not very funny, not funny at all. As he cries out to his analyst, "Doctor Spielvogel, this is my life, my only life, and I'm living it in the middle of a Jewish joke! I am the son in the Jewish joke—*only it ain't no joke!*" (*PC,* 36–37).

The tone of Portnoy's anguished cry, which accelerates as his plea continues, suggests the way in which excess is a dominant theme in the novel and controls much of its form. Roth here takes everything to extremes—deliberately. If he overdoes obscenity, as many readers have complained, he does so, he says, "to raise obscenity to the level of a subject" (*RMAO,* 19). But he also does it to realize its comic potential: outrageousness can be and often is funny. It shocks us out of our ordinary complacency or easy acquiescence in accepted norms of behavior, and the surprise can be salutary. That may be why Kafka found Joseph K.'s predicament in the opening chapters of *The Trial* funny: thoroughly conditioned by customary forms of behavior and himself utterly committed to the ordinary, Joseph does not know what to make of the unusual events that beset him one morning. In *Portnoy's Complaint* (written while Roth was teaching Kafka at the University of Pennsylvania and also writing *When She Was Good*)[4] Roth submits both his hero and his reader to a series of outrageous situations that not only baffle and perplex but in their very outrageousness strike the reader, if not the victim, as funny. Compounding the comedy is that Portnoy, the victim, recognizes the comic aspects in the situation, even as he struggles to free himself from them.

Unlike *When She Was Good* or the later chapters of *The Trial, Portnoy's Complaint* does not deal with life-and-death problems; however serious and threatening they may appear to Alexander Portnoy, his problems cannot be equated with Lucy Nelson's or Joseph K.'s. The man in top hat and tails slips on a banana peel and feels genuine pain, but to us onlookers the scene is funny, not painful. Only on reflection do we realize the pain involved and begin to sympathize, as we do after reading and reflecting on *Portnoy's Complaint.* Meanwhile the accumulating episodes of outrage and excess evoke laughter as their initial response, even as their narrator, who is also their major subject, comes closer and closer to real despair. Moral imperatives, such as those found in *Letting Go* or *When She Was Good,* are not abandoned in this novel; on the contrary, they become if anything even more pronounced. But they conflict with Portnoy's equally fierce determination to indulge in hedonistic delights. The collisions between the pleasure principle and the reality principle (to adopt appropriate Freudian terminology) are richly comic, with depths that reward investigation.

Essentially a *Bildungsroman,*[5] *Portnoy's Complaint* begins at the beginning, with Portnoy as a little boy. But unlike, say, Joyce in *A Portrait of the Artist as a Young Man,* Roth departs from a conventional lineal development and interweaves incidents from various points in his subject's life. Partly this development is dictated by the novel's basic structure, the analysand's monologue, but it is also the result of Roth's desire to juxtapose events in a particularly significant way, as we shall see.[6] At the outset Portnoy presents us with the dominant fact of his young life: "She was so deeply imbedded in my consciousness that for the first year of school I seem to have believed that each of my teachers was my mother in disguise" (*PC, 3*). He goes on to describe rushing home from school to see if he could catch his mother before she had managed to transform herself. He never does catch her, of course, but he says his failures only intensified his respect for her powers. The point of this childish fantasy—and its many permutations—lies at the heart of Portnoy's problems, as the definition of "Portnoy's Complaint" (the epigraph to the novel) indicates: "It is believed by Spielvogel that many of the symptoms can be traced to the bonds obtaining in the mother-child relationship."

Sophie Portnoy as the archetypal Jewish mother has been scrutinized and criticized often enough,[7] but she nonetheless remains an important and all-powerful personality throughout the novel, especially in the first half, dealing mainly with Portnoy's early years. If she seems more of a caricature than a character, an aspect of Roth's strategy of excess, much of her description and dialogue still has the ring of authenticity. Her anxieties certainly appear real, and they succeed only too well in transferring themselves, one way or another, to her otherwise-normal, healthy young son, who does his best to resist. In the episode concerning the polio season, her anxieties are reflected in the staccato cadences of her speech and in her relentless questioning: "Open your mouth. Why is your throat red? Do you have a headache you're not telling me about? You're not going to any baseball game, Alex, until I see you move your neck. Is your neck stiff? Then why are you moving it that way? You ate like you were nauseous, are you nauseous?" (*PC, 33*). And so on. The excessiveness of Sophie's anxieties in the exasperating cross-examination of her son is not far removed from the proverbially overprotective tendencies of the stereotypical Jewish mother. When portrayed baldly in this fashion, such women's excessiveness becomes even more pronounced, and sympathetic laughter results.

Not that Portnoy himself laughs much, although he does show some sympathy for his mother and for his terribly frustrated, worried, and overworked father, who suffers from chronic, severe constipation. No, Alex does not laugh much; he is too busy recounting his many complaints and pleading for help. Powerfully afflicted with guilt from every conceivable source—mother, father, sister, lovers—he struggles fruitlessly to alleviate the burden he carries. From the very beginning he seems unable to understand why he should be accused of wrongdoing, for example, when his mother periodically locks him out of their apartment (but not without providing little Alex with galoshes and a lunch to take with him). "What can I possibly have done!" he cries, mystified (*PC,* 14). And why should his mother threaten him with a bread knife when he doesn't want to eat? To add to the mystery: why doesn't his father stop her (*PC,* 16–17)?

For consolation, to seek some relief in physical pleasure, Alex during adolescence resorts to "whacking off"—excessively, of course, like everything else. His candor in recounting his experiences is surpassed only by his graphic descriptions. Granted, adolescence is a wild and wildly disturbing stage in growing up, and many boys have experiences not unlike Portnoy's. Not unlike—but not quite like either:

> I actually begin to set new records for myself. Before meals. After meals. *During* meals. Jumping up from the dinner table, I tragically clutch at my belly—diarrhea! I cry, I have been stricken with diarrhea!—and once behind the locked bathroom door, slip over my head a pair of underpants that I have stolen from my sister's dresser and carry rolled in a handkerchief in my pocket. So galvanic is the effect of cotton panties against my mouth—so galvanic is the *word* "panties"—that the trajectory of my ejaculation reaches startling new heights: leaving my joint like a rocket it makes right for the light bulb overhead, where to my wonderment and horror, it hits and hangs. . . . I am the Raskolnikov of jerking off. (*PC,* 19–20)

Portnoy's adventures in masturbation are succeeded—and surpassed— by his adventures later in heterosexual lovemaking. They begin, naturally, with his first attempt to have sex. His school friend Smolka arranges for him and Arnold Mandel, another classmate, to visit the notorious Bubbles Girardi, an 18-year-old girl who has been expelled from high school and whose favors Smolka has already enjoyed. When they arrive at her house, she is ironing clothes in the living room in her slip. Already excited, Portnoy and Mandel wait while Smolka talks her into taking on his two friends. At first she demurs; then she agrees, but only to jerking off one of the two boys and only if he keeps his pants on while she does. Portnoy wins the coin toss—and "the right to get the syph!" as he believes (*PC,* 177).

What happens afterward is both hilarious and, in its way, poignant. But before bringing the reader—or, rather, Portnoy—to climax, Roth interweaves a series of narratives having to do with Bubbles Girardi's home life (*PC,* 166); Alex's fantasies on the aftermath of his experience (*PC,* 167, 171); his sister's fiancé, Morty Feibish (*PC,* 169–71); and the early and later lives of his friends Smolka and Mandel (who afterward legally changes his name to Ba-ba-lu *PC*, 172–76). Suspense is just one function of this strategy; Roth also contrasts Portnoy's upbringing with that of his less fortunate friends to show the surprising outcomes of each: Ba-ba-lu becomes a salesman in his father-in-law's business and leads a bourgeois family life; Smolka becomes a Princeton professor. A sentimental picture of Jesus ascending to heaven tacked up in Bubbles's kitchen sets off a tirade against organized religion and an apostrophe to socialism—and Morty Feibush. Portnoy's fantasies reveal the fear underlying his adventuresomeness. He imagines he has contracted syphilis and his penis falls off with a "clink" right in front of his mother, whose screams bring his father rushing out of the bathroom with his pants around his knees and the *Newark News* clutched in his hand (*PC*, 167).

Portnoy does not contract syphilis from Bubbles, only a terrific case of chagrin. Having waited anxiously for the momentous occasion of having sex with an actual girl, he discovers—as he will later in Israel—that he cannot get an erection, that indeed he cannot even *find* his shriveled penis. When he finally succeeds in both, he is so long in ejaculating that Bubbles gives him up and he has to complete the job himself—whereupon his sperm jets directly into his eye. Believing he is permanently blinded, he indulges in yet another fantasy, complete with histrionics suited to his hysteria. He imagines he enters his parents' home with a cane and a Seeing Eye dog that infuriates his mother: "A *dog*? In my house? Get him out of here before he makes everything filthy!" When at last she realizes what's happening, she cries out to her husband, "Jack, Alex is home with a dog—he's gone blind!" "Him, blind? . . . How could he be blind, he doesn't even know what it means to turn off a light." "How?" his mother screams. "*How? Tell us how such a thing—*" "Mother, how? How else? Consorting with Christian girls" (*PC*, 181–82).

"Consorting with Christian girls" is another dominant theme in the book. From adolescence on Alexander Portnoy finds the attraction of gentile women irresistible, if not almost fatal. As a boy he dreams of The-real McCoy as either a burlesque queen (*PC*, 131) or a lithe young blond skating with her friends on the frozen pond he also frequents (*PC*, 144–51). He rehearses introducing himself to the girl on the pond, inventing obviously gentile names for himself but troubled by an ineradicable feature of his face—his nose—which he is sure will give him away. So preoccupied is he with his diction, his alias, and his excuse for his big nose ("old hockey injury? Fell off my horse while playing polo one Sunday morning after church—too many sausages for breakfast, ha ha ha!") that he misjudges his approach to the shoreline where the girl is sitting and he goes hurtling, chipping a front tooth and fracturing his knee (*PC,* 164). Again, this is not a fatal accident, but it is sufficient to justify his comment "With a life like mine, Doctor, who needs dreams?" (*PC,* 165).

Those are the beginnings. Greater adventures follow, for to Portnoy, whatever it meant to his forebears—gold in the streets or a chicken in every pot—America is "a *shikse* nestling under your arm whispering love love love love love!" (*PC,* 146). After all, as a child his earliest movie memories are of Ann Rutherford and Alice Faye, not Barbra Streisand or Carol Kane. Whatever he thinks of gentile America as a whole—and the usual Christmas displays fill him with revulsion (*PC,* 144)—*shikses* are something else. They are enough to make him think fondly of stereotyped families in which sons go to places like UCLA or Northwestern; fathers have white hair, possess deep voices, and never use double negatives; and mothers say things like "I do believe, Mary, that we sold thirty-five cakes at the Bake Sale" (*PC,* 145).

But Portnoy's Jewish heritage is not as easy to slough off as he thinks. He discovers this fact, much to his surprise, at college, after a prolonged affair with Kay Campbell, "The Pumpkin," a girl whose interests, intellectual and otherwise, seem so thoroughly to coincide with his own. As they dream of a cozy married life together, Kay coolly rejects the absurdity, as she views it, of her conversion to Judaism, which Alex suggests partly in jest. Her reaction is enough to dampen his ardor, and he soon ends the relationship, much to Kay's distress. On the other hand, his introduction to her family back in Iowa indicates early in the relationship the profound differences—not only in upbringing—between them, when he is invited to spend his first Thanksgiving away from home with her and her parents. Astonished by the family's civility, he has trouble recognizing himself as "something called 'a weekend guest'" instead of *bonditt* (outlaw) or *vantz* (bedbug). For the first 24 hours in Iowa he says "Thank you" to whatever anyone says to him, even to inanimate objects like chairs or dinner napkins. "Would my mother be proud of her little gentleman!" he muses. "Polite even to the furniture!" (*PC,* 220).

Being at ease in America among the *goyim* is a desideratum of Portnoy's life that he finds all but impossible to experience, try though he does. His revenge—revenge also against the anti-Semites in his father's insurance firm who keep him from rising to a higher managerial level in the company—is to screw as many of their daughters as possible. Comic as they are, Alex's escapades thus reveal a dark underside.

Another case in point is Portnoy's affair with the super-WASP Sarah

Abbott Maulsby, appropriately dubbed "The Pilgrim" because of her New England origins and rearing. The epitome of everything Portnoy seems to want in a woman—beautiful, adoring, refined, and gentile—he nevertheless rejects her, and not only or mainly because of her aversion to fellatio.[8] She is just another means, he sees, of the way he can discover "America"—or, rather, conquer it: "As though my manifest destiny is to seduce a girl from each of the forty-eight states" (*PC*, 235; as a child of the 1940s, having no scores to settle with Eskimos or Orientals, he excludes Alaska and Hawaii). He knows all the words to the songs of the various armed services—"The Marine Hymn," "The Caissons Go Rolling Along," even the songs of the U.S. *Navy* Air Corps and the Seabees. Trying to be thoroughly Americanized, he flaunts a superficial patriotism, demanding as a reward *his* GI bill, "real American ass! The cunt in country-'tis-of-thee!" (*PC*, 236). That is part of his driving force; that is why, finally, he cannot marry Sarah, for despite her many sterling qualities—her charm, devotion, beauty, and place in American history—he could never feel true "love" for her. He is too intolerant of her frailties, jealous of her accomplishments, and resentful of her family. "No, not much room there for love," he concludes (*PC*, 240).

No, not much room there—or anywhere, it seems—for love. Portnoy is, by his own admission, too restless, too horny, too "cunt-crazy" to find a place in his heart for love (*PC*, 102). His predicament is agonizing, and the only comfort he finds is that in his early thirties he is not (like Paul Herz) "locked into a marriage with some nice person whose body has ceased to be of any genuine interest to me," someone whom he has to get into bed with every night and "fuck out of obligation instead of lust" (*PC*, 102). His desires are boundless, and boundlessly tormenting: "What a mysterious business it is!" he says to Dr. Spielvogel. "The endless fascination of these apertures and openings! You see, I just can't stop! Or tie myself to any *one*. . . . How can I give up what I have never even had, for a girl, who delicious and provocative as once she may have been, will inevitably grow as familiar to me as a loaf of bread? For love? What is love?" (*PC*, 103–4).

Clearly Portnoy does not know what love is; mesmerized by sex, he has not the merest conception of love, which he calls weakness, convenience, apathy, guilt, and so forth (*PC*, 105). And yet sex does not entirely satisfy him either. Having found in Mary Jane Reed—whom he picks up one evening in New York—an extremely attractive and sexually adroit young woman who performs feats he had previously only dreamed of, he finally

abandons her in a hotel room in Athens, shortly after engaging with her
in what he considers the ultimate sexual degradation. For more than a
year she had pleasured him in every possible way, culminating in sex *à
trois* with a prostitute in Rome. If anyone were capable of satisfying Portnoy's cravings, surely it would seem to be "The Monkey," as Mary Jane
is nicknamed, owing to some earlier perversion before she met him and
went on "to grander things" (*PC,* 106).

Though he vehemently denies it, Mary Jane claims it is love that drove
her to do the things Portnoy demanded, however degrading. And it is
love that drives him away, as it drove Gabe Wallach away from Martha
Reganhart. Briefly, however, during an idyllic weekend in Vermont
when Portnoy and Mary Jane play at being married, it seems as if she
could almost fulfill all his needs *and* be his wife. But Portnoy is too
slippery, and love and marriage terrify him. The Monkey's hillbilly background (she was born and raised among coal miners in West Virginia) is
a constant source of embarrassment, even as her physical attractions are a
constant source of delight. Portnoy tries in vain to educate her, corrects
her language, and gives her books to read—for example, *U.S.A., The
Grapes of Wrath, An American Tragedy,* and *Notes of a Native Son.* His
purpose, he says, is to save her, to teach her compassion, "to bleed a little
for the world's sorrows." They will then be "The perfect couple: she puts
the id back in Yid, I put the *oy* back in *goy*" (*PC,* 209).

It doesn't work; they are not the perfect couple. The Monkey is willing
enough, in every way (unlike The Pumpkin, she would probably gladly
convert, though the question never arises). She recognizes in Portnoy a
"breakthrough" in her relationships with people; her love is genuine,
deep, and unfortunately excessive. As she says on the way to a dinner at
Gracie Mansion with Portnoy, after a terrible quarrel, "I love you, Alex!
I worship and adore you! So please don't put me down, please! Because I
couldn't take it! Because you're the very best man, woman, or child I've
ever known! In the whole animal kingdom! Oh, Breakie, you have such
a big brain and a big cock and I love you!" (*PC,* 212). She then proceeds
to demonstrate the depth of her love by performing fellatio there, "no
more than two hundred feet from *The Lindsays'* mansion," despite Portnoy's frantic outcries about plainsclothesmen and cops everywhere in the
vicinity.

Genuinely, deeply, and extremely in love, Mary Jane at 29, nearly 30,
wants desperately to get married. That, of course, is enough finally to
scare Portnoy off. Note that it is in the context of his parents' wish for
him to settle down with a wife and provide them with grandchildren that

The Monkey is first introduced. However unstructured and rambling the monologue appears, the juxtaposition is significant and the humor submerged. (Roth wisely resists writing a full-length scene of Portnoy introducing The Monkey to his parents, let alone one broaching to them the idea of marrying her.) As preposterous as the idea may seem (*PC,* 201), the long affair with Mary Jane is as close as Alex ever gets to marriage. But this son, accomplished as he is, is not "perfect": he will not give his parents what they need to fulfill the dreams of their later years.

It is not only their dream. As a boy Alex himself dreamed of a typical middle-class, Jewish-American home life, complete with wife and kids and Sunday-morning softball games. And at night "three solid hours of the best radio entertainment in the world": Jack Benny and Fred Allen and Mrs. Nussbaum and Phil Harris and on to Kenny Baker. And then to bed, fast locked in the arms of "Mrs. A. Portnoy, that kind and gentle (and in my sugary but modest fantasy, faceless) woman" (*PC,* 246–47). What, then, happened to that dream? What killed it, leaving Portnoy complaining to his analyst about his loneliness and isolation? His own explanation is that the desire of others—Mary Jane, his parents—that he be or become a saint is too much for him to bear. Yet he rejects any feeling of responsibility: "No, any guilt on my part is *comical*! I will not *hear* of it!" (*PC,* 249).

What, then, is he doing on a psychiatrist's couch? What has his long, anguished monologue been about if not guilt—heavy, persistent, crushing guilt? Guilt that has left him, at last, impotent in the land of his fathers, Israel. Guilt that is, like everything else in his experience, excessive in the extreme. But though he rejects the imputation of guilt as "comical," Portnoy recognizes its potential—no, its actuality. He had thought his suffering, like others', would be different: "[I]s *this* human misery? I thought it was going to be loftier! *Dignified* suffering! *Meaningful* suffering—something perhaps along the line of Abraham Lincoln. Tragedy, not farce! Something a little more Sophoclean was what I had in mind" (*PC,* 251).

Portnoy seems unaware of the close affinities between tragedy and farce, or the ways one can merge into the other.[9] "It surely never crossed my mind," Portnoy says to Dr. Spielvogel, "that I would wind up trying to free from bondage nothing more than my own prick. LET MY PETER GO! There, that's Portnoy's slogan. That's the story of my life, all summed up in four heroic dirty words. A travesty! My politics, descended entirely to my putz!" (*PC,* 251). He is wrong, for the story of his life is more, much more than that, although his sexual escapades tend to overwhelm other aspects of his existence and to command the limelight along with the humor. Though he claims he wants to liberate his libido, to "put the id back in Yid" (PC, 124), his anxieties run deeper, and his predicament is more severe, as he discovers with a new twist of ironic comedy in Israel.

There Portnoy has two encounters with Israeli women—one with an army lieutenant, the other with a kibbutznik—and both end in disaster, at least as he conceives disaster. Unable to have or maintain an erection, Portnoy believes he is being punished for his desertion of Mary Jane Reed in Athens, who has threatened to commit suicide if he doesn't marry her. But that is only part of the cause. In Israel he rediscovers his Jewish identity, which comes smashing home to him. He also discovers a different kind of woman: Naomi is strong both in her convictions and in her ability to present them. A six-footer, she is also physically powerful, as Portnoy finds out. It is she who shows Alex what he truly is: a sick, pitifully poor excuse for a human being. She attacks him at his most vulnerable point: not his masculinity as such but his stature, or lack of it, as a person. She also severely criticizes his self-deprecating humor used to disguise his immaturity and unhappiness. She recognizes that he seems to take some special pleasure, or pride, in making himself the butt of his own jokes. "I don't believe you actually want to improve your life," she concludes. "Everything you say is somehow always twisted, some way or another, to come out 'funny.' All day long the same thing. In some little way or other, everything is ironical, or self-depreciating" (PC, 264).

Naomi hits home, as no one yet has ever done. Moreover, she recognizes the wastefulness: a "highly intelligent man," Portnoy could make a real contribution, instead of dissipating his abilities as he has done. Shaming him thus, she leaves him, kicking him hard just below the heart ("The blow I had been angling for?") in response to his last groveling plea: "at least let me eat your pussy. I know I can still do that" (PC, 270).

## Bruno Bettelheim's "Discovery"

In "Portnoy Psychoanalyzed" Bruno Bettelheim makes several cogent observations about Portnoy's condition.[10] Subtitled "Therapy Notes Found in the Files of Dr. O. Spielvogel, a New York Psychoanalyst," the essay appears as a kind of spoof, but it scores several very palpable hits. For example, after the first "hour" (for Bettelheim, each chapter, or section, of the novel is equivalent to an analytical session) Spielvogel notes that Portnoy "simply cannot relate to other persons" (Bettelheim, 3). In his affliction, or illness, Portnoy "exploits everyone because he loves no one" (Bettelheim, 5). The reason he loves no one is directly related to his abject fear of life. It is this fear, not her supposed strength, that Portnoy identifies with in his mother, as Spielvogel remarks after the fourth hour (Bettelheim, 6). Moreover, Portnoy's "promiscuity is one big effort to keep from his parents what they so much want [a grandchild], while making certain he is punished for it by getting nothing that is meaningful to him. . . . he does not see that his promiscuity, particularly with gentiles, is one big reassurance that he is not having incestuous relations with his mother. By keeping his women ever-changing and meaningless to him, he remains faithful to his mother—not because she won't let him go but because he won't let go of her" (Bettelheim, 6–7).

Portnoy's fixation on his mother is not oedipal, or genital, Spielvogel concludes, but oral, "his wish to remain the suckling infant forever" (Bettelheim, 9). Although Portnoy recognizes in Naomi many physical features that resemble his mother's, especially his mother as a young woman, he is mistaken in thinking that fear of incest causes his impotence. In Spielvogel/Bettelheim's analysis the cause is different, and Portnoy's failure earlier with the lieutenant tends to confirm the point. No longer a Jew in a gentile world, Alex in Israel loses the pattern of demanding and receiving without ever giving. Without his customary excuses, "he is nothing—[he] cannot even manage an erection" (Bettelheim, 9).

Naomi's rejection forces Portnoy at last to confront the truth about himself and his sickness: that his insistent demands—that whatever he wants he must be given immediately—are not valid. Naomi's rejection, even more than his impotence, drives him to seek help at last. And Portnoy's growing insight gives Spielvogel hope—despite much initial skepticism—that psychoanalysis may help his patient after all. Hence, the "Punch Line" that ends the novel: "So. . . . Now vee may perhaps to begin. Yes?" (*PC,* 274).[11]

## Roth's Linguistic Virtuosity

Portnoy's oral fixation is demonstrated above all in the form of the novel—his endless talk—and in the evident delight he takes in words. His is more than the intellectual's playfulness with language, which Sheldon Grebstein relates to the stand-up comic's *spritz,* the "spray" or "outpouring" of words that gains momentum and energy as it goes along and leads to total freedom from inhibition (Grebstein, 154). Hence, the abundance of coarse language in the novel. But Roth's witty and humorous use of language in *Portnoy's Complaint* transcends his stated desire to raise obscenity to the level of a subject. That may be a by-product, but it is hardly the main function of his work.

The various kinds of linguistic virtuosity Roth exhibits here extend well beyond those Grebstein has documented. As Patricia Meyer Spacks has said, the book's comedy is, despite its subject matter, "the high comedy of style. It often derives from the same contrast between innocence and experience which shapes the action, a contrast exemplified in incongruities between language and subject" (Spacks, 628). Spacks analyzes as an example Portnoy's first encounter with The Monkey (*PC,* 158), noting how the comedy derives from tonal manipulation, "the close blending of a wonder amounting almost to awe with the deflating self-awareness which recognizes the ludicrousness of the situation" (Spacks, 628). Other examples might be cited, such as Portnoy's account of his mother's attempt to make him urinate (*PC,* 133) and (in a darker mode) his story of Ronald Nimkin and his mother (*PC,* 96–99, 120). Roth fully and frequently exploits the discrepancies between language and subject, as he does those between expectation and consequence.

One of the most effective devices in the latter regard is Roth's use of metaphor, the primary linguistic means of yoking apparently unlike subjects to offer a surprising new collocation. In *Portnoy's Complaint* these yokings are almost invariably funny in themselves but gain further from the cadences, tone, and contexts in which they are couched. For example, in speaking of his parents Portnoy expresses his outrage in terms that derive directly from his mother's kitchen: "Doctor, these people are incredible! These people are unbelievable! These two are the outstanding producers and packagers of guilt in our time! They render it from me like fat from a chicken!" (*PC,* 36).[12] Another example gains not only from extending the metaphor in graphic detail but also from employing unexpected and excessive repetition at the end:

Sometime during my ninth year one of my testicles apparently decided it had had enough of life down in the scrotum and began to make its way north. At the beginning I could feel it bobbing uncertainly just at the rim of the pelvis—and then, as though its moment of indecision had passed, entering the cavity of my body, like a survivor being dragged up out of the sea and over the hull of a lifeboat. And there it nestled, secure at last behind the fortress of my bones,

leaving its foolhardy mate to chance it alone in that boy's world of football cleats and picket fences, sticks and stones and pocketknives, all those dangers about which I was warned and warned and warned. And warned again. And again.
And again. (*PC,* 37–38)

The nautical metaphor reappears later on as a conceit (self-pitying Jewish sons are "on the biggest troop ship afloat . . . rolling through heavy seas of guilt," and so on; *PC,* 118–19). Although varied to avoid monotony, repetitions abound throughout the novel, because in Portnoy's family "nothing is ever said once—nothing!" ("my mother would tell me—and tell me—*and tell me*"; *PC,* 99). Conscious that he may be guilty of exaggeration—"Do I exaggerate? Am I doing myself in only as a clever way of showing off? Or boasting perhaps?" (*PC,* 102)—Portnoy nevertheless indulges himself, deriving the maximum humor by judiciously spacing his most outrageous examples, as in the wildly distorted account of another mother's successful son—Alex's friend Seymour, a doctor. The tale is related, of course, by Sophie Portnoy to *her* son. In Sophie's account Seymour is "the biggest brain surgeon in the entire Western Hemisphere. He owns six different split-level ranch-type houses made all of fieldstone in Livingston, and belongs to the boards of eleven synagogues, all brand-new and designed by Marc Kugel. . . ." But that is only the beginning. Taking his family on a tour all over Europe—all 7,000 countries, "some of them you never even heard of, that they made them just to honor Seymour"—the doctor performs impossible brain surgeries in every single city "in hospitals that they also built for him right on the spot," where they pumped into the operating room the theme song from *Exodus,* "so everybody should know what religion he is." That's how important Alex's friend Seymour is today! *"And how happy he makes his parents!"* (*PC,* 99–100).

This out-Falstaffs Falstaff. Although the rhetoric resembles the fat knight's story of the robbery at Gad's Hill, which heaps exaggeration on exaggeration as it gathers momentum,[13] the purpose here differs. The last sentence, only seemingly gratuitous in its emphasis, conveys the aim. Sophie is, after all, a Jewish mother, as the local references in her account of Seymour's astonishing success abundantly indicate. But her conclusion comes in the form of a stunning and humorous non sequitur, just as Portnoy/Roth intends.

Linguistic exaggeration, a prevalent form of excess in the novel, also appears orthographically in Portnoy's penchant for what Grebstein calls

one of his "high-volume, high-speed techniques" of interjecting imagined
newspaper headlines to announce some imagined catastrophe or other
(Grebstein, 165). Among the examples Grebstein cites are these:

ASST HUMAN OPP'Y COMMISH FOUND HEADLESS IN GO-GO
GIRL'S APT! (*PC*, 161)

ASST HUMAN OPP'Y COMMISH FLOGS DUMMY, Also lives in Sin, Reports Old School Chum. (*PC*, 175)

JEW SMOTHERS DEB WITH COCK, Vassar Grad Georgetown Strangula-
tion Victim; Mocky Lawyer Held (*PC*, 240)

But this tabloid rendition, like Portnoy's penchant also for slogans ("LET
MY PETER GO!"), is just one form of linguistic exaggeration; uppercase
letters, like italics, appear throughout the novel to indicate raised voices,
heavy emphasis, high volume, or all of these, as in Mrs. Portnoy's warning to her son when he leaves for college (*PC*, 188–89).

## Melodrama and Fantasy

By this time Portnoy's histrionic flair is patent, and he comes by it
honestly: the Portnoy household in which he grew up indulged in melodrama the way overeaters indulge in ice cream. The exaggeration of a
legitimate dramatic form, melodrama is another type of excess in the
novel, and episodes are sometimes piled one on the other. Early in his
monologue, for example, Portnoy dramatizes his mother's warnings
against eating french fries (*PC*, 32–33) and follows up immediately with
her behavior during polio season (*PC*, 33). His father's "tumor test" (*PC*,
25–26) is a frequent occasion for melodrama, and 14-year-old Portnoy's
revolt against the High Holidays (*PC*, 60–64) is typical of the emotional
tensions aroused in the family almost daily ("There is no good reason for
me to be crying, but in this household everybody tries to get a good cry
in at least once a day"; *PC*, 25).

The emotional cataclysms naturally extend beyond the family confines
as Alex grows older, and they are often interwoven with fantasies that are
themselves melodramatic, as Portnoy's encounter with Bubbles Girardi
shows. While still a boy, Portnoy learned that "nothing was ever simply
nothing but always SOMETHING, that the most ordinary kind of occurrence could explode without warning into A TERRIBLE CRISIS, this
was to me *the way life is*" (*PC*, 96). If that was true of ordinary occur-

rences, what about extraordinary ones, such as Portnoy's escapade with
The Monkey and Lina, the Roman whore? After it is over Mary Jane
accuses Portnoy of delivering her into evil. She screams at him with a fury
and poignancy that are surpassed only by her use of graphic detail:

> All you ever talk about and think about is tits! *Other people's tits*! Mine are so
> small and everybody else's in the world you see are so *huge*—so you finally get a
> pair that are *tremendous,* and what do you do? *Nothing*!
> Nothing is an exaggeration, Monkey—the fact of the matter is that I couldn't
> always fight my way *past* you—
> I am not a lesbian! Don't you dare call me a lesbian! Because if I am, *you made
> me one*! (PC, 138).

Spacks says that what is most real about Portnoy, however, are his
fantasies. Incapable of true intimacy, he makes everyone in the book seem
his projection (Spacks, 634).[14] In one sense Spacks is right; in another
sense Roth clearly distinguishes between Portnoy's narrative of actual
events and his vivid fantasy life. Portnoy's vision of being punished in
hell for his abominations is a good example. Imagining the Devil as Rabbi
Warshaw, his fantasy smoothly flows into a detailed account of his bar
mitzvah and out again, though not without a little incidental fantasy
thrown in for good measure, as young Portnoy imagines himself—that
paragon among 13-year-olds—carried adoringly, like the Torah, up and
down the aisles of the congregation (PC, 201–3). What, then, is his
diabolical punishment? To be chained to a toilet in hell, dressed up like
a Las Vegas hood, and condemned to masturbate for eternity. Why, he
asks—"For loving a saucy girl?" Warshaw's reply thunders back at him:
"Loving? *You*? Too-ey on you! *Self*-loving, boychick, that's how I spell it!
With a capital self! Your heart is an empty refrigerator! Your blood flows
in cubes! I'm surprised you don't clink when you walk! . . . What *you*
did with *your* promise! Disgusting! Love? Spelled l-u-s-t! Spelled s-e-l-f"
(PC, 203).

So much for what in Portnoy's fantasy Warshaw calls "poetic justice"
(compare Spielvogel/Bettelheim's analysis). But the novel ends with a
different fantasy of retribution, one reminiscent of *The Trial,* combining,
as Spacks says, both the comedy and the horror of the book (Spacks, 635).
Concluding his account of impotence in Israel with Naomi, Portnoy returns to his feelings of degrading Mary Jane Reed in Rome. He imagines
himself before an unearthly magistrate who accuses him of his crime
bluntly and, naturally, in capital letters. At first meekly and then with
increasing energy, Portnoy tries to defend himself, comparing his alleged

crime with some far worse by others he knows from his experience as an assistant commissioner in New York. Growing more and more indignant, he wonders what would happen if he so much as dared to tear from his mattress the tag that says "Do Not Remove Under Penalty of Law" (PC, 273). The disproportion of the guilt makes him more than want to scream, though it does that too. It also makes him imagine the police coming after him, surrounding him, ordering him to come out with his hands up—and then his defiance, ending in a prolonged and anguished cry.

This is Portnoy's concluding "primal scream," as others have noted. By this time Roth modulates his comedy into something else, certainly something that is no longer quite so funny, no longer quite so ribald. Portnoy at last experiences real pain, just as Nathan Zuckerman does near the end of The Anatomy Lesson, when his fantasies overcome him and hurl him to the bedrock of existence, literally smashing his face on a granite tombstone. Thus, life and death, comedy and tragedy blend into each other, and Portnoy's manifold conflicts at the end of the novel remain unresolved. Roth has much further to go, as his subsequent novels show, before he finds a way to get his heroes off the "larger hook" that Gabe Wallach and, here, Alexander Portnoy find themselves on. In the voyage of comic adventure he and they—as Dr. Spielvogel's punch line indicates—have only just begun.

# Chapter Six

# Roth Agonistes:

## Philip Roth as Critic and Autobiographer

Long before *Portnoy's Complaint* was published, Philip Roth defended himself in public speeches, debates, symposia, and journal articles against the charges of anti-Semitism and self-hate. *Reading Myself and Others* contains versions of these encounters with his critics; so does *The Facts: A Novelist's Autobiography*. Like his fiction, these accounts are filled with a combination of moral earnestness and humor, often hilarious humor. But the humor, like the sharp wit that often accompanies it, does not diminish the seriousness of Roth's purpose. As in the work of other writers, whether in satire or not, comedy serves to heighten seriousness by eschewing solemnity and providing perspective.

## Critical Roth

To begin at the beginning, one opens *Reading Myself and Others* in the middle, where Roth places one of his earliest—and best—essays, "Writing American Fiction." It appeared in *Commentary* in March 1961 but was based on a speech delivered earlier at Stanford University in a symposium sponsored by *Esquire* on "Writing in America Today." For Roth, the subject was fascinating and his dilemma acute: given the real-life events one had to contend with daily in these United States, events that by their very nature strained credulity and seemed utterly fantastic, how could a writer of fiction hope to compete?

The first incident to illustrate his argument, or, rather, to derive his argument from, is the case of the Grimes murders in Chicago in the mid-1950s, when Roth lived there. The sisters, Pattie and Babs, went off one night to see an Elvis Presley movie and never returned. Weeks later their unclothed bodies were discovered in a roadside ditch in a forest west of Chicago. By this time the case had become a media event: one newspaper ran a foot high drawing of the two girls in four colors, "like Dixie Dugan on Sundays" (*RMAO*, 117). Television interviews of high school classmates and others followed. Finally a skid-row bum of 35, Benny Bedwell, confessed to killing the girls after he and a friend had cohabited with them for weeks. Media coverage then intensified: the girls' mother denied they could have slept with the men; two nuns at the girls' school were interviewed; Benny's mother and Mrs. Grimes were brought together for news photographers; "The Benny Bedwell Blues" became a popular song.

It was still not over. Bedwell, out on bail, drove around in a pink Cadillac, held a press conference, and got a job singing in a Chicago nightclub for $2,000 a week. A newspaper ran a contest entitled "How Do You Think the Grimes Girls Were Murdered?" and gave a prize for the best answer. From all over the state, money flowed to Mrs. Grimes, who redecorated her house. Someone gave her a brand-new kitchen, and she bought two parakeets, which she named—predictably—Pattie and Babs. At this point, Roth reports, Bedwell was extradited to Florida, where he was charged with raping a 12-year-old girl.

Though the story was not over even yet, Roth ends there, because at about that time he left Chicago.[1] But he makes his point that an American writer in the middle of the twentieth century "has his hands full trying to understand, describe, and then make *credible* much of American reality. It stupefies, it sickens, it infuriates, and finally it is even a kind of embarrassment to one's meager imagination" (*RMAO*, 120). Who, for example, could have invented Charles Van Doren? Roy Cohn and David Schine? Sherman Adams? Dwight David Eisenhower? he asks.[2]

The next example Roth uses is the television debates between John F. Kennedy and Richard M. Nixon, candidates for president in 1960. After mimicking Nixon's speaking style (which *Our Gang* satirized more fully a decade later), Roth confessed that it was a little easy—too easy—to ridicule him, and that in any case to do so was not his point; rather, his aim was to focus on the astonishment that the spectacle provoked. The television debates produced professional envy in him, he confessed: "All the machinations over make-up and rebuttal time, all the business over whether Mr. Nixon should look at Mr. Kennedy when he replied, or should look away—all of it was so beside the point, so fantastic, so weird and astonishing, that I found myself beginning to wish I had invented it" (*RMAO*, 120–21). But then, he adds, he wishes that *someone* had invented it, and that it was not real and with us.

Roth was not alone in this feeling, though he gave it perhaps the wittiest expression. He quotes from Benjamin DeMott, also writing in *Commentary,* who said there seems to be a kind of "universal descent into unreality. . . . [E]vents and individuals are unreal, and . . . power to alter the course of the age, of my life and your life, is actually vested nowhere" (*RMAO*, 121). Others Roth cites bore similar witness—for example, Edmund Wilson, who said that after reading *Life* magazine on America he felt he did not belong to the country depicted there.

Roth goes on to consider the fiction of some of his contemporaries, such as Norman Mailer, J. D. Salinger, and Bernard Malamud, who in different ways also seem to suffer from the affliction caused by American "reality." For Mailer "our era has provoked such a magnificent disgust that dealing with it in fiction has almost come to seem, for him, beside the point" (*RMAO*, 123). Mailer's life became a substitute for his fiction, or it did then, as *Advertisements for Myself* shows, and he became "an actor in the cultural drama." Confronting the times, what had Salinger to offer? Holden Caulfield, who ends up in a sanitarium, and Seymour Glass, who ends up a suicide. Neither answered Roth's pressing question, which most of his own fiction raises: how are we to live in this world? "The only advice we get from Salinger," Roth says, "is to be charming on the way to the loony bin" (*RMAO*, 126). As for Salinger's other alternative, the way of Zen, this seemed a cop-out more than anything else.

A "spurning of our world," though of a different order, occurred in Malamud's work as well. Roth takes exception to the statement often attributed to Malamud (but out of context) that "All men are Jews." Moreover, the Jews of *The Magic Barrel* and the Jews of *The Assistant*, Roth says, are not the Jews of New York and Chicago. Even Malamud's first novel, *The Natural*, was hardly baseball as it is actually played—in Yankee Stadium or anywhere else. True, some of Malamud's best work, such as *The Fixer*, was still to come, and in any case Roth was explicitly not saying that Malamud had spurned *life* or an examination of its difficulties: "What it is to be human, and to be humane, is his deepest concern. What I do mean to point out is that he does not—or has not yet—found the *contemporary* scene a proper or sufficient backdrop for his tales of heartlessness and heartache, of suffering and regeneration" (*RMAO*, 127–28). Later, of course, Malamud did find in the contemporary American scene (note, for example, *The Tenants* and *Dubin's Lives*) as well in czarist Russia fitting subjects for his fiction.

## Roth On Roth

But what of Roth as a critic of his own work? Here he seems almost immediately to have gone on the defense, necessarily so, since he was vigorously and repeatedly attacked—often, it seems, for the wrong reasons by the wrong people, although on occasion by some very important people, like Irving Howe, whose critical reappraisal of Roth's work infuriated the author as it also wounded him.[3] But before Howe's reappraisal appeared, Roth was busy fending off what seemed to him irrelevant and misguided criticisms from others, many of whom were far removed from literary criticism or from literature altogether.

In "Writing about Jews," based on remarks delivered in 1962–63 in Iowa; in Hartford, Connecticut; and at Yeshiva University, Roth took on the conservative Jewish establishment and its criticism of his work as "dangerous, dishonest, and irresponsible" (*RMAO,* 149). He specifically defended his stories "Epstein" and "Defender of the Faith." For Roth, the fact that Epstein was a Jew was not nearly so important as the fact that he was a man: "I write the story of a man who is adulterous to reveal the condition of such a man. If the adulterous man is a Jew, then I am revealing the condition of an adulterous man who is a Jew" (*RMAO,* 152). For Roth, it was as simple as that. But not for his critics, particularly those who assembled at Yeshiva University to hear him speak, along with Ralph Ellison and Pietro di Donato, on "The Crisis of Conscience in Minority Writers of Fiction." After the three writers delivered their formal statements, the audience zeroed in on Roth and began grilling him mercilessly, until Ellison interceded and the symposium ended—though not Roth's grilling, which continued even afterward, as he describes the occasion (*TF,* 125–30).

Decades later the audience's reaction to Roth and his work may seem extreme, although Roth now considers it a lucky break: "I was branded," he says in *The Facts* (130). But what was his defense that the audience either did not understand or could not accept? In the written version of his talk he argues that fiction is not written "to affirm the principles and beliefs that everybody seems to hold, nor does it seek to guarantee the appropriateness of our feelings" (*RMAO,* 151). Fiction frees us from "the circumscriptions that society places upon feeling"; it allows both the writer and the reader "to respond to experience in ways not always available in day-to-day conduct; or, if they are available, they are not possible, or manageable, or legal, or advisable, or even necessary to the business of living" (*RMAO,* 151). Literature, in short, provides for an "expansion of moral consciousness" that is of considerable value to individuals and to society.

What is so inflammatory about that? Nothing, of course. But that is not what the audience at Yeshiva was listening to or for. Like the rabbis who had written to complain of Roth's stories in *Goodbye, Columbus,* they were antagonized by the Lou Epsteins, the Nathan Marxes, and the Sheldon Grossbarts who populated Roth's fiction. Why was Roth betraying his people in the ways he did? Why did he shame them so—he, who showed so little knowledge of "the tremendous saga of Jewish history" (*RMAO,* 154)? Why did he have to write of Jews committing adultery, of violating personal and religious integrity? For one thing, writers write out of their own backgrounds; for another, they write to explore the depths of human experience and human capability—wherever such explorations may lead. The writer of fiction writes neither sociology nor propaganda, which Roth's nonliterary critics seemed to want him to do—or at least to produce the kind of thing for which Roth elsewhere roundly criticizes Leon Uris with respect to *Exodus.*[4]

As *Portnoy's Complaint* was being published and reviewed, Roth anticipated some of the criticism he was certain he would get, and did get. In an interview in the 23 February 1969 *New York Times Book Review,* on the page following Josh Greenfield's review of the novel, Roth commented on several of the book's more notorious aspects. Regarding his use of obscene language he said that obscenity was and had been "a usable and valuable vocabulary" since James Joyce, Henry Miller, and D. H. Lawrence and that the same was true of sexuality as a subject (*RMAO,* 17). Whereas in *When She Was Good* language of the kind Portnoy used was utterly beside the point, in *Portnoy's Complaint* obscene language was "very nearly the issue itself." Portnoy uses the language he does not because it's the way people talk but because he wants "to be saved." Roth admits that this is an odd, perhaps mad way to seek personal salvation but maintains that "investigation of this passion, and of the combat it precipitates with [Portnoy's] conscience, is what's at the center of the novel" (*RMAO,* 19). Portnoy's anguish arises from a refusal to be bound by taboos, which he experiences as "diminishing and unmanning." "The joke on Portnoy," Roth says, "is that for him breaking the taboo turns out to be as unmanning in the end as honoring it. Some joke" (*RMAO,* 19). Roth fully expected that not only Jews but also gentiles would be offended by his novel, and he was right.

Years later Roth was still talking about his experience in writing *Portnoy's Complaint* and trying to explain what he had done and why. In "Imagining Jews" (1974) he begins: "Alas, it wasn't exactly what I'd had in mind" (*RMAO,* 215). As a student in the 1950s and afterward, Roth believed that literary activity was a form of ethical conduct; by contrast, "the postwar onslaught of a mass electronically amplified culture" seemed diabolical. Insofar as he thought about gaining fame as a writer, he thought it would come to him as it came to Gustave von Aschenbach in Mann's *Death in Venice,* that is, as honor. Never was a writer more disappointed—or, should we say, deluded. With the publication of *Portnoy's Complaint,* Roth's fame spread everywhere, but "for being everything that Aschenbach had suppressed and kept a shameful secret right down to his morally resolute end" (*RMAO,* 216). Far from receiving Honor, with a capital *H,* Roth received stinging derogation. He left immediately for Yaddo, a retreat for writers near Saratoga, New York, as the media took over his life and reinvented it. At one point everyone—even his editor, who called him at Yaddo—was convinced Roth had suffered a nervous breakdown and was institutionalized.

Such are the dangers of writing a confessional novel, or, to be more precise, a novel in the form of a confession: people were convinced that Portnoy was Roth and vice versa. Now it is true that in his later work, especially the Zuckerman trilogy, Roth plays games with autobiography; if we listen to Zuckerman writing to Roth at the end of *The Facts,* he too plays games with autobiography. That, however, was by no means the main cause of the scandal—or the best-seller—that *Portnoy's Complaint* became. Nor was the comic treatment of masturbation, "a dirtier little secret than even Alexander Portnoy had imagined" (*RMAO,* 220). According to Roth, the historical moment was right for this kind of novel, coming "at the end of a decade that had been marked by blasphemous defiance of authority and loss of faith in the public order" (*RMAO,* 221). Whereas such a book might not have been even tolerated a few years earlier, its appeal in 1969 was irresistible to many, though not all, readers. Roth still had the conservative Jewish establishment to contend with.

Whether or not Alexander Portnoy's Jewish identity was the "key element" in making him "a more interesting case than he might otherwise have been at that moment" (*RMAO,* 222) is perhaps debatable. But without question his Jewish identity raised the ire of many Jewish leaders. As Roth puts it in his essay, "[G]oing wild in public is the last thing in the world that a Jew is expected to do. . . . He is not expected to make a spectacle of himself, either by shooting off his mouth or shooting off his semen, and certainly not by shooting off his mouth about shooting off his semen. That pretty much takes the cake. And in fact it did" (*RMAO,* 222).

In many ways publication of Roth's notorious novel was an act of defiance. More important, it was also an act of liberation, not so much from Judaism or Jewish subjects—Roth continued to be interested in both, as his subsequent work shows—as from literary influences that had inhibited his particular genius. As he says in *The Facts*, "[*Portnoy's Complaint*] had rather less to do with 'freeing' me from my Jewishness or from my family . . . than with liberating me from an apprentice's literary models, particularly from the awesome graduate-school authority of Henry James . . . and from the example of Flaubert" (*TF*, 156–57). He had now found his own voice or, rather, recognized it fully (he had already been using it in *Goodbye, Columbus* and in parts of *Letting Go*). *Portnoy's Complaint* could not be repeated, in form or content, as Roth and his critics knew; it was a terminus ad quem for the confessional novel. After detours, or diversions, in *Our Gang* and *The Great American Novel,* Roth resumed his proper subject and voice.[5]

## Roth on Other Writers

Placed as a companion piece to "Portnoy's Fame—and Mine," which is the first part of "Imagining Jews," the essay entitled "Heroes Jewish Writers Imagine" is a critique mainly of Saul Bellow,[6] Bernard Malamud, and Norman Mailer. Valuable as Roth's insights into these writers are, they also illuminate the achievement of *Portnoy's Complaint.* The point he makes is that for Bellow, Malamud, and less obviously Mailer, an important connection exists between (a) the Jew and conscience and (b) the gentile and appetite (*RMAO,* 229). Bellow's second novel, *The Victim,* clearly shows the relationship between the Jewish protagonist and his ethical concerns; *Henderson the Rain King* shows the libidinous greed of its protagonist, whose insistent "I want!" is the voice of "the id—raw, untrammeled, uncompromising, insatiable, and unsocialized desire" (*RMAO,* 227). As for Augie March, he is an "non-Jewish Jew," more closely identified with Chicago and Cook County than with specifically Jewish ethical codes of conduct and conscience (*RMAO,* 225–26). In *Herzog* and *Mr. Sammler's Planet* Bellow returns to the world of the victim, to the Jew, "the man of acutely developed sensibilities and a great sense of personal dignity and inbred virtue, whose sanity in the one book, and whose human sympathies in the other, are continuously tried by the libidinous greed of the willful, the crazed, and the criminal" (*RMAO,* 227).

The tendencies identified in Bellow's work are even more schematically represented in Malamud's, giving his work, Roth says, "the lineaments of moral allegory. For Malamud, generally speaking, the Jew is innocent, passive, virtuous, and this to a degree that he defines himself or is defined by others as a Jew; the Gentile, on the other hand, is characteristically corrupt, violent, and lustful, particularly when he enters a room or a store or a cell with a Jew in it" (*RMAO*, 230–31). The primary illustration of all this is *The Assistant,* but *The Fixer* also illustrates the point, emphasizing as it does even more the physical brutality gentiles inflict on Jews. In *Pictures of Fidelman,* however, Malamud strays off course, or, rather, turns the tables on himself and "take[s] a holiday from his own obsessive mythology: he imagines as a hero a Jewish man living without shame and even with a kind of virile, if shlemielish, forcefulness in a world of Italian gangsters, thieves, pimps, whores, and bohemians" (*RMAO*, 237). But for Roth it does not work; *Fidelman* lacks the kind of "internal narrative tension" and "continuous sequential development" that provide the necessary counterforce to runaway fantasy. After "Last Mohican," the first in the series of stories that comprise the novel, the book "takes on the air of unchecked and somewhat unfocused indulgence" (*RMAO*, 238). If Malamud thought Fidelman's experience with Susskind in that story freed him for what follows, essentially a "libidinous and disordered life" in which "nothing much is at stake or seriously challenged," then he was seriously guilty of what Roth calls "magical thinking" (*RMAO*, 238). Instead of dramatizing the struggles toward release, Malamud inserts a chapter break, and the freedom is henceforward assumed.

Of course, *Pictures of Fidelman* began as discrete stories only later gathered together as a novel, whose title indicates its somewhat disconnected nature. Entering an art gallery, we don't see paintings in a tightly organized narrative structure. Still, Roth has a point. As for Mailer, he seems more interested in vicious acts as they affect the well-being of the violator rather than the violated (*RMAO*, 232), and a Jewish protagonist for novels like *The Deer Park* and *An American Dream* is scarcely conceivable. Although Mailer once contributed a series of Talmudic *responsa* to *Commentary* (a point not noted by Roth), he is rarely identified as a Jewish-American writer in the way that Bellow and Malamud are (a point noted by Roth, who might also have included himself). Nevertheless, the ethical associations Roth perceives in all three writers—and in Jerzy Kosinski, whom he glancingly links with them—are extremely well taken.

That brings Roth back to *Portnoy's Complaint.* His "lusting Jew" is, given the foregoing discussion, an "odd type" to say the least (*RMAO*, 243). Here again Roth defends himself against charges of anti-Semitism and even Nazism, as Marie Syrkin levels them in the pages of Norman Podhoretz's *Commentary.* For Syrkin, the kind of sexual desires Portnoy has "is unimaginable to anyone but a Nazi" (*RMAO*, 245). Imagining Jews by Jews is very much to the point, Roth argues, and has been certainly since the Holocaust, as contemporary American fiction demonstrates. Comparing his book to *The Victim* and *The Assistant,* Roth finds in all three, despite their different approaches, "nightmares of bondage, each informed . . . by a mood of baffled, claustrophobic struggle" (*RMAO,* 245). He concludes that the task for the Jewish novelist is not "to forge in the smithy of his soul the *un*created conscience of his race" (emphasis his) but "to find inspiration in a conscience that has been created and undone a hundred times over in this century alone" (*RMAO,* 246). Out of this "myriad of prototypes," imagining a Jew becomes problematic, even if one can, with conviction, accept the appellation in the first place—also a problematic act. For as serious Jewish-American novelists reveal in their choices of subject and emphasis, "there are passionate ways of living that not even imaginations as unfettered as theirs are able to attribute to a character forthrightly presented as a Jew" (*RMAO,* 246).

Although Roth has spent a good deal of time and energy discussing Jewish-American writing—his own and others'—he is by no means parochial in his interests or obsessed by this subject. Other essays, as well as his editing activities, amply testify to the fact. In "Imagining the Erotic," for example, he collects three essays on writers quite different from himself and makes perceptive as well as witty comments about them. For a 1972 *Esquire* colloquium on "Which Writer under Thirty-Five Has Your Attention and What Has He Done to Get It?" Roth cited Alan Lelchuk and *American Mischief.* Roth called this first novel "a brilliant and original comedy on the subject of the immediate present" (*RMAO,* 195). What he found "fresh and intriguing" about it was "not the concern with obsession, extremism, outlandishness, and injustice," all of which appear in the book, but "the *robust delight* that the contemplation of confusion arouses" in Lelchuk (*RMAO,* 195). Roth describes escapades involving the "erogonist" Dean Bernard Kovell and the terrorist Lenny Pincus, comparing Lelchuk's achievement with Hawthorne's *The Scarlet Letter* and Dostoyevski's *Crime and Punishment.* In context the comparisons do not seem extravagant, and Roth is not blind to Lelchuk's shortcomings, especially in the second half of the book, where "Lelchuk's imagination runs away with him, though not far enough" (*RMAO,* 198). Recognizing his potential as well as his achievement, Roth says that if Lelchuk is already impatient with himself, "exuberantly hacking and tearing away at himself . . . , trying to see what else he can do," he will find out, "though the battlefield be strewn with chunks of his own tough hide" (*RMAO,* 200).

On Milan Kundera, the next novelist he takes up, Roth is similarly witty and perceptive. Here he deals with a much larger corpus, although the essay was written as an introduction to Kundera's collection of stories *Laughable Loves,* published in English translation in 1974. At about this time Roth had begun taking a serious interest in Eastern European writers, many of them unknown to or overlooked by Anglo-American readers. His essay begins with a discussion of *The Joke* (1967), the novel Kundera published as opposition was mounting against the repressive Communist regime that would culminate in the "Prague Spring" and eventually, for Kundera, expulsion from the writers' union and exile from Czechoslovakia.

In analyzing the novel Roth mentions his own visits to that country and the ironic encounters he had there with writers like Miroslav Holub,[7] but his major focus is on Kundera. He contemplates *The Joke* as a piece of "socialist realism," the only approved artistic mode permitted, defined as "writing in praise of the government and the party so that even *they* understand it" (*RMAO,* 205). The government and the party in Czechoslovakia in those days did not understand *The Joke,* a novel that ironically, Roth notes, conforms closely to Stalin's prescription for art: "socialist content in national form." As evidence he adduces the two most esteemed books written by Czechs in this century, Kafka's *The Trial* and Hašek's *The Good Soldier Schweik,* in whose tradition *The Joke* nicely fits. But Stalin was dead by then, and in any event the author of *The Joke* could hardly have appealed to him. Roth concludes that Kundera must instead have received from reality "strong verification for what was, after all, only a literary invention," some consolation, at least, to a writer "so attuned to harsh irony, and so intrigued by the startling consequences that can follow from playing around" (*RMAO,* 205).

Discussion of *The Joke* leads directly into *Laughable Loves,* since Ludvik Jahn's revenge against the political friend who turned his back on him is related to the sexual intrigues that characterize many of the stories in the collection. Roth draws comparisons with Mailer's characters and Yukio Mishima's, whose virility is also often put into the service of rage: Jahn's revenge is to seduce the wife of his erstwhile friend. But unlike Mailer or Mishima, Kundera seems amused by "the uses to which a man will think to put his sexual member, or the uses to which his member will put him," an attitude that wisely leads him away from any kind of "mystical belief or ideological investment in the power of potency or orgasm" (*RMAO,* 206).

After considering Kundera's amusement with "erotic enterprises and lustful strategies" in "The Golden Apple of Eternal Desire," the Dr.

Havel stories, and others, Roth finds a kind of Chekhovian tenderness in "Let the Old Dead Make Room for the Young Dead." It is "Chekhovian" not merely because of its tone or its concern with old selves dying but because "it is so very good" (*RMAO,* 207). Occasionally, simple declarations of value can impress far more than fulsome praise. After reviewing several more stories, Roth says, "What is so often laughable, in the stories of Kundera's Czechoslovakia, is how grimly serious just about everything turns out to be, jokes, games, and pleasure included; what's laughable is how terribly little there is to laugh at with any joy" (*RMAO,* 208). The deadly farce in Roth's early fiction has a similar effect; Kundera was a kindred spirit.

But not Frederica Wagman—the third writer Roth includes in "Imagining the Erotic." Although Roth was partly responsible for getting Wagman's first novel published, *Playing House* (1973) is unlike anything in Roth's fiction. A novel that is a "love song to childhood incest," it is also an exemplum, "a perverse validation of that universal taboo . . . perverse because it says: 'Little girl, thou shalt not know the bliss of being the ravished kid sister—otherwise the longings for the big bad brother will be a torment forevermore'" (*RMAO,* 212). This woman's pain seems worlds apart from the anguish of Alexander Portnoy. But Roth is sensitive to her futile struggle, the sense of the living damned she represents, and the literary worth of the novel that in 1974 was a runner-up (in French translation) to the Prix Medicis Etranger.

## Roth as Autobiographer

Roth has always been generous in giving interviews, and in them he reveals a good deal about his own work and his views of others'. He also says something about his personal life—though, guarding his privacy, not much—and he strongly disavows any kind of "public" life. As a result, the media have had to invent one for him, as he writes in "Imagining Jews." He alludes to Leonard Lyons's repeated references in 1969 to Roth's alleged romance with Barbra Streisand, whom he had never met and whom by the time of that essay had still not met.

In *The Facts* Roth decided to talk about his personal life at length and in detail. He explains this decision in a prefatory "Letter" to his alter ego, Nathan Zuckerman, the character he invented in *My Life as a Man* and developed in *Zuckerman Bound* and *The Counterlife.* He claims that his motives were mainly therapeutic, that they had little to do with trying to prove "that there is a significant gap between the autobiographical

writer that I am thought to be and the autobiographical writer that I am,"
or with proving "that the information that I drew from my life was, in
the fiction, incomplete" (*TF,* 3). No; what he was attempting, he says,
was to overcome the confusion that beset him a few months earlier, when
he could no longer understand where he was or what he was, what he was
doing or why he was doing it. The "old strategies" no longer worked for
him, either for the business of daily life or for "the specialized problems
of writing" (*TF,* 5).

In an effort to "repossess life," to recover from a breakdown—a severe
depression following a prolonged physical ordeal that began in the spring
of 1987—Roth traced back the "multiple origins," or series of moments,
that constituted his personal history. Hence, *The Facts,* his autobiography, his attempt "to transform myself into *myself"* (*TF,* 5), emerged to
render experience as it was, not transformed through the alembic of fiction. He calls it his counterlife; just as in *The Counterlife* Zuckerman and
his brother were both miraculously revived from death, Roth hoped he
could do the same for himself, by providing "the antidote and answer to
all those fictions that culminated in the fiction of you [Zuckerman]" (*TF,*
6). *The Facts,* then, was to be "the structure of a life without the fiction."

Roth realizes that there is something disingenuous in proposing to
present himself "undisguised," without fiction. He knows that calling his
autobiography *The Facts* begs more questions than it answers. He knows
too that "facts" are never as simple as they seem or purport to be—as he
is here purporting them to be: "Memories of the past are not memories
of facts but memories of your imaginings of the facts" (*TF,* 8). He wonders too if his basic motivation for writing is not, more profoundly, to
ameliorate grief for his mother, who died "inexplicably" in 1981, and to
hearten him as he observes his 86-year-old father awaiting death. Remembering—reinventing—the past provides consolation insofar as one relives
the time when "we were all there," when death—one's parents' or one's
own—was "unperceivable and unsuspected," even "unconceivable," because one's parents were there "like a blockade" (*TF,* 9).

In this letter, or self-justification, to the fictional Zuckerman Roth
tries to be as straightforward and honest as he can be, or can seem to be.
He freely admits that to protect some of the living he has deliberately
altered a few names or identifying details, as he grew "increasingly
squeamish about confessing intimate affairs of mine to *everybody"* (*TF,* 10;
emphasis his). But that is hardly a major consideration; in any case he
knows the book will leave *him* exposed in ways he would rather avoid.
His real concern is whether the book is any good. He asks Zuckerman to
be candid.

He is. "Don't publish," Zuckerman advises (*TF,* 161). For some 35 pages he argues his point, or rather points, in the afterword that concludes the (published) volume. His comments offer an amusing perspective, actually a continuation or extension of some of the points Roth makes in his letter. Zuckerman maintains that Roth needs him as much as he needs Roth, for in fiction Roth can afford to be "more truthful without worrying all the time about causing direct pain": "You try to pass off here as frankness what looks to me like the dance of the seven veils—what's on the page is like a code for something missing. Inhibition appears not only as a reluctance to say certain things but, equally disappointing, as a slowing of pace, a refusal to explode, a relinquishing of the need I ordinarily associate with you for the acute, explosive moment" (*TF,* 162). In short, Roth is not an autobiographer; he's a "personficator." Roth's ability lies not in personalizing his experience but in "personfying" it, embodying it in the representation of someone other than himself. Zuckerman claims that Roth's fictional world is far more exciting than the world of facts from which it derives. As an example he cites the parallel episodes of the elder Roth's reaction to *Portnoy's Complaint* as compared with the elder Zuckerman's reaction to *Carnovsky* (in *Zuckerman Unbound*). Whereas Roth's father took pride in all of his son's accomplishments, Zuckerman's condemned his son's work with a fierce curse and provided Roth with "the opportunity to pull out all the stops on a Jewish deathbed scene," something Roth's temperament doubtless found "irresistible" (*TF,* 163).

Art is judged by criteria that are aesthetic; autobiography, by criteria that are moral or ethical. The two must not be confused, but in *The Facts,* consciously or not, Roth seems to obscure the distinction, Zuckerman argues: "Think of the exclusions, the selective nature of it, the very pose of fact-finder" (*TF,* 164). Through his alter ego Roth thereby provides a critique of his own performance, a sharp assessment of "this fictional autobiographical projection of a *partial* you" (*TF,* 172). To Zuckerman *The Facts* is Roth's decorous or reserved way of talking about himself, of presenting himself as a victim as opposed to someone who has a real need for combat, as when he accepted the invitation to speak at Yeshiva University. "With autobiography there's always another text, a countertext, if you will, to the one presented," Zuckerman says. "It's probably the most manipulative of all literary forms" (*TF,* 172).

So be it. Zuckerman may be right, and we should read *The Facts* as fiction. Either way, it is funny: Roth fortunately cannot abandon his sense of humor while he writes, whatever he writes. In *The Facts* his main comic device is first to arouse expectations and then to reverse them. For example, his relationship with "Josie,"[8] whom he met while a student and then an instructor at the University of Chicago, involved endless quarrels, lies, deceptions, misunderstandings, entrapments, escapes, and everything else imaginable along with some that are not. So how does he end the chapter, ironically titled "Girl of My Dreams"? "Reader, I married her" (*TF*, 112).

For in the realm of the imagination Josie outdid him, Roth acknowledges with both admiration and rue. Perhaps this fact more than anything else explains how the two came to be married. The deception Josie adopted to "confirm" her pregnancy in 1959 was identical to the one Maureen Johnson uses to trick Peter Tarnopol into marriage in *My Life as a Man*. Those scenes in the novel are one of the few instances in which Roth did not try to reshape actual events in the interest of being more interesting. "I couldn't be more interesting," he admits; "I couldn't have been *as* interesting. What Josie came up with, altogether on her own, was a little gem of treacherous invention, economical, lurid, obvious, degrading, deluded, almost comically simple, and best of all, magically effective. To reshape its smallest facet would have been an aesthetic blunder" (*TF*, 107).

The trick was for Josie to obtain from an obviously pregnant black woman in Tomkins Square Park, near where they lived, a urine sample to use as her own for a rabbit test. After accepting Roth's marriage proposal, contingent upon her having an abortion, Josie immediately followed up with another deception. A good actress as well as fictionalist, Josie so fascinated Roth that after he learned two years later (again, like Peter Tarnopol) about the deceptions he continued to be "mesmerized" by her "overbrimming talent for brazen self-invention." How could "a half-formed, fledgling novelist hope ever to detach himself from this undiscourageable imagination unashamedly concocting the most diabolical ironies?" he asks (*TF*, 111). How indeed!

Roth's marriage, fictionalized in *My Life as a Man*, was constantly stormy. Even after he managed a legal separation, the war continued. He simply could not get free of Josie or her demands on him for security, alimony, respect. She was determined, he says, to make a man of him, and in the process came close to destroying him altogether. How devious his wife could be, and was, Roth shows in a number of incidents—for example, the time he took Josie's 12-year-old daughter, Helen, to dinner and the theater. "While we waited in our seats for the play to begin," he recalls, "I was served from the aisle with a subpoena. I immediately recognized the polite gentleman who was serving me; previously he had served me politely while I was at the dentist's" (*TF,* 142). Josie had an uncanny way of uncovering Roth's every movement, it seems, and an incorrigible desire to extract from him the maximum amount of guilt as well as alimony.

In 1968, after they had been separated for six years, news came that Josie had been killed in an automobile accident. Roth's reaction epitomizes the relationship: "How could she be dead if I didn't do it?" (*TF,* 151). Disbelief mingled with relief; for a while he was sure it was all a plot to get him to say something that would convince the judge, hiding behind the door to the next room, that his heart was flint, that he should be made to cough up more alimony. Demurring on Helen's request that he identify the body at the morgue, Roth offered to make the funeral arrangements and was astonished that he could now afford a taxi ride uptown to the funeral parlor. At the service, ironically presided over by one of the anti-Roth New York rabbis (Josie had converted to Judaism), he fantasized: "When I saw the casket, I said to Josie, 'You're dead and I didn't have to do it.' Whereupon the late Jew replied, 'Mazel tov'" (*TF,* 152). This sounds more like a scene from Bernard Malamud than Philip Roth, but such was Roth's state of mind at the time, one supposes.

Nevertheless, Josie had her revenge. Writing *My Life as a Man* became one of the most difficult pieces of fiction Roth ever attempted: "Writing it consisted of one false start after another and, over the years it took to finish it, very nearly broke my will." The only thing worse than writing it, Roth says, would have been to endure the marriage without afterward being able to reimagine it into "a fiction with a persuasive existence independent of myself" (*TF,* 152). While trying to complete the novel he wrote three other books, none of them quite as successful as *My Life as a Man,* which ranks among his best.

But in *The Facts* Roth's relationship with his wife, fascinating, funny, and dreadful as it appears, is only part of the story. Roth's early years, fictionalized in stories like "The Conversion of the Jews," held a fascination too. Roth remarks, for example, on the three years of training preparatory to his bar mitzvah, explaining how the afternoons spent in Hebrew school contrasted with the experience of public school and revealed something significant to him about being Jewish. Whereas he would have given anything to be outdoors playing ball instead of being cooped up in the dingy Hebrew school, he recognized that underlying everything was a "turbulence," a "bubbling, energetic unruliness." This turbulence was not only far removed from what he experienced in the "airy, orderly public school, where I was a bright American boy from nine to three"; it was also far removed from the exacting ritual laws he was being instructed in and asked to observe. This energy, or what he otherwise calls "a nervous forcefulness decidedly *irrepressible*" (*TF*, 122) that pulsated through daily life, he intimately associated with being Jewish.[9] For him it led to "unpredictably paradoxical theater" as his friends at parties during college and graduate school found in his mimickings and as his readers find in his fiction.

The story of Roth's early love affair with the girl he here calls Gayle Milman, a prototype in some ways for Brenda Patimkin in *Goodbye, Columbus*, also reveals Roth's predilection for dramatic juxtapositions and the coupling of alien perspectives. Ever since his graduation from Bucknell and during the two years spent in graduate school and the army, Roth had been carrying on "an obsessional passion" shared equally with Gayle. After the army and his decision to return to Chicago, however, Roth decided to give up Gayle and the affair he felt would impede his "voyage out," that is, out of Newark and "the safe enclosure of Jewish New Jersey." "I wanted a harder test," he says, "to work at life under more difficult conditions" (*TF*, 89). The irony is that Gayle had "an enigmatic adventure of her own to undertake" (*TF*, 89) and, after graduating from college, went to Europe, where for more than a decade she was, he learned, "the most desirable woman of *any* nationality between the Berlin Wall and the English Channel" (*TF*, 90). Meanwhile the "outward-bound voyager" who was the young Philip Roth, who refused to surrender his precious independence to any vestige of the world he felt he'd outgrown, became the thrall to a woman who sealed him into "a joyless existence, rife with the most preposterous, humanly meaningless responsibilities" (*TF*, 90). The woman was, of course, his wife, "Josie." By his own admission Roth had got everything "backward."

There are poignant aspects to his early life too, as in the scenes involving his hardworking, very able, deeply devoted, and loving father. One errs badly in making simplistic identifications between the elder Roth and Jack Portnoy, although similarities between them exist. For example, both worked for large insurance companies and suffered from religious and other prejudices that prevented them from rising higher on the corporate ladder. But between Roth and his father was a loving bond quite unlike the antagonisms that developed between Alex and Jack Portnoy, although Roth remarks on the potential for conflict with his father as he got older. This was avoided, he says, by entering Bucknell after a year at Rutgers in Newark. Young Philip was worried about the expense of going away to school, but his father, magnanimous as ever, said during their visit to the college, "You want to go here, you're going" (*TF*, 47).

## Roth's *Patrimony*

Zuckerman's criticisms of Roth as autobiographer hardly pertain to Roth as biographer and memoirist in *Patrimony: A True Story,*[10] the book he began writing when he knew his father was afflicted with a large brain tumor that eventually would take his life. One of Roth's most moving prose pieces, it recounts in detail the extremely close relationship he shared with Herman Roth, especially following his mother's sudden death in 1981. But even here the deep poignancy and elegiac qualities are punctuated with comedy as Roth refuses to sentimentalize his father. Instead, he pays the highest tribute to the man he loved ever more deeply by presenting him as he was—stubborn, opinionated, generous with others, tight with himself, energetic, forceful, absurdly critical but also fiercely loyal to family and friends. For example, Bessie Roth once confided to her son that since his retirement her husband had become almost impossible to live with. She who had run her home and raised two sons now had a new boss who dominated her and their life together in ways that had become unbearable. As Roth recognizes, all this was the result of his father's no longer working in another job. Having formerly directed a staff of 40 at Metropolitan Life, he now had only one person to supervise—she who had never before wanted or needed supervision—and it was driving her crazy.

After his wife's death Herman was bereft as Philip had never seen him. But like the hard worker he was, he undertook his duty as he saw it and wasted no time about it. No sooner had the family returned from the cemetery than Herman began going through his wife's closets and drawers in the bedroom to dispose of her things—this while family and friends stood elsewhere in the apartment waiting for him to join them. Philip finally had to pull Herman out of the bedroom, where to his surprise he found his father neither hysterical nor dazed but "simply doing what he had done all his life: the next difficult job."[11] Eventually Herman overcame his loss sufficiently to enjoy living in Florida with an old friend, Bill Weber, also a widower, on whom he focused his characteristic concern and criticism for Bill's welfare—as Herman perceived it.

Within a few years Herman struck up a relationship with a woman named Lil, to whom he became devoted and toward whom he also became, inevitably, judgmental. But it was Lil who stood by Herman during the difficult time of his illness, when the brain tumor (first diagnosed wrongly as Bell's palsy) afflicted him. Roth does not flinch from describing the pathetic spectacle of his father, his face badly distorted, his hearing seriously affected, and his sight failing. But he does not dwell on the pathos. Nor does he dwell unduly on his own torment, as powerful as it is real, which emerges as he watches this sad deterioration in his father's health. In the book the caring son stands revealed as clearly and vividly as does the afflicted father, though other family members, such as Philip's brother, Sandy, and his family, remain only sketches.

*Patrimony* gives us a good idea of what Roth's family life was like as he grew up in Newark, attended college, and became a successful writer and celebrity, all to the immense satisfaction of his devoted father, who, throughout everything—up to the very end, when Philip undergoes quintuple bypass heart surgery—still regarded him, first and forever, as his son. One of the most touching moments, for instance, comes near the end, when the tumor has taken almost all its toll on the 88-year-old father, who berates his son for not telling him about the surgery: "I should have been there," he said, at first in a breaking voice and then more sternly and furiously (*P*, 231). In many ways incorrigible, Herman Roth insists on offering advice and admonitions, oblivious of how un-needed or unwanted they are, as when he continues to lecture his grand-son Jonathan, who has just started a new job. In reply to Sandy's request to cease and desist, Herman writes a letter that is in a very real sense his *apologia pro vita sua*, explaining that there are two types of people, "People who care, and those that don't, People who *do* and people who Procras-tinate and never *do* or *help*" (*P*, 80). He goes on to describe himself as one of those who *care* and *do*. He is not defensive; on the contrary, he shows characteristic self-confidence, his poor spelling and punctuation (the only things he apologizes for) in no way detracting from his argument. An inveterate *hocker* (nagger), he signs his name accordingly, though quali-fying it as a "Misnomer": "it should be the carer," he writes, adding a postscript:

> I will always continue to
> Hock and Care. Thats me
> to people I care
> for. (*P*, 81–82)

Philip is not a *hocker*, but, as the book shows, he is very much a "carer." Agonizing over whether to let his father undergo difficult and problem-atic brain surgery for the tumor or to let nature take its course, he calls on various friends, not all of them doctors, for advice. He guards his father from the worst aspects of the situation but not from the essentials. It is the greatest testimony to each man and to their relationship that

Philip is neither overprotective nor brutally candid. If his father could be and often was insensitive to others' feelings, forcing his advice and opinions on them, Philip rarely feels the need to act likewise. When he does, he surprises both himself and his father, as when he insists that the old man get up, put on his shoes, and go out for a walk with him. Other emotions also surprise him, as with his feelings about his father's will. Earlier Philip had said everything should be left to his brother, Sandy, and his sons, but now, his father's death imminent, he discovers to his dismay that he regrets that decision; he wants his share of the "financial surplus" that against all odds his father had accumulated over the years: "I wanted the money because it was his money and I was his son and I had a right to my share" (*P,* 104). Renouncing his patrimony, he cannot now renounce his renunciation but instead savors the "comedy of [his] own automatic brand of elevated stupidity" (*P,* 106).

The real patrimony, Roth discovers later, is something else. After a painful, debilitating biopsy, his father comes to stay for a week with Philip and Claire Bloom in their Connecticut home. Constipated since his hospital stay, he asks Philip to get him some prune juice. At lunch one day when his grandson Seth and his wife, Ruth, visit, Herman excuses himself and does not soon return. Concerned, Philip follows him to his room, finding his father in the midst of a terrible accident. Herman has "beshat" himself. Shit is everywhere—in his discarded clothes, on the floor, in the shower stall—and the poor man is nearly beside himself with shame. Comforting him, Philip first tends to cleaning him up and putting him to bed for a rest and then proceeds to clean up the mess left behind. Despite the odor and everything else he must overcome, he feels a strange satisfaction: "I thought I couldn't have asked for anything more for myself before he died—this, too, was right and as it should be." He cleans up his father's shit because it has to be cleaned up, but afterward he feels things "as never before": once past the disgust and nausea and phobias, he finds, "there's an awful lot of life to cherish" (*P,* 175). Then, as he dumps a garbage bag of soiled clothes and linens into the trunk of his car, he recognizes what his real patrimony is: not the money he had renounced, not the tefillin (phylacteries) his father had left in the locker room of the Y, not his grandfather's coveted shaving mug, but the shit: "And not because cleaning it up was symbolic of something else but because it wasn't, because it was nothing less or more than the lived reality that it was" (*P,* 176).

When the end comes in October 1989 and Herman is rushed to an emergency room, Philip must decide whether or not to let his father be placed on a breathing machine to keep him alive. The living will Herman had signed notwithstanding, for Philip the decision is almost impossible. How do you sit by and let your father die, knowing that equipment is available to prolong life? But by then Herman's life had shriveled to nearly nothing, as Philip well knew, and although the old man is unconscious, his son whispers to him, "Dad, I'm going to have to let you go" (P, 233). He repeats the words until finally he believes them himself.

After Herman dies and is buried in a shroud, Philip has a dream that his father comes to him complaining that he should have been buried in a suit. "You did the wrong thing," he says. Philip later realizes the dream's significance, that his father alluded to the book he was then writing, this book, which with the "unseemliness" of his profession he had been writing all the time his father was ill. Further, the dream told him that, if not in his life or in his books, then in his dreams, he would forever be Herman Roth's little son, with a little son's conscience, just as his father would remain alive there, "not only as my father, but as *the* father, sitting in judgment on whatever I do" (P, 238).[12] "You must not forget anything," the book concludes. It appears Philip has forgotten nothing essential, nothing that is not true.

## Chapter Seven

# Fantasy as Satire, Satire as Fantasy in *Our Gang*

Ever an accomplished mimic, Roth knew in 1960, when he first parodied him in print, that he could imitate Richard Nixon's style and vocal mannerisms to humorous and satiric effect.[1] But it was not until 10 years later that he produced a full-length comic satire on the man, then in his first term as president of the United States, and on the people surrounding him. As the subtitle indicates, *Our Gang, Starring Tricky and His Friends* (1971) is, unlike Roth's other books, in the form of a playscript or movie scenario, mostly in dialogue, with two chapters as dramatic monologues. It originated in the pieces published in the *New York Review of Books,* which form the work's first two chapters.[2] Subsequently Bantam Books published the book in paperback editions, including the "Watergate Edition" (1973) and the "Pre-Impeachment Edition" (1974), each with a new preface by the author. Like Roth's other books, *Our Gang* has been translated into many languages, but it is generally regarded as a minor work, or one of Roth's "least significant" fictions (Rodgers, 107).

Roth's critics nevertheless concede that the book is often amusing and its satire sharp. As Dwight MacDonald said in his *New York Times* review, *Our Gang* is "a political satire that I found far-fetched, unfair, tasteless, disturbing, logical, coarse and very funny—I laughed out loud sixteen times and giggled internally a statistically unverifiable amount.[3] Of course, Dwight MacDonald, hardly a Nixon lover, would. But his judgment, like his reactions, is apt: the book has all the strengths and weaknesses he indicates. Moreover, MacDonald's later comparison to Swiftian satire, invited by Roth's first epigraph from *A Voyage to the Houyhnhnms,* is justified. Like his illustrious forebear, Roth indulges in fantasies and distortions—often gross distortions, such as President "Dixon's" attitude toward the My Lai massacre, or his skull sessions in football uniform—to drive home his points. But unlike Swift, Roth uses a sledgehammer rather than a scalpel; subtlety is rare in *Our Gang.* Then again, Roth was obviously outraged and angry, for those were outrageous and infuriating times.

In his own comments on the book Roth defends his brand of humor by linking it to the tradition of American political satire as represented by James Russell Lowell's *Biglow Papers* and David Ross Locke's "Nasby Letters," to H. L. Mencken's "Gamalielese," and to the broad comedy of Olsen and Johnson, Laurel and Hardy, Abbott and Costello, and other slapstick comedians (*RMAO,* 44–47). The "ferocity" of political satire in our earlier history, especially in the period before and after the Civil War, is, he says, practically forgotten today, when scarcely any satiric writing exists, apart from newspaper cartoons. As for decorum, that is precisely what Roth means to attack, or, rather, what hides behind it: "All I'm saying, of course, is that the level of comedy in *Our Gang* isn't exactly what it is in *Pride and Prejudice*—in case anyone should fail to notice" (*RMAO,* 46). Roth's strategy is to "dislocate" readers and get them to view familiar subjects in a different way.

Roth's second epigraph, from George Orwell's "Politics and the English Language," clearly indicates the aim of his satire. Orwell sees a connection between "the present political chaos" and "the decay of language"; he says any improvement in the political condition might well start from "the verbal end." Through his exaggerations and distortions, Roth hoped to enlighten readers to the kinds of verbal chicanery that Nixon and his associates were guilty of, that is, to the devices of language these politicians used to deceive their audiences in pursuit of their goals. To the extent that his parodies are effective, Roth succeeds. On the other hand, he did not expect the world to change as a result of his efforts. Falling back on the status of satire as literature, Roth maintains that "Satire is moral rage transformed into comic art—as an elegy is grief transformed into poetic art" (*RMAO,* 53). Or, as W. H. Auden put it in his elegy on Yeats, "poetry makes nothing happen." Those who, like Dwight Mac-Donald, were predisposed to see and deplore the verbal licentiousness of Nixon and his administration could revel in Roth's satire; those inclined in the opposite direction would reject it, as, of course, they did (and some still do).[4]

None of this is to deny the humor evident in Roth's satire, or the comic artistry he employs variously in various chapters. If the novel lacks coherence and unity in its overall conception, the ingenuity displayed in the development of specific scenes or situations shows the range of Roth's wit, which is considerable. And if *Our Gang,* like *The Great American Novel* that followed, is eccentric to the main current of Roth's fiction, it should be judged as such, except insofar as it provides further evidence of the power of his mimicry and his talent for comedy.

The launching pad for Roth's satire is Nixon's statement on abortion, made on 3 April 1971 and printed in large capital letters opposite the beginning of chapter 1. There Nixon denounces what he calls "abortion on demand" and states his personal belief in "the sanctity of human life—including the life of the yet unborn." The brief opening chapter, "Tricky Comforts a Troubled Citizen," contains a dialogue between Tricky and an unnamed person who raises questions about Lieutenant Calley's role in the My Lai massacre, particularly in light of the abortion statement and President "Dixon's" attitude toward Calley's conviction. The Citizen is concerned that Calley may have committed an abortion, or what amounts to the same thing, if one of the 22 Vietnamese civilians killed was a pregnant woman. Before the Citizen can even ask the question, odd as it sounds, Dixon anticipates (what he thinks are) some of its implications and begins the sanctimonious double-talk that typifies much of his discourse throughout the interview and the novel:

Well, in the wake of the public outcry against that conviction, the popular thing—the most popular thing by far—would have been for me, as Commander-in-Chief, to have convicted the twenty-two unarmed civilians of conspiracy to murder Lieutenant Calley. But if you read the papers, you'll see I refused to do that, and chose only to review the question of his guilt, and not theirs. As I said, I'd rather be a one-term President [and do what I believe is right than be a two-term president by taking an easy position like that]. And may I make one thing more perfectly clear, while we're on the subject of Vietnam? I am not going to interfere in the internal affairs of another country. If President Thieu has sufficient evidence and wishes to try those twenty-two My Lai villagers posthumously, according to some Vietnam law having to do with ancestor worship, that is his business. But I assure you, I in no way intend to interfere with the workings of the Vietnamese system of justice. I think President Thieu, and duly elected Saigon officials, can "hack" it alone in the law and order department.[5]

Roth captures the rhythms and cadences, as well as the clichés and repetitions, characteristic of his subject. At the same time—and more important—he reveals the outrageous twists in logic that Dixon tries to make plausible or persuasive through the use of pietistic language.

But the Citizen, gullible and agreeable though he may be, is not put off from asking his question about the possible abortion. The conversation thus leads into still-more-tortuous twists of logic, replete with other verbal pieties. Dixon's allusions to his own background as a lawyer tend to highlight rather than conceal his duplicity. In the end, more sanctimonious than ever, Dixon promises that if after a thorough investigation he finds "in the evidence against the lieutenant anything whatsoever that I cannot square with my personal belief in the sanctity of human life, including the life of the yet unborn," he will disqualify himself as a judge and turn the entire matter over to the vice-president. This seems to satisfy the Citizen, who concludes, "I think we can all sleep better knowing that" (*OG*, 10).

It is not until much later that Roth focuses his satire on Vice-President "What's-his-name" and his fondness for alliteration. Meanwhile Tricky holds a press conference (chapter 2) that opens with another question on his "San Dementia" statement of 3 April. Here Roth spares neither Dixon nor the reporters. The representatives of the media he names "Mr. Asslick," "Mr. Daring," "Mr. Shrewd," "Miss Charmin'," "Mr. Catch-Me-in-a-Contradiction," "Mr. Fascinated," and so on, according to their various characteristics. Mr. Asslick's first question, for example, compares the 3 April statement with Martin Luther King's "I Have a Dream" speech. Responding, Dixon quickly catapults into a reductio ad absurdum, which he treats with the utmost seriousness. Recalling King's assassination and those of "John F. Charisma" and his brother, Robert, he refuses to be intimidated by "extremists or militants or violent fanatics"; he insists he will bring justice and equality not only to every fetus but to microscopic embryos as well. If ever there was a group in this country that was "disadvantaged," he says, it is not the ethnic minorities, the hippies, or anyone else, all of whom have their advocates, but "these infinitesimal creatures up there on the placenta" (*OG*, 12–13).

From then on Dixon gets into one absurdity after another as he or a reporter raises such issues as troublemaking fetuses, "Prenatal Power," and the voting rights of embryos—all of which Dixon, along with his interlocutors, treats seriously. At the end, after considering (and evading) a question by Mr. Practical about the mechanics of bringing the vote to the unborn, and similar questions by Mr. Fascinated and Mr. Reasonable, Dixon downplays possible challenges by Governor Wallow and Senator Hubert Hollow in the 1972 presidential election: "the fact is that I have never heard either of these gentlemen, for all their extremism, raise their voices in behalf of America's most disadvantaged group of all, the unborn" (*OG*, 23). He therefore is confident that "when election time rolls around," the embryos and fetuses will remember their champion and vote accordingly.

But not everything runs as smoothly as Tricky expects, and he must face another "crisis," the subject of chapter 3. Dressed in the football uniform he wore at Prissier College, he meets with his closest advisers, or "coaches," similarly costumed. They gather in a blast-proof locker room built beneath the White House. The present crisis involves an uprising by the Boy Scouts of America, who because of his 3 April statement publicly protest that "Trick E. Dixon favors sexual intercourse. Favors fornication—*between people!*" (*OG,* 30). Was ever anyone so misunderstood? Was ever a president so put upon?

For President Dixon, the crisis is real. "Gentlemen," he addresses his coaches, "you can go to war without Congressional consent, you can ruin the economy and trample on the Bill of Rights, but you just do not violate the moral code of the Boy Scouts of America and expect to be reelected to the highest office in the land!" (*OG,* 28). His Political, Spiritual, Military, Highbrow, and Legal Coaches propose or discuss several expedients. During this long dark night of the soul, after wrangling together long and hard over those on their respective hit lists—including Jane Fonda, the Berrigans, Joan Baez, and the Black Panthers—Dixon finally comes to a decision. To divert attention from the Boy Scouts, who will be ruthlessly suppressed, he will announce an invasion of Denmark, where the renegade baseball player Curt Flood has fled. Flood is chosen over the others because of his attack on baseball's reserve clause (and the consequent threat to the game as we know it) and because he is a lesser-known celebrity, someone ripe for vilification without becoming a hero or a martyr. In short, for their purposes he is a "natural" (*OG,* 78).

This chapter, "Tricky Has Another Crisis," is the longest in the book and, truth be told, the most tiresome. Roth's vitriol knows little restraint. Although the basic conception is funny—the "skull session" in the underground locker room—the humor is often strained and obvious. Nevertheless, several of his jokes score well. For example, during the discussion of the hit lists the Political Coach mentions a film Hollywood is planning to make about the Berrigans. The image of Bing Crosby as Father Berrigan "in a collar crooning to Debbie Reynolds in her habit about b-b-b-b-lowing things up" becomes funnier as Dixon fears that "Not even Lenin could have devised a more sure-fire method of converting the American working class into bomb-throwing revolutionaries" (*OG,* 67). Then the Legal Coach astonishes the rest by mentioning among those on his hit list none other than Johnny Carson. His plan is to indict Carson only to have him acquitted afterward, thus helping the jury feel good about the other convictions, which will then "look better all around." Dixon likes the idea and suggests that when Carson is freed he could introduce him at a press conference with "*H-e-e-e-re's* Johnny!" But Roth unwisely milks his humor: "and he could come out and do his cute little golf stroke! He could make jokes about being in jail with the other conspirators. Maybe he could even wear a ball and chain and a striped suit!" (*OG*, 75).

With the decision reached to invade Denmark, President Dixon addresses the nation in "The Famous 'Something Is Rotten in the State of Denmark' Speech," as chapter 4 is subtitled. A master parody of Nixon's public speaking style, the speech includes visual aids; for example, Dixon uses a map to point out little Denmark, specifically Elsinore, the site of Hamlet's castle, which U.S. Marines, wading ashore at midnight, have liberated "without firing a single shot" (*OG*, 89). The main enemy, however, is the "Pro-Pornography" government of Denmark, a country that since the eleventh century has had expansionist policies directed against North America. Dixon cites the landings of Erik the Red and Leif Eriksson, both in violation of the Monroe Doctrine. And so on. Throughout the speech, Roth is obviously satirizing Nixon's Vietnam, Laos, and Cambodia policies, but in the full context of the novel the satire unfortunately tends to trivialize the serious and tragic events of those years, as Dixon cites many actual events, not imagined ones. Only the geography is different (*OG*, 92).

Roth salvages humor, however, by moving on to a parody of Nixon's famous "Checkers" speech. After an account of his early life as a struggling young lawyer in Prissier, California, Dixon discusses the current state of American justice, the need to alleviate courtroom crowding (hence the "Justice in the Streets Program"; *OG*, 101), the Boy Scouts uprising ("it was necessary to kill only three in order to maintain law and order," or "one and one-half Scouts dead per diem"; *OG*, 106), and the link between the uprising and the fugitive Charles Curtis Flood. Finally, to apprehend Flood, Dixon says he ordered a surprise helicopter raid on a suspected hideout on the island of Zealand. The mission, though fraught with danger, was accomplished with "split-second timing" and "without sustaining a single casualty" (*OG*, 124–25). The "large dark object" identified as Curt Flood was, however, replaced "at the very last minute" by a big black Labrador retriever taken into custody and transported to Elsinore "in order to keep faithfully to the plan." But under his orders, Dixon says, interrogation has since been stopped and the dog set free on a leash to roam the castle grounds (*OG*, 126).

The speech ends with a peroration in praise of "Operation Courage," a quotation from William Shakespeare about Denmark, and a promise to do whatever else may be necessary to "purge Denmark of corruption" (*OG*, 128). But the next chapter finds Tricky Dixon assassinated, his body stuffed in the fetal position into an oversized plastic baggie filled with water—"satiric retribution" or "parodic justice," as Roth calls it (*RMAO*, 54), for his advocacy of the unborn. As Vice-President What's-his-name profusely alliterates in a series of addresses to various organizations, his words are interrupted with contradictory or noncommittal news reports concerning the president's death. Again the media are satirized, with an additional parody of Billy Graham in "The Eulogy Over the Baggie (As Delivered Live on Nationwide TV by the Reverend Billy Cupcake)" (*OG*, 176–83).

Following the format of network television when it reports a calamity of national importance, movement in this chapter—like its wit—is rapid. Shifting the focus from one scene to another, Roth's intention is to satirize "the discrepancy between official pieties and the unpleasant truth"—certainly not to advocate Nixon's assassination, as some might misunderstand (*RMAO*, 56). He succeeds admirably, as reports from "Morton Momentous" in Chicago, "Peter Pious" in Los Angeles, "Ike Ironic" in New York City, and the anchorman's summing up show (*OG*, 150–54). The chapter reaches a climax when "Brad Bathos" describes from "down here in the streets of Washington" the thousands and thousands of people pouring into the city and surrounding the White House (*OG*, 162–71). The solemnity of his words and their tone suggest that these are mourners come to pay their respects to the dead leader; in fact, they are people clamoring to confess to the assassination.

But Dixon, though dead, is not out. Chapter 6, "On the Comeback Trail; or, Tricky in Hell," shows him once again making his imitable public address, this time to the legions of the damned. Campaigning against Satan for the leadership of Hell, he attacks his opponent for being outdated, for raising empty hopes, and for being neither imaginative nor aggressive enough. Satan may be satisfied with the status quo, but Dixon is not. In an era of "rapid and dramatic change" a new administration and new lies are needed: "[Y]esterday's lies are just not going to confuse today's problems. You cannot expect to mislead people next year the way you misled them a year ago, let alone a million years ago" (*OG*, 191). To back him for the job as Devil, Dixon points to his record. Not even Satan, with the support of all his legions, could have accomplished in the United States what he did in a mere thousand days as president, sowing "seeds of bitterness and hatred between the races, the generations and the social classes" that will plague Americans for years to come (*OG*, 192). He also points to his achievements in Southeast Asia, where with the help of others and the U.S. Air Force he turned that part of the globe "into nothing less than Hell on earth" (*OG*, 193).

As for his earlier shortcomings, Dixon asserts that a new administration will see a new Dixon. No longer burdened by "conscience, caution and consideration for one's reputation" as he was while on earth and president of the United States, he sees Hell as "a great challenge and a great opportunity." He can therefore promise the denizens of the underworld—"where no holds are barred and nothing is sacred" (*OG,* 194)—that he will become the Dixon he could only dream of becoming while on earth. But before concluding his "opening statement" in what is apparently to be a debate with Satan (an element Roth does not develop), Dixon reviews the famous "Job case" to show how ineffectual his opponent has been and to warn all the demons of Hell that the champions of Righteousness will not stop with one soul; appeasement will not work. This is all the more reason to elect Dixon and "launch a new offensive in this battle for the minds and hearts and souls of men," for, if elected, he will "see Evil triumph in the end," ensuring that "our children, and our children's children, need never know the terrible scourge of Righteousness and Peace" (*OG,* 200).

These excerpts show that, ingenious as the conception of a campaign speech in Hell may be, Roth's satire is too heavy-handed and broad. The humor, hardly more than incidental in this final chapter, falters badly. Perhaps that is why Roth did not continue the debate with Satan. Instead, he quotes some verses from the Book of Revelation. Like the opening lines from Nixon's antiabortion statement, it is printed in capital letters:

THEN I SAW AN ANGEL COMING DOWN FROM HEAVEN, HOLDING IN HIS HAND THE KEY OF THE BOTTOMLESS PIT AND A GREAT CHAIN. AND HE SEIZED THE DRAGON, THAT ANCIENT SERPENT, WHO IS THE DEVIL . . . AND BOUND HIM FOR A THOUSAND YEARS, AND THREW HIM INTO THE PIT, AND SHUT IT AND SEALED IT OVER HIM, THAT HE SHOULD DECEIVE THE NATIONS NO MORE.

Sadly, Roth feels compelled to appropriate another's fantasy and indulge in a kind of wishful thinking rather than invent a more stringent irony with which to end his political satire.

## Chapter Eight

# Tour de Farce:

## The Comedy of the Grotesque in
*The Great American Novel*

What Roth began in *Portnoy's Complaint* and, in a different mode, *Our Gang*, bloomed—as a mushroom cloud may be said to bloom—in his tour de farce[1] *The Great American Novel*. Here (to change metaphors) Roth let out all the stops. Perhaps he needed to so that he could get on with *My Life as a Man*, which he was then struggling to write.[2] He puts it differently in his remarks on the novel, written when the book came out. The social phenomena of the 1960s attack on venerable American institutions and beliefs, together with the emergence of a "counterhistory, or *countermythology*, to challenge the mythic sense of itself the country had when the decade opened" (*RMAO*, 89), gave him a handle by which to take hold of baseball, "of all things," and place it at the center of a novel. He did not intend to demythologize baseball, a sport which did not interest him very much; rather, he discovered in baseball a way to dramatize the struggle between the "benign national myth of itself that a great power prefers to perpetuate" and the "nearly demonic reality . . . that will not give an inch in behalf of that idealized reality" (*RMAO*, 90). But baseball too gets demythologized, Roth's demurrer notwithstanding.[3] And as Roth indicates earlier in his comments, he needed now to relax the constraints he had felt, consciously or otherwise, since the beginning of his career, on being a "serious" writer. He had, finally, to "let go."

He therefore also acknowledges the influence upon him, first as a boy, then as a man and a writer, of Henny Youngman, Jake the Snake, and his older brother's friend Arnold G., "an unconstrained Jewish living-room clown whose indecent stories of failure and confusion in sex did a little to demythologize the world of the sensual for me in early adolescence" (*RMAO*, 81). Roth was now ready to try to *be* the reckless, conscienceless writer critics had accused him of being. He was willing to be "deliberately, programmatically perverse—subversive not merely of the 'serious' values of official literary culture . . . but subversive of my own considerable investment . . . in seriousness" (*RMAO*, 86–87). *The Great American Novel*, from its title onward, shows how willing he was.

But let us not take Roth's unseriousness too seriously. Without question, much in *The Great American Novel* is as perverse, as outrageous—not to say outlandish—as Roth or anyone else could wish. It revels in its own bad taste and grotesquerie. Much of its humor is low, very low, often "black." If Roth denies any redeeming value, social or otherwise, in the novel (*RMAO*, 76), that does not mean it lacks any. He may have deliberately set out to write something for the sheer "fun of it," but no writer—least of all Roth, committed as he is to the moral imperatives he reveals elsewhere—can utterly eliminate them from his work, try as he may.

Thus, while his comedy often makes its point, or points, Roth's exuberant spirit must not be denied. No *necessary* conflict exists here, and we should not try to invent one, even if Roth seems to in his own comments. The "spirit of farce, the nature of the Comic" may lie at the heart of Roth's "comic inventiveness," as Donald G. Watson suggests. But they are not inimical to other motives. "To destroy gleefully the fixed and orthodox clichés of normality, to oppose the craziness of reality [one of Roth's favorite themes] with the craziness of fantasy, to attempt to renew by burying the old"—these are not trivial pursuits. Within the traditions of "carnivalesque" comedy that Watson identifies, "which respects no boundaries and cares only to expose the folly of business–as–usual," Roth assesses American institutions and values.[4] Let the novel now speak for itself.

## Prologue: "Call me Smitty"

Roth begins at once by invoking—and parodying—epic traditions and eminent precursors: "Call me Smitty," his first sentence, directly takes off from Melville's *Moby-Dick* and sounds the keynote of literary satire in this "Prologue." The superannuated sportswriter, Word Smith, intends to set history straight or, better, recover it, and in the process write "The Great American Novel." The only one alive who is willing to recall the defunct Patriot League, third of baseball's major leagues, he will unfold a saga of national shame and disgrace—the annihilation for political and other reasons of a once-proud and accomplished organization. The Patriot League had included such teams as the Kakoola Reapers, Tri-City Greenbacks, Terra Incognita Rustlers, Aceldama Butchers, Asylum Keepers, and Ruppert Mundys. Where have they disappeared to? Where even are the cities that once boasted their laurels and floated their pennants? Gone, the teams are gone, and the cities have changed their names. Where Smitty is concerned, however, the teams and those who owned or managed them are by no means forgotten. Yet only he, it seems, is left to tell their story.

And he tells it well, forgoing (under doctor's orders) a heavy and favored predilection for alliteration that punctuates passages and permeates paragraphs prevailing in the prologue. But first he establishes his bona fides. He knows his craft, having practiced it for most of his 87 years as the writer of a daily column called "One Man's Opinion." He has more than a nodding acquaintance with the masterpieces of literature as well. In fact, Hawthorne's preface to *The Scarlet Letter,* he says, gave him the idea for this lengthy prologue, in which he also refers to the work of Chaucer, Mark Twain, and others. A prominent section recounts Smitty's experience in Florida with Ernest Hemingway, whose style Smitty recaptures accurately and tellingly. Their conversation about "Literatoor" inevitably gets around to The Great American Novel, which "Hem" believes has not yet been written. And when it is written, he says, Smitty—whom Hemingway calls "Frederico"—will write it.

Smitty therefore considers "My Precursors, My Kinsmen" in the prologue. The first is Nathaniel Hawthorne, with whose *The Scarlet Letter* Smitty's novel has this affinity: the Ruppert Mundys (the main subject of his novel) wear a large scarlet *R* on their uniforms. But unlike Hawthorne, Smitty claims more than "the authenticity of the outline"; he contends for the authenticity of "the whole thing!"[5] He was there, he saw and heard it all, or had it reported to him by "reliable informants." *The Adventures of Huckleberry Finn* is another important precursor: "Listening to Huckleberry Finn ramble on is like listening to nine-tenths of the baseball players who ever lived talk about what they do in the off season down home" (*GAN,* 38).[6] The link involves not only the oral tradition but the "tall tales" of the old Southwest, which *The Great American Novel* contains in abundance.[7] The picaresque tradition also connects them, although here a whole team instead of Huck and Jim comprises the picaros.[8] Finally, Melville's *Moby-Dick* provides Smitty with numerous parallels to baseball; for example, citing the most famous double-play combination in baseball, he asks, "Who are Flask, Starbuck, and Stubb, Ahab's trio of first mates, if not the Tinker, Evers, and Chance of the *Pequod*'s crew?" (*GAN,* 41) What happened to the *Pequod* happened to the Ruppert Mundys and the entire Patriot League and will, he prophesies, through a different kind of pollution happen to the whole planet. But first, Smitty tells his tale.

## The Patriot League and the Ruppert Mundys

He tells it in the manner of the great eighteenth-century novelists, such as Fielding, who fashioned novels like epics, prefacing each chapter with a synopsis of events recorded in the ensuing pages. Chapter 1 briefly describes the history of the World War II. General Douglas D. Oakheart became president of the Patriot League in 1933, when the sensational pitcher Gil Gamesh broke into the majors with the Tri-City Greenbacks. (Throughout this novel, Roth enjoys inventing allegorical names or adopting mythological ones for his fictitious characters and mingling them with historical figures.) Gamesh began demolishing records—until he ran up against the likes of Michael ("Mike the Mouth") Masterson, the rigid and righteous umpire that General Oakheart believed was alone capable of handling the brash, outspoken, and wildly conceited ballplayer ("I can beat anybody, I'm an immortal!" *GAN,* 67). When Masterson inadvertently ruins Gamesh's chance for a perfect "perfect game" (81 strikes in a row) by missing the call on the last pitch, Gamesh takes revenge by throwing a ferociously fast pitch that hits the umpire on the Adam's apple, destroying his voice forever. Swearing "I'll be back," Gamesh is banished from baseball, while Masterson spends his life madly demanding that Gamesh be tried for attempted murder.

This period also marked the decline of the Ruppert Mundys,[9] the contribution of Port Ruppert, New Jersey, to the teams of the Patriot League. By the outbreak of World War II their golden age had ended, as had the long life of their owner, Glorious Mundy, 1839–1931. The franchise was now in the hands of his greedy sons, who began dismantling its treasures. After selling the phenomenal Luke Gofannon (lifetime batting average .372) and the other stars of the great teams of the 1920s, the Mundy brothers climaxed their decimation of the team by leasing their ballpark to the War Department as an embarkation camp. From then on the Ruppert Mundys played all their games on the road; they never had a home-field advantage, never heard the cheers of their local supporters ("Rupe-it rootas"), never got last licks.

Not that there was much left to cheer, though once a Rupe-it roota, always a Rupe-it roota. With most of the able-bodied gone to the various services, ballplayers were hard to find and the Mundys had to settle for as motley a crew as ever took the diamond. "Batting first and playing shortstop, No. 1: Frenchy ASTARTE. ASTARTE," begins chapter 2, and so on down the lineup. A French-Canadian who understood only French, 39-year-old Astarte had played first in Georgia and then in the Cuban and other Latin American leagues before being traded to Tokyo, Japan, "the only player ever traded out of his own hemisphere (and the only player traded back)" (*GAN,* 97). If Astarte was a star in Asia, where he played against men half his size, he was hardly one in the Patriot League, where his "specialty" was dropping high infield flies. Just such an error in the last game of 1942 allowed two Rustler runners to score, costing the Mundys the game and seventh place in the league. Finishing last led directly to the team's departure from Port Ruppert and permanent exile on the road. But the next player in the lineup had his troubles too, as did all the Mundy regulars.

"Batting second and playing second base, No. 29: NICKNAME DA-MUR. DAMUR" (*GAN,* 100). Only 14 years old, Damur was the youngest player in the majors, as well as the skinniest, weighing a mere 92 pounds. "Indeed, so slight was he," Smitty reports, "that on the opening day of the '43 season, a base runner barreling into second knocked Nickname so high and so far that the center-fielder, Roland Agni, came charging in to make a sensational diving two-handed catch of the boy." The field umpire called "Out!" until he remembered that it was the ball, not the player, that had to be caught and instantly reversed his decision (*GAN,* 101–2). Although the derision that followed compounded Damur's eagerness to get a nickname for himself worthy of a major league player, all his attempts at something like Cappy, Gabby, or Dusty failed; instead, he was christened Nickname by the team's peacemaker, Jolly Cholly Tuminikar.

"Batting in third position, the first baseman, No. 11, JOHN BAAL. BAAL" (*GAN,* 103). The strong man of the Ruppert Mundys, Big John was said never to have hit a home run while sober. He had played with every team in the league before being sent to jail for swindling a rookie out of his World Series winnings by using loaded dice in a game of craps. He was now out on parole in the custody of the Mundys' benevolent manager, Ulysses S. Fairsmith, an ancient and deeply religious man who refused to enter a ballpark on Sunday and who, later in the season, furloughed himself to Africa (as he had done years before to Japan) as a baseball missionary.[10] Grandson of "Base" Baal and son of "Spit" Baal, Big John had a long and notorious legacy in the sport. For example, his father, "Spit," served up a ball so juicy (in the years when doctoring the ball was allowed) "that by the end of an inning the catcher had to shake himself off like a dog come in from romping in the rain" (*GAN,* 105). But it was the "stringy stuff" (from phlegm or from blowing his nose on the ball) that antagonized batters most of all—until in the 1902 World Series Baal was found coating the ball with earwax. That did it. From then on, "anointed" balls were forbidden and Baal headed south, where he founded the Mosquito Coast League of Nicaragua. At least there you could rub anything you wanted to on a ball before pitching it, and there, amid the heat and filth, the toothless Indians and jugs of raisin wine, Big John Baal was born.

Hothead, or "Hot," Ptah, the catcher, batted fourth. The most irritating player in baseball, he was the most despised of the Ruppert Mundys despite his physical handicap—he had only one leg, which doubtless contributed to his crabby disposition. He delighted in tormenting batters until they cried out in protest to the umpire behind home plate. Although he had an excellent throwing arm, his artificial limb hampered him: "having that leg made out of wood caused him to lurch like something on a pogo stick when he came charging after a bunt, and he was not exactly death on fly balls popped back to the screen behind home plate" (*GAN,* 112). He could hit the ball right up against the left-field fence, but his plentiful doubles and triples resulted only in singles, and his singles in nothing but outs. His feats were matched by the Mundys' right fielder, Bud Parusha, who had only one arm. He did not even have the stump of a second arm (like Pete Gray of the St. Louis Browns),[11] so that when he caught a fly ball he had to extract it from his glove with his teeth until he could grip it again with his ungloved hand and throw it back into the infield. Unfortunately, the ball would sometimes get stuck in his jaws, and it required the aid of two other fielders to extract it, one kneeling on his chest and the other working the ball free. This did not happen often, but it occurred always in the same tense situation—with the bases loaded, resulting inevitably in "an inside-the-mouth grand-slam home run" (*GAN,* 120).

The other starters on the team included Mike "the Ghost" Rama, the left fielder whose incorrigible tendency to chase fly balls into the wall often ended in knocking himself out. Wayne "the Kid" Heket was at 50 the oldest player in baseball. His reflexes all but gone, he necessarily modified the way he played third base. "At my age," he told Smitty, "you just got to cut down, no question about it. You just got to give up somethin', so I give up goin' to my left." He let those balls go for the consideration of the shortstop, Astarte: "The way I see it now, if a feller

hits it to my left, he got hisself a single and more power to him. If a'
course the Frenchman wants to try and get it, well, that's his business
and I don't propose to interfere. His ways is his ways and mine is mine"
(*GAN,* 116). Always an excellent mimic, Roth obviously profited much
from listening to the players' tapes in the library at Cooperstown.

Exceptional among the Ruppert Mundys was Roland Agni, whose
given name, deriving from the hero of the Old French epic, suggests the
quality of the man and his abilities. An excellent hitter and fielder, how
did he wind up batting eight—and for the Ruppert Mundys? He owed
it to his parents, who were intent on teaching the young man humility,
for Roland knew he was good; like Gil Gamesh earlier, he believed he
was the best: "in four years of varsity play in high school, he had batted
.732 and regularly hurled shutouts when he wasn't in the outfield rob-
bing the other team of extra-base hits" (*GAN,* 123). To curb Roland's
overweening pride and to teach him a much-needed lesson, his father
rejected bids from 23 major league teams, as well as 40 offers of college
scholarships. He then telephoned the Mundy front office in Port Ruppert
and was overjoyed, his son downcast, when the Rupperts agreed to his
terms: Roland must bat eighth in his first year, rise no more than one
position in the batting order in each succeeding year, and be paid no more
than the lowest-paid member of the team. When the front office suggested not paying him at all, Mr. Agni was delighted. And so the anguish of Roland Agni (Agonistes; sacrificial lamb) commenced.

The Mundys had a variety of pitchers as well, "every last one of them
flabby in the middle, arthritic in the shoulder, bald on the top" (*GAN,*
127). Chico Mecoatl, for example, a sore-armed right-handed reliever
from Mexico, occasionally had to throw the ball underhand, so bad was
his pain. Every time he had to raise his arm to throw overhand, a "little
bleat of pain" passed between his lips. His yelp, like his throwing style,
became legendary. He seldom got anyone out but kept loading the bases
until the sun set and the game could be called on account of darkness and
the fans all went home. But not the Mundys: doomed to stay on the road,
traveling from one ballpark to another, they never went home to Mundy
Stadium in Port Ruppert, New Jersey.

Swinging around the league for the first time in 1943, the Mundys
were honored in every Patriot League city with a parade and a pregame
welcoming ceremony (*GAN,* 133). Theirs, after all, was a *patriotic* sacrifice. But because of wartime shortages, the vehicle that escorted them
from the train station was more often than not borrowed from the sani-
tation department. The music that played from a loudspeaker mounted

on the truck was Gene Autry singing and playing "Home on the Range," appropriate for the occasion besides being President Roosevelt's favorite song.

The Mundys' many and varied experiences on the road provide targets for Roth's satire. After a loss to the Kakoola Reapers, they are adopted by the "Mundy Mommys," three elderly ladies, "wrinkled little walnuts in identical hats, shoes, and spectacles" (*GAN*, 148), who take all but two of them home for some tender loving care—and a home-baked pie of their choice (Roth's sequel to Philip Wylie's "Momism"). Although Nickname Damur wanted to go along too, Big John prevented him, taking him instead to the "pink 'n' blue" district of the city, where he experienced another kind of "mommy" (*GAN*, 147–60). In August, while in Asylum, Ohio, the Mundys board a bus to the world-famous mental institution out in the country to play a three-inning exhibition game against a team composed of its inmates and coached by one Dr. Traum, the chief psychiatrist. Justification for the game lay in its therapeutic value, as far as the hospital was concerned, for it afforded the patients a "chance to make contact, if only for an hour or so, with the real world they had left behind" (*GAN*, 168). As for the players, who despised exhibition games in the regular season, they were compelled to play because of the publicity value to the sport.

The game provides some of the funniest moments in the book. Roth depicts the Lunatics, as the Mundys call them, with as much deftness as he did the Portnoys (whom they don't quite resemble), capturing their idiom and postures equally well. For example, at the start of the third inning the Lunatic pitcher and catcher cannot agree on what pitch to throw to Big John Baal. The pitcher rejects the signals from his catcher with increasing vehemence; when he refuses the fifth call, the catcher erupts into sarcastic rejoinder, and by the sixth time he becomes outspokenly defensive. Parodying paranoiacs, Roth precisely conveys the catcher's frustration using appropriate language and cadences: "'In other words,' the catcher screamed, 'I'm wrong *again*. But then in your eyes I'm *always* wrong. Well, isn't that true? Admit it! Whatever signal I give is *bound* to be wrong. Why? Because *I'm* giving it! I'm daring to give *you* a signal! I'm daring to tell *you* how to pitch! I could kneel here signaling for the rest of my days, and you'd just stand there shaking them off and asking God to give you strength, *because I'm so wrong and so stupid and so hopeless and would rather lose than win!*'" (*GAN*, 175). The issue is resolved (after 10 more rejected signals) in a manner utterly distasteful and utterly hilarious, as in desperation the catcher uses not a finger but his penis to send a signal to the pitcher. Only after he is led away in tears, crying "He made me do it," does the game resume.

Another uproarious incident occurs when, hoping to avoid a shutout, Dr. Traum substitutes a pinch runner at first base. The runner is as neurotic as any of his teammates, constantly arguing with himself about how long a lead to take, whether to steal second, and—when the ball is finally hit by the batter—whether or where to run, since he can't see where the ball is. Again Roth expertly captures the base runner's comic dilemma, here through an interior monologue that ends, after many hesitations and debates, with the man running for all he's worth toward home and then praising God for letting him get there (*GAN,* 179–80). But the real reason the runner scores is that his teammate, an inveterate kleptomaniac, had secreted the ball while standing in the batter's box. Hence, no one can see the ball, and that is why Dr. Traum stopped the hitter as he was rounding third base and argued with him to give up the ball hidden in his shirt.

Outrageous as the game and the grotesque comedy it engenders may be, more follows, as the Ruppert Mundys exult in their victory—a rare occurrence in this year of exile—and a shutout to boot. The episode recalls the fishing trip the inmates take in Ken Kesey's *One Flew over the Cuckoo's Nest,* except that there the patients are the heroes and the comedy is not as anthracite in either color or texture. If Roth's farce seems overdone, then the point of farce, which is to exaggerate reality, is missed. Roth's unrestrained exuberance surpasses the fine excesses of *Portnoy's Complaint.* If farce originally meant "stuffed," full of forcemeat and herbs (Watson, 108), then this fiction, like *Our Gang,* is nothing if not "farced." It is not the deadly farce of *Letting Go* or *When She Was Good,* since the satire is less grim, though not less cutting, and better—or worse—comes in the succeeding chapters. Chapter 4, for example, entitled "Every Inch a Man," introduces a feud between two midgets whom one of the more commercially minded owners, Frank Mazuma, signs for his team, the Kakoola Reapers.

Mazuma resorts to hiring a midget, Bob Yamm, as a pinch hitter when in September of that wartime season his team is battling the Asylum Keepers for sixth place. His strategy is to have the 40-inch, 65-pound graduate of the University of Wisconsin, who had never even played the game, crouch at the plate, keeping his bat on his shoulder, thus presenting to the opposing pitcher a strike zone "not much larger than a match box" (*GAN,* 189). Walks inevitably follow, and wins. When the other owners begin remonstrating, General Oakheart telephones Mazuma to remind him of "the dignity of the game and the integrity of the league (and vice versa)" (*GAN*, 191). Mazuma responds by calling a press conference. There the impeccably dressed and well-spoken Bob Yamm reminds the reporters of midgets' rights, especially in that time of national emergency, when the rights and freedom of every American were at stake. His words and his bearing carry the day, winning the hearts of Americans everywhere. Midgets become the talk of the nation, Sunday papers run feature articles, and Mrs. Yamm appears on Martita McGraff's daytime radio show—Roth's superb parody of the talk shows of that or any other era (*GAN*, 194–96).

Things change when another midget, O.K. Ockatur, shows up in Mazuma's office for a tryout as a pitcher. Three inches shorter than Yamm, Ockatur is his antithesis in every respect. Whereas Yamm is smooth and attractive, Ockatur is craggy and ugly. Above all, he fiercely hates all men taller than he, including, or perhaps especially, Bob Yamm. Conflict is inevitable, and it comes when Ockatur insults his teammate on the afternoon they are to be photographed shaking hands outside the Reaper dugout. In another media parody Roth presents events through newspaper reports, involving crazy headlines (*GAN*, 199).

When the Mundys come to town the next day and Bud Parusha hits a fluke home run, Mazuma arranges to trade Ockatur for the one-armed outfielder, thus resolving the conflict on his team between the two midgets but also precipitating a crisis for the Mundys. Who was now going to play right field? One by one, the Mundys' reserves—Wally Omara, Mule Mokos, Applejack Terminus, Joe Garuda, Red Kronos, and the rest—decline to play the position on a regular basis. They are too old, too tired, too enfeebled; they prefer to sit on the bench instead of standing on their feet to see their team lose. In the end Specs Skirnir is drafted, despite his fear of breaking the glasses he has still not got used to after wearing them for a decade.

With Ockatur playing for the Mundys and Yamm for the Reapers, the inevitable happens. To celebrate the arrival of his new outfielder, the ever-enterprising Frank Mazuma organizes "Welcome Bud Parusha Day," which includes some outlandish "special events" that end in disaster. The final catastrophe results when the Reapers fail to discover how to extract the ball from their new teammate's jaws; thus, instead of claiming an easy 8–0 victory they are tied 8–8 going into the bottom of the ninth. With the bases loaded and two outs, the newly reinstated Bob Yamm comes to the plate as a pinch hitter. The crowd roars in anticipation; however, the Mundys then counter by sending in their new relief pitcher, O.K.

Ockatur. The face-off between the two midgets has arrived—with terrible consequences for both. Facing an unfamiliar 0–2 count, Yamm determines not to look at another called strike, which would send the game into extra innings. Not only his pride but "the pride of respectable, honest, hardworking midgets everywhere, the average American midget whose dignity he embodied and trust he bore" are at stake. Thus, Smitty brings the moment to its climax as Ockatur, deciding to "waste" a pitch, throws a high, hard ball toward the plate. Thinking the pitch is going to break down and away, Yamm swings and misses, as the ball keeps on coming, and when it hits him between the eyes, he is permanently blinded. Little is heard of Ockatur again (*GAN*, 235–36).

From here the novel moves into a still-darker realm of comedy in two chapters on "The Temptation of Roland Agni." Classified 4–F (physically unfit) by his draft board for no apparent reason and apparently doomed to spend his life playing for the grossly inept Ruppert Mundys despite leading the league in batting, Agni in desperation one fine September evening steals into the bunker beneath Tycoon Park in Tri-City. There the Tycoons' owner, Mrs. Angela Whittling Trust, lives in an apartment, and Agni is determined to persuade her to get him traded to the Tycoons. Her team is neck and neck with the Aceldama Butchers vying for the league lead, and Agni knows that with his help the Tycoons will win the pennant. A long conversation with Mrs. Trust ensues, during which she rehearses her lifetime in baseball with various lovers, among them Ty Cobb, Babe Ruth, and Luke "the Loner" Gofannon—the greatest love of her life, who loved triples more than he loved home runs—or her. Since her husband's death 10 years ago, however, she has reformed. She no longer takes lovers but has become the "responsible human being" her husband, on his deathbed, asked her to be, thenceforth dedicating her life to fighting the Communist conspiracy to destroy baseball.

For this reason Mrs. Trust turns down Agni's plea. Were he to leave the Mundys, the team would collapse, the first step in the destruction of the league—and then all of baseball. What follows is Roth's satire on McCarthyism. If, as Glorious Mundy and Ulysses S. Fairsmith had said, the religion of America is baseball, then the destruction of baseball is the destruction of America. Or, as Angela Whittling Trust puts it to Agni, what holds this country together is not the stars and stripes; it is baseball. To destroy America, she argues, the Communists and their agents are attempting to destroy the major leagues. Their target is the weakest link in the majors—the Patriot League—and the weakest link within that league is the Mundys (*GAN*, 262). She then explains that the idea of dispossessing the team of its home ballpark originated not with the play-boy Mundys but in a conspiracy within the War Department, infiltrated as it was, like the State Department and even the Patriot League, with Communists.

Distasteful and outdated as Roth's anti-McCarthyism satire now seems, he sinks to still-lower humor in his representation of the Jews who own the Tri-City Greenbacks, the team to which Agni turns next in his effort to escape the Mundys. Not that Roth is done with the so-called Communist conspiracy: more follows in later chapters with the sensational return of Gil Gamesh, now a double agent for the Kremlin; the abject confession by John Baal; and the accusations against others among the "Mundy Thirteen"—Astarte, Damur, Demeter, Mecoatl, Ockatur, Ptah, Tu-minikar, to name a few. By then, however, most of the humor has drained from the novel, and not much remains in the continuing temptation of Roland Agni to get himself traded from the Mundys. Nevertheless, the contretemps between Abraham Ellis, the owner of the Greenbacks, and his little son Isaac, who has advanced ideas of his own about how baseball should be played, is often funny.

If Roth's descent into ethnic humor, complete with heavy accent and overtly anti-Semitic comments, has at best limited appeal (compare Siegel, 190), the humor improves somewhat with satire against the Jewish intellectualism manifest in Isaac's theories, charts, graphs, and formulas on how to play the game. But even here Roth goes overboard, as he does elsewhere when he treats the subject of blacks in baseball. Over the years, Isaac's influence on the players is mainly detrimental. In the name of baseball's hallowed traditions, they resist his theories, and even his father appeals to him to cease and desist. But the little genius cannot or will not do so, with the result that not only the players, who start trying to reason things out at the plate, but also the fans wind up exhausted at the end of a game at Greenback Stadium, where the latter saw "a perfectly competent ball club struggling in vain against eighteen men—the nine on the opposing team and the nine on their own" (GAN, 273).

It is to the Greenbacks, then, that Agni next appeals, arriving at their doorstep in the middle of the night. But despite the maternal ministrations of Mrs. Ellis as well as Isaac's keen interest, Ellis cannot strike a deal. He is stymied by the person who answers the telephone in the Mundy front office, the black janitor, George Washington, who earlier had negotiated the trade of Bud Parusha for O.K. Ockatur. Now, claiming that the Mundys "don' *need* no mo' players" (GAN, 282), he refuses a trade and insists on cash instead—in the amount of $250,000. The dialogue between Ellis and Washington, both in heavy accents, is cruder and coarser than almost anything else in the novel. The janitor is the *"shvartze,"* and Ellis is simply "Jew." Contempt on both sides is apparent, and all decency vanishes.

If his father is unable to strike a deal, Isaac is not so easily deterred. Genius that he is, he spends his time in a laboratory behind the scoreboard in Greenback Stadium not only splitting atoms but also inventing a new Breakfast of Champions, or "Jewish Wheaties," as they come to be called. These can work wonders on the Mundys or any other team that uses them, Isaac claims. And so they do when he convinces Agni to spike his teammates' breakfast cereal with them each morning. Planning to bet on the Mundys to win and thus raise the $250,000 needed to buy Agni, Isaac argues that with Agni's physical prowess and his brains "there'd be nothing like it in the history of the game" (*GAN,* 285).

The scheme almost works. Revitalized, the Mundys go on an unprecedented late-September winning streak, and Isaac does too. Disaster strikes, however, on the last day of the season, when the Mundys play against the Tri-City Tycoons. Their recent performance having been so impressive, the once-despised ball club is cheered all the way to the stadium. General Oakheart wires Mr. Fairsmith (lately returned from darkest Africa), asking to join him on the train to Tri-City. On the morning of the game the general, festooned with ribbons, welcomes all the players to breakfast in the dining car. Amid this greatness Agni loses his nerve, and the Mundys lose the game—in front of Oakheart, Commissioner Kenesaw Mountain Landis, and even Eleanor Roosevelt, who attends on behalf of her husband, otherwise occupied in the War Room in Washington. Without the Jewish Wheaties, the Mundys are again the Mundys they used to be, and old Mr. Fairsmith is gathered to his maker. As for Isaac Ellis, who by then had won enough to buy Agni, he greedily bet everything on the game. With all the money he figured he would win, he could then buy not only Agni but the whole franchise. But with every cent now gone, he has to go back to splitting atoms, and Agni to being a Mundy forever. Their concluding conversation, filled with recriminations on both sides (*GAN,* 314–16), is not, to say the least, at all edifying.

The last chapter, except for an epilogue, concerns "The Return of Gil Gamesh; or, Mission from Moscow." Roth hurriedly brings his mock epic to a close, but not without further satiric blasts at McCarthyism, the House Un-American Activities Committee led by Congressman Martin Dies, and several literary precursors: O.K. Ockatur is revealed as Captain

Smerdyakov, Hot Ptah as Major Stavrogin, and a Kakoola grocer as Colonel Raskolnikov of the Russian Secret Police—"the number one underground espionage agent in the United States" (*GAN,* 332–33). (More lit. wit—the Russian names derive from characters in Dostoyevski's novels.) Behind all the machinations to destroy baseball is Gil Gamesh, who returns and persuades Mrs. Angela Whittling Trust, who in turn persuades General Oakheart, of his reformed character and his sincere anti-Communist zeal. Needless to say, Gamesh lies, but his lies pay off: he gets himself appointed as the new manager of the Ruppert Mundys for the 1943 season. When during a game in Kakoola All-American Agni uncovers Gamesh's plot and threatens to expose him, the manager counters with a threat of blackmail involving the Jewish Wheaties. But before either can take definitive action, two rifle shots ring out from the scoreboard. Both men fall, Agni dead, Gamesh badly wounded in his left shoulder. The assassin, the forever vengeful Mouth Masterson, is at once the target of a barrage of bullets from the Kakoola mounted police. Although one of their 256 bullets had actually grazed Mike's ear, it is a heart attack, brought on by the excitement of the assassination attempt, that kills him. Roth finds most targets for satire irresistible.

In the end Gamesh returns to Moscow, where he is seen during May Day parades standing next to Stalin in 1949 or Khrushchev in 1953, until he is executed as a double agent by the Russians in 1954. Meanwhile the Patriot League, found riddled with Communists and fellow travelers, is dissolved, its records expunged from the books of baseball. General Oakheart runs for president on the Patriot Party with Bob Yamm as his running mate in 1948, 1952, and 1956, when their private plane mysteriously disappears without a trace and both are presumed dead. Steadfastly refusing to cooperate with the Dies subcommittee, Word Smith is found in contempt of Congress and sentenced to a year in prison—and sentenced also to a life of vainly persuading others of the existence as well as the past glories of the Patriot League.

In an epilogue Smitty prints several rejection letters he has received from various (unnamed) publishers to whom he has sent his manuscript—Roth's way, obviously, of attempting to anticipate and thereby disarm criticism while indulging his gift for parody. Though most press readers find the book distasteful, not all do, and at least one appreciates its humor:

Dear Mr. Smith:
——Book blew my mind. Great put-down of Estab. Wild and zany black humor à la Bruce & Burroughs. The Yamms are a gas. I'd publish tomorrow if

I was in charge here. But the Money Men tell me there's no filthy lucre in far-out novel by unknown ab't mythical baseball team. What can ya' do? Fallen world. (*GAN,* 378)

Smith resorts to writing Chairman Mao Tse-tung in the hope that China will be interested in publishing his work, as the United States became interested in publishing Solzhenitsyn's—for both writers, Smitty implies, are despised in their native countries because they refuse "to accept lies for truth and myth for reality" (*GAN,* 380). Some comparison! Some chutzpah!

*The Great American Novel,* of course, did not have to await Chairman Mao's response to see the light of print. Although critics, including some most sympathetic to Roth's work, have seen it as a "false step" in his career (Rodgers, 121), and although the book, like *Our Gang,* runs counter to the main current of Roth's fiction, it is hardly without artistic merit, wit, or humor.[12] Operating on a number of levels, *The Great American Novel* incorporates social, economic, political, religious, literary, and still other strains of satire. However "far-fetched," according to one of Smitty's rejection letters, it is, the book tries, as Roth says, to establish "a continuum between the credible incredible and the incredible credible" (*RMAO,* 91). Insofar as it succeeds, it succeeds in demythologizing a good number of more or less cherished beliefs, compelling anyone who cares about them to take another look at the objects ridiculed. Fantasy by its very nature enlarges life; satiric fantasy blows life up through caricatures in order to blow them out. Though limited in appeal, the grotesque has its uses—and its humor. It is, finally, not with Solzhenitsyn, as Smitty thought, that comparisons with *The Great American Novel* should be made, but with the paintings of Hieronymus Bosch.

## Chapter Nine

# Playing with Autobiography:

*My Life as a Man*

In *My Life as a Man* Nathan Zuckerman makes his first appearance as an alter ego or, rather, as an alter ego for an alter ego, for here he is a surrogate novelist for a surrogate novelist for Philip Roth. The structure of this novel has thus led several critics to refer to the work as a set of Chinese boxes, or a fiction within a fiction within a fiction.[1] The justice of this description also points to the wit that is everywhere inherent in this work, which Roth had much difficulty writing.[2] But although three other novels intervened, write it he did, and it is one of his best and most important books. It is also one of his funniest, despite its darker side, which reveals the depths Roth had begun to plumb in his fiction.

## "Useful Fictions"

The novel opens with "A Note to the Reader" announcing that the two stories in part 1, grouped as "Useful Fictions," and part 2, the autobiographical piece called "My True Story," are drawn from "the writings of Peter Tarnopol." From the outset Roth thus attempts to distance the work from himself—an important consideration insofar as several crucial events, such as Tarnopol's disastrous marriage to Maureen Johnson, closely parallel Roth's experiences. In *The Facts* Roth tries to distinguish between fiction and autobiography, but resemblances between "fact" and "fiction" not only tantalize the imagination; they also raise questions about why authors write as and what they do.

In "After Eight Books" Roth suggests an answer to such questions when he discusses the role of certain characters in a writer's "personal mythology," or the "legend of the self" that is a "useful fiction." Often "mistaken by readers for veiled autobiography," these fictions are "a kind of idealized architect's drawing for what one may have constructed—or is yet to construct—out of the materials actuality makes available" (*RMAO*, 106). If Tarnopol's fiction is thus his *idea* of his fate, then *My Life as a*

*Man* is Roth's idea of *his* fate, his imagined reconstruction or reordering of events, his attempt to make art out of reality. That his is a comic art in no way diminishes its accomplishment, just as his humor in no way diminishes his seriousness.

"Salad Days," the first of the two "Useful Fictions," depicts young Nathan Zuckerman growing up in Camden, New Jersey, and recalls the early life of Alexander Portnoy—except that here Zuckerman's mother is a devoted, nonthreatening woman and his father is a hardworking, ambitious "shoedog." The same conflict of generations develops between the darling son and the protective parents, only this time it is Zuckerman's father who is the insistent, demanding parent, not the mother. For example, over such trifles as signing his name the senior Zuckerman orders his son to do better: "This is the way they teach you to sign your name, Natie? . . . Who the hell can read something that looks like a train wreck! Goddam it, boy, *this is your name*. Sign it *right!*" (*MLAM,* 4). By the time young Nathan enters college as an English major, he fully asserts himself, however, indulging in "college sarcasm" toward his mother and refusing to complete ROTC against his father's best advice. By his senior year he is totally under the sway of Miss Caroline Benson, his teacher, who had taught him as a freshman to pronounce the *g* in "length," the *h* in "whale," and other assorted niceties. Even being drafted into the army fails to dispel his dream of leading a life similar to hers, a life of books, culture, and genteel manners.

On the other hand, there is Sharon Shatzky, the 17-year-old daughter of Al "the Zipper King" Shatzky, the tall, red-haired, green-eyed, rangy Amazon whom Nathan turns "overnight" from "the perfect little lady," "a lovely lovely child," into the "most licentious creature he'd ever known" (*MLAM,* 22–24). All this happens in the four-week interval between Nathan's graduation from college and his induction into the army, and practically under the noses of the four adoring parents. This "startling metamorphosis" is rivaled in Nathan's recollection only by his mother's change into the Maiden Bereft when his older brother, Sherman, left home for the navy, or by Sherman's own remarkable switch after the navy from a hip jazz musician living a bachelor's life in New York into an orthodontist married to flat-chested Sheila and living conventionally in the suburbs. But these are nothing compared with the metamorphosis Nathan himself will undergo after his discharge from the army and his later life as a budding writer and teacher.

That is the subject of the second story, "Courting Disaster (or, Serious in the Fifties)," introduced in the last two paragraphs of the first story.

Adversity would overtake Nathan: "He would begin to pay . . . for the vanity and the ignorance, to be sure, but above all for the contradictions: the stinging tongue and the tender hide, the spiritual aspirations and the lewd desires, the softy boyish needs and the manly, *magisterial* ambitions" (*MLAM,* 30–31). As Peter Tarnopol (writing this) says, the account of Zuckerman's suffering calls for "a darker sense of irony, a grave and pensive voice to replace the amused, Olympian point of view" (*MLAM,* 31). That becomes the tone and the stance of "Courting Disaster." It treats Nathan's encounter with Lydia Ketterer, the unbeautiful siren that is the disaster Zuckerman inexplicably courts, renouncing the sexually dazzling (if intellectually boring) Sharon Shatzky in the process.

Maintaining fictional license, Tarnopol alters Nathan's life in several details, endowing him with a sister, Sonia, instead of a brother, and a father who is a bookkeeper instead of a shoedog. These changes and others, hardly more than variations on a theme, emphasize the fictions as fictions, and as such provide another "idea," or view, of Zuckerman's (or Tarnopol's or Roth's) fate. Ensconced now as a youthful instructor at the University of Chicago and delighting in his newfound freedom, his orderly life, and above all his nascent career as a writer and intellectual, Nathan seems more than satisfied with his "full, independent, and honorable" existence (*MLAM,* 50). Only the recurrent migraine headaches, which began in the army, mar his otherwise-perfect happiness—that is, until he meets Lydia Ketterer.

The meeting occurs during the second semester, when he teaches a course in creative writing during night school. Nathan's preparation for the class typifies his earnestness and pretentiousness. He writes a lengthy introductory lecture on "The Strategies and Intentions of Fiction," replete with references to and quotations from Aristotle's *Poetics,* Flaubert's correspondence, Dostoyevski's diaries, James's critical prefaces, and assorted Great Books of Literature. The response to his two-hour discourse, which leaves all but one of his students dazed into speechlessness, is scarcely what Zuckerman expects. A thin, middle-aged woman wearing a dark suit and a pillbox hat rises to ask politely, "Professor, I know that if you're writing a friendly letter to a little boy, you write on the envelope 'Master.' But what if you're writing a friendly letter to a little girl? Do you still say 'Miss'—or just what *do* you say?" (*MLAM,* 62). The question breaks the class up, its laughter directed at the questioner, not the lecturer, but it effectively punctures Zuckerman's pretentiousness. Like the migraine headaches, the episode is a fit prelude to Nathan's relationship with Lydia, which plunges him into a life such as he not only had never known but could never have imagined, least of all for himself.

"Courting Disaster" actually begins with Zuckerman's comment on his marriage to Lydia: everything later on is placed in that perspective. "No, I did not marry for conventional reasons; no one can accuse me of that," he says. Not fear of loneliness or the desire to have a helpmate, a cook, or a companion motivated him; nor did lust. "No matter what they may say about me now, sexual desire had nothing to do with it," he insists. On the contrary, though Lydia was pretty enough, her body was, from first to last, "unremittingly distasteful" (*MLAM,* 33).

Why, then, does Nathan choose her? The question is recurrent, not only in "Courting Disaster" but in its sequel, "My True Story." Again Nathan's migraine headaches and Mrs. Corbett's embarrassing question provide clues. Nathan's profound sense of guilt, deriving in part from an overweening belief in himself, fostered by doting parents, and in part from his until-then "charmed" existence, leads directly to brutal, largely self-inflicted punishment. The punishment and the pain last for years, blighting his existence and wrecking his career, even after Lydia dies. The only thing they do not destroy is his wit, or his sense of himself, like Portnoy, caught in a kind of cosmic joke from which he vainly tries to extricate himself while at the same time marveling at the variations and permutations his predicament can take in the hands of his tormentor.

For example, unattractive as she is, Lydia attracts Nathan powerfully, partly because she had suffered from childhood onward (her father had raped her, her first husband was a brute), and partly because she seemed to him so brave. Moreover, she was a survivor: "Not only that she had survived, but *what* she had survived, gave her enormous moral stature, or glamor, in my eyes" (*MLAM,* 70). The stories she wrote for his class were filled with details of her life, which Zuckerman found compelling. In other words, in contrast to his own sheltered existence this woman had *lived.* The imp of the perverse thus seems to latch tightly onto Nathan: wanting what Lydia has endured, he allows this attraction to overmaster the very real repulsion he also feels for her. He forces himself to overcome physical distaste to the extent that he performs cunnilingus on her "dry, brownish, weatherworn" vagina the morning after their first night of lovemaking. But though the act apparently gave little pleasure to either of them, he says that "at least I had done what I had been frightened of doing, put my tongue where she had been brutalized, as though . . . that would redeem us both" (*MLAM,* 72). Nathan later realizes that this notion was "as inflated as it was shallow." It grew, he believed, out of "serious literary studies": "Where Emma Bovary had read too many romances of her period, . . . I had read too much of the criticism of mine" (*MLAM,* 72). As often during a week as he could manage, he "took the sacrament" without, however, conquering either his "fearful repugnance" or his shame at feeling repelled.

Another example of Nathan's self-torture involves Monica, Lydia's child by an earlier marriage, who usually spent Sunday afternoons with Nathan and her mother. For Zuckerman those hours provided some of the most exquisite agony he experienced: "To watch the cycle of disaster repeating itself was as chilling as watching an electrocution—yes, a slow electrocution, the burning up of Monica Ketterer's life" (*MLAM,* 78). Sunday after Sunday he attends the "[s]tupid, broken, illiterate child" who literally did not know her right hand from her left, and he thinks: "Monica. Lydia. Ketterer. . . . 'What am I doing with these people?' And thinking that, could see no other choice for myself but to stay" (*MLAM,* 78). The final irony, years later, is that after her mother's suicide Monica becomes Nathan's lover, and they live in Italy. She has blossomed into an attractive, devoted, not-unintelligent young woman, though sometimes morose. But for Zuckerman, the dreams of following Miss Benson's example as a professor of literature or as a famous author have long since vanished from his imagination.

At one point in this narrative—told, unlike "Salad Days," in the first person—Zuckerman considers how ridiculous his "worship of ordeal and forbearance and the suppression of the sexual man" might seem (*MLAM,* 81). Even the literary mode of presentation may strike some, he says, as the funniest thing of all—"the decorousness, the orderliness, the underlying sobriety, that 'responsible' manner I continue to affect" (*MLAM,* 81). So much has changed since the 1950s, and Zuckerman has changed too. Through it all, he is unable to stifle the sense that he is now living someone else's life, not the life he planned for, worked for, was made for (*MLAM,* 84). Wanting to go home, he feels much like Joseph in Kafka's *The Trial* and experiences the "panic of the escaped convict who imagines the authorities have picked up his scent—only I am the authority as well as the escapee" (*MLAM,* 85). Unfortunately, he lacks the emotional or moral wherewithal to extradite himself. Although America has changed, he has not, at least not in that respect. His humiliation is too deep. He knows he should either leave Monica or return with her to America, but he cannot. He is the victim, it seems, of his own literary education; indeed, "Courting Disaster," like "My True Story," which follows, is filled with literary allusions. Nathan explains the irony or paradox of his situation as being unable to believe fully in the hopelessness of his predicament, while being convinced that the last line of Kafka's *The Trial* also applies to him: "it was as if the shame of it must outlive him!" (*MLAM*, 86).

Characteristically, having once formulated it, Zuckerman now rejects the Kafka reference, insisting that he is not a character in a book, "certainly not *that* book. I am real. And my humiliation is equally *real*" (*MLAM*, 86). But he *is* a character in a book, if not Kafka's, then Tarnopol's, as Tarnopol is a character in Roth's book. As the Chinese boxes unfold, the characters in "My True Story" also have something to say about Zuckerman and the "Useful Fictions" Tarnopol has written, just as Zuckerman later has something to say about Roth's autobiography in *The Facts*. If the reader begins to feel like someone in a hall of mirrors at a fun fair, that seems to be precisely Roth's intention in *My Life as a Man*.

## "My True Story": Reactions to Tarnopol's "Useful Fictions"

"My True Story" begins with a brief biographical sketch of and by the author, Peter Tarnopol. It is dated September 1967, a year after his wife's death, and is written, like everything that follows, at Quahsay, an artists' colony in Vermont, where Tarnopol has retreated to come to grips with his experience, specifically his obsession with Maureen, his wife of 10 years. Coming to grips with experience, exorcising an obsession, or trying to make sense of what has happened means for a writer—for this writer, at least—writing. In Tarnopol's case it means writing—first as fiction (the two "Useful Fictions"), then as autobiography—about the events that occupy, if not overwhelm, his imagination.

It is not the first time Tarnopol has tried to do this. The successful author of a first novel, *A Jewish Father,* he (like Roth) has been trying for years to write the story of his marriage into fiction, hoping thereby "to understand how I had fallen into this trap and why I couldn't get out" (*MLAM*, 104). From very early in his marriage he has struggled with the problem. His description of the effort also says something of the difficulties of much artistic composition. Trying to penetrate the mystery of his experience, he composes draft after dissatisfying draft of "the single unfinished chapter" that was driving him mad:

How I struggled for a description. (And, alas, struggle still.) But from one version to the next nothing of consequence ever happened: locales shifted, peripheral characters (parents, old flames, comforters, enemies, and allies) came and went, and with about as much hope for success as a man attacking the polar ice cap with his own warm breath, I would attempt to release the flow of invention in me by changing the color of her eyes or my hair. Of course, to give up the obsession would surely have made the most sense; only, obsessed, I was as incapable of not writing about what was killing me as I was of altering or understanding it. (*MLAM,* 105)

In actuality Roth was both capable and incapable of not writing about what was killing him: during his marriage he produced several books, and after his wife's death, while struggling with *My Life as a Man,* he wrote three others. But the statement stands as both fictional and biographical truth: writing *My Life as a Man,* Roth says, involved "one false start after another," and it nearly broke his will (*TF,* 152).

It almost breaks Peter Tarnopol's. At Quahsay (which resembles Yaddo, Roth's favorite retreat) he abandons fiction (as Roth did later, for similar reasons, when he wrote *The Facts*). Instead he writes his "true story," in five chapters, starting with "Peppy" (his boyhood nickname). But meanwhile he has produced two other stories, "variants" of the chapter, or book, he is trying to write, and sent them to his sister, Joan, who in turn has sent them to two of her friends, publishers of a literary magazine called *Bridges.* From all three he gets reactions, as later he gets some from his brother, Morris; his psychiatrist, Otto Spielvogel (imported from *Portnoy's Complaint*); his lover, Susan; and even one of his students, Karen Oakes, with whom he has a brief affair while teaching at the University of Wisconsin.

In a letter to Joan that accompanies the stories, Tarnopol analyzes the stories himself, thus becoming the first of his several critics. If "Salad Days" is "something like a comic idyll honoring a Pannish (and as yet unpunished) id," then "Courting Disaster" is "a legend composed at the behest and under the influence of the superego." To complete the trilogy, to give the ego its day in court, the nonfiction narrative Tarnopol is writing might be regarded as "the 'I' owning up to its role as ringleader of the plot," the central figure in the "conspiracy-to-abscond-with-my life" (*MLAM,* 113). Joan responds immediately and directly: "Thanks for the long letter and the two new stories, three artful documents springing from the same hole in your head," she says. "Is there no bottom to your guilty conscience? Is there no other source available for your art?" (*MLAM,* 114–15). Good questions, those, and before she finishes Joan urges Peter again to "drill for inspiration elsewhere." She dismisses his concern for her reaction to her fictional counterparts in the stories: "I know you can't write about me—you can't make pleasure credible" (*MLAM,* 115). Joan is a happily married, hedonistic, and very successful woman, and these attributes are utterly foreign to her brother.

Joan encloses two more critiques, one from Lane Coutell, associate editor at *Bridges,* and the other from his wife, Frances, who runs the magazine. They take diametrically opposed views of the stories. As Joan says, "Fiction does different things to different people, much like matrimony" (*MLAM,* 116). Lane likes "Salad Days" very much because it reads (to him) like a frontal attack on the "prematurely grave and high-minded author of *A Jewish Father,*" a novel he found "much too proper a book." "Courting Disaster," on the other hand, seems a throwback to the same "misguided and morbid 'moral' imagination" that produced Tarnopol's overrated novel (*MLAM,* 116–17). By contrast, Frances views "Salad Days" as "smug and vicious and infuriating, all the more so for being so *clever* and *winning*" (*MLAM,* 117). She hates what the author does to Sharon Shatzky. "Courting Disaster," however, is to her "absolutely heart*rending.*" Moved to tears, she finds the wife, the husband, and the daughter all unforgettably and "painfully true" (*MLAM,* 118).

Roth presents the Coutells as two satirized types: Lane, the sophisticated, smart-ass exemplar of the literati; Frances, the shrill, perplexed feminist (she adds a postscript to Joan: "You're an older woman, tell me something. What's the matter with men? What do they *want*?"). Morris Tarnopol's comments are not unlike Joan's, though they are couched in references to contemporary literature (Saul Bellow's *Herzog,* Norman Mailer's *An American Dream,* Arthur Miller's play, and Bernard Malamud's third novel): "What is it with you Jewish writers? Madeleine Herzog, Deborah Rojack, the cutie-pie castrator in *After the Fall,* and isn't the desirable shiksa of *A New Life* a kvetch and titless in the bargain? And now, for the further delight of the rabbis and the reading public, Lydia Zuckerman, the Gentile tomato. Chicken soup in every pot, and a Grushenka in every garage. With all the Dark Ladies to choose from, you luftmenschen can really pick 'em" (*MLAM,* 118). Like Joan, Morris too ends with a plea to Peter to forget Maureen and stop wasting his talent on "that Dead End Kid."

But, of course, Peter can't. He must tell the story of Maureen and his marriage to her. He is obsessed; what obsesses him is what obsessed Zuckerman. He wants to know why he did what he did: what drove him, first to take up with so obvious a loser as Maureen Johnson; then to marry her; then against all reason, when the marriage was clearly a mistake and, what's more, a fraud, to cohabit with her for three years before getting a

legal separation. And so he goes on to tell his "story," asking himself, as
Morris earlier had asked, "*Why*, Peppy? Why are you destroying your
young life for *her?*" (*MLAM*, 124). The answers, partly suggested in
"Courting Disaster," don't come easy, and at the end Tarnopol is no more
sure of himself than when he began.

## Maureen's Antithesis: Susan Seabury McCall

Like any good, modern novelist, Tarnopol does not follow a straight
lineal development in his narrative. His account loops back and forth on
itself, juxtaposing characters and events not only for their dramatic impact but for the illumination such juxtapositions offer. For example, before going into agonizing detail about his marriage to Maureen in
"Marriage à la Mode," Tarnopol spends a chapter on his long affair with
Susan Seabury McCall and explains why, after Maureen's death, he decides not to marry her. Susan seems to be everything, or almost everything, any man could want. Good-looking, rich, well mannered,
adoring, and an excellent cook, she provides a welcome port in the storm
that has become Peter's life even during his separation from Maureen. If
Maureen represents the extreme of irrationality, violence, and aggressiveness, Susan embodies her antithesis; neither finally will do, however.
Susan is too submissive, too compliant: all the comforts she supplies
notwithstanding, she is essentially boring. Besides, once burned, twice
shy: Tarnopol is not again going to risk marriage—or the stringent divorce laws of New York State as they were in the 1960s.

Susan's frigidity also contrasts with Maureen's. Neither woman is able
to experience orgasm, but whereas Maureen repels Peter, Susan does not.
Indeed, Susan and Peter work hard at sex. Here Roth shows how well he
can develop humor out of pathos, farce out of poignancy, as in the description of their lovemaking. "What a thing it was to watch the appetite
awaken in this shy and timid creature!" Peter exclaims. "And the daring—for if only she dared to, she might actually have what she wanted!"
He sees her on the very brink of success, her pulse beating in her throat,
her jaw strained upward, her eyes yearning: "a yard, a foot, an inch to
the tape, and victory over the self-denying past!" But all this "honest
toil"—his and hers, for Peter also works as hard as he can—is to no avail.
Valiant and persevering as they are, by the third year of the affair both of
them "were the worse for wear and came to bed like good workers doing
overtime night after night in a defense plant: in a good cause, for good
wages, but Christ how we wished the war was over and won and we could
rest and be happy" (*MLAM*, 133–34).

Both Susan and Maureen attempt suicide, filling Tarnopol with more guilt, but Maureen's attempt gives him an unexpected moral edge that enables him at last to separate from her (an aspect treated later in this chapter). Susan's case is different; Peter is struck by the terrible sadness of her situation, her unsuccessful attempts to be brave when he announces that since he cannot or will not marry her, they must break off their relationship—for although Susan never mentions them, Peter knows she wants marriage and children, and he believes she has a right to both, if not with him, then with someone else. When she breaks down and returns home to her mother in Princeton, Peter visits her and is again struck by her fragile beauty. He has to fight hard against his impulse to return to her, realizing that it is her "vulnerability and brokenness, [her] *neediness*" that draw him, not love. Here comments by Mrs. Seabury ("Sexual vanity"), Dr. Spielvogel ("Rescue fantasies . . . boyish dreams of Oedipal glory"), and his brother ("Fucked-up shiksas, . . . you can't resist them, Pep") all help to confirm his belief (*MLAM*, 168).

If Peter cannot resist such shiksas, he has no trouble resisting "rich, pretty, protected, smart, sexy, adoring, young, vibrant, clever, confident, ambitious" Jewish princesses, such as Dina Dornbush, the Sarah Lawrence senior with whom he has been having a passionate love affair when he meets Maureen. He gives up Dina for Maureen because "[Dina] was a girl still, who had just about everything. I, I decided at twenty-five, was beyond 'that.' I wanted something called 'a woman'" (*MLAM*, 178). With two failed marriages and a turbulent childhood behind her, Maureen "had been around," whereas Peter "hadn't been anywhere, really" (*MLAM*, 177). Besides, he liked "something taxing" in his love affairs, "something problematical and puzzling to keep the imagination going . . . something to think about" (*MLAM*, 179). In Maureen he gets more, much more, than he bargained for.

## Maureen

The social and historical moment has something to do with it too, Peter recognizes. He met Maureen in the 1950s, a deadly earnest period, with the draft still on and "maturity" very much an issue among young Americans. This was a prefeminist era, when men were expected to give women "the value and the purpose that society at large withheld—by marrying them" (*MLAM*, 169). Rationalization or not, such was the operative zeitgeist, Tarnopol claims, during his encounter with Maureen. Together with his own predilections and proclivities described earlier, or his "aberrant, if not pathological, nature" (*MLAM*, 171), everything was conducive to Peter's precipitous decline into the arms of matrimony with Maureen, a woman whose mission, she decides, is to make a man of him—come what may.

Maureen has her work cut out for her, for when she meets him, Peter, though a confident 25 is in fact naive, a true innocent. He has not the slightest idea of what life with Maureen would be like or of what the dangers to him, personally and professionally, might be in hooking up with someone so deeply disturbed, so ready for violence (she gives as good as she gets), and so heavily dependent on others, especially men, for whatever satisfactions she can find. By the time Peter becomes aware of the impossibility of continuing their affair, it is too late. He tries to throw Maureen out of his apartment, but three days later she is back on his doorstep, "wan and scrappy looking as a street urchin" (*MLAM*, 183). Fights inevitably ensue, as do recriminations and pleas; then Maureen plays her trump: she is two months pregnant.

As Tarnopol says, anyone could have seen that coming a mile away (*MLAM*, 181). Though naive, he is not that naive, and he refuses to believe her. He insists that Maureen prove she is pregnant by having a urine test done at a local pharmacy. It is here that, exactly as Roth's first wife had done,[3] she demonstrates the imagination, the sheer inventiveness, that later astonishes Peter. Maureen deceives him by finding a pregnant black woman and obtaining a sample of her urine to use in the rabbit test. The trick works. Incredible as it seems, since they had not had intercourse in ages, Peter accepts responsibility for the child. It never occurs to him that anyone else could be the father. An inveterate liar, Maureen couldn't lie "about something as serious as fatherhood. *That* I couldn't believe," he says (*MLAM*, 192).

So much for Peter's maturity and his understanding of how life imitates art. As he goes on to comment, reality and fiction were still so mixed up in his mind that he knew of no other way to judge the one but by the other: "Stuffed to the gills with great fiction—entranced not by cheap romances, like Madame Bovary, but by *Madame Bovary*—I now expected to find in everyday experience that same sense of the difficult and the deadly earnest that informed the novels I admired most." At the heart of his "model of reality," deduced from reading the masters, was *intractability*: "And here it was, a reality as obdurate and recalcitrant and (in addition) as awful as any I could have wished for in my most bookish dreams" (*MLAM*, 194).

Literate Tarnopol (like Roth) is also a master of lit. wit, as many allusions to "the masters" indicate. But lit. wit is no substitute for mother wit, as the novel also abundantly reveals and Tarnopol's fate demonstrates. When he discovers before Maureen knows it that the rabbit test has proved positive, Peter takes a long walk deciding what to do. He concludes—wrongly, as he later realizes—that the only "manly" thing is to go back to the apartment and, pretending he knows nothing about the test, propose marriage. He is motivated by the fear that if he does not marry Maureen, she will do herself in, "And that was unthinkable—I could not be the cause of another's death" (*MLAM,* 193). Further, by proposing before Maureen knew the test results, Peter could appear as though he were acting out of choice, not necessity. In that way, he feels, their union might have some chance of success. Wrong again!

Maureen is so overjoyed and, in her turn, so taken in by the apparent sincerity of the proposal that she agrees to an abortion. That leads to her second deception, an action she performs with consummate skill, when she pretends to have had the surgery and returns to the apartment evidently shaking with illness and fatigue. All this is in behalf of getting Peter to assume his "manly" duty, the course Maureen maintains even as the marriage fails, a separation is arranged, and Peter is saddled with financially crippling alimony.

Tarnopol has wanted to experience reality in all its obduracy and intractability, expecting it to "take place at an appropriately lofty moral altitude, an elevation somewhere, say, between *The Brothers Karamazov* and *The Wings of the Dove*" (*MLAM,* 194). Ironically, he gets intractability, all right, but instead of the intractability of serious fiction he gets the intractability of soap opera: "Resistant enough, but the wrong genre" (*MLAM,* 195). The soap opera he and Maureen play out lasts for several more years, until her sudden death (as with Roth's wife) in an automobile accident. Many of the scenes are indeed operatic, inspiring comedy amidst pathos, such as Maureen's revelation during a suicide attempt of how she deceived Peter with the urine test (*MLAM,* 208–10). On another occasion years afterward, when Maureen has steadfastly refused to divorce him, insisting that he return to her and be "a man" (*MLAM,* 268), she again deceives Peter into thinking she has relented. But it is only another ploy, one that ends in violence and disaster for them both (*MLAM,* 274 ff.).

## Dr. Spielvogel Again

By this time, having broken down completely, Peter is in the care of Dr. Spielvogel. Unlike the Spielvogel in *Portnoy's Complaint,* this Spielvogel is a developed character, one who participates significantly in its action—and in its humor. Again lit. wit is operative, as in the description of Spielvogel three years after Tarnopol casually meets him at a social gathering. Both men have changed: while Tarnopol was battling Maureen, Spielvogel was battling cancer. His pasty skin, his limp, and other features suggest the figure of Dr. Chillingworth in Hawthorne's *The Scarlet Letter*. "Appropriate enough," Peter thinks, "because I sat facing him as full of shameful secrets as the Reverend Arthur Dimmesdale" (*MLAM*, 203). Among the shameful secrets Peter confesses are his brief transvestitism (*MLAM*, 210), his habit of leaving his sperm around in people's houses and on library books (*MLAM*, 211), and his total unmanning—or so it seems to him—by Maureen (*MLAM*, 213).

Literally crying for help, Tarnopol puts himself in Dr. Spielvogel's hands—only to be invited to consider how much Maureen may remind him of his mother. The question throws Tarnopol back: "Psychoanalytic reductivism was not going to save me from the IRT tracks," he feels (*MLAM*, 213). Nevertheless, he allows Spielvogel to pursue the issue further, much further, until he all but accepts the hypothesis of a "phallic threatening mother" (*MLAM*, 216) and begins treating his adoring, amazed, and terribly hurt parent with coldness and disdain (*MLAM*, 218). Spielvogel questions Tarnopol's happy childhood, suggesting a sinister aspect underlying his mother's "competence and vigor and attentiveness," which have led to his patient's "castration anxiety" (*MLAM*, 214).

Roth here not only satirizes Freudian theories of childhood development; he opposes to it an interesting and humorous theory of his own.[4] The trouble with "Mrs. Tarnopol's little boy" was not her threatening behavior but just the opposite: in Peter she had nourished the belief that he could win whatever he wanted, that he led a "charmed life." Thus, unprotected against "the realities of setback and frustration" (*MLAM*, 215), he was totally unprepared for Maureen. This theory also explains Peter's astonishment when he learns about the urine trick and his difficulty in turning it into fiction: Most likely the reason he could not make it seem credible is that he could hardly believe it himself—"HOW COULD SHE?" he thinks. "TO ME!" (*MLAM*, 208).

## The Artist as Narcissist

Later Spielvogel attempts to convince Tarnopol that he is essentially narcissistic. The issue arises when Spielvogel writes an article entitled "Creativity: The Narcissism of the Artist" for a professional journal with a small circulation. The essay is what Tarnopol, enraged, regards as a thinly veiled portrait of himself. He confronts his therapist, and for several sessions they argue about the essay. Spielvogel forcefully takes the position that he had every right to do what he did, since he was writing a scientific paper. Moreover, he maintains that Tarnopol's anger and distress are the result of his ambivalent attitude about his own "specialness" (*MLAM*, 249) and of the blow the article delivers to his narcissism (*MLAM*, 251). Tarnopol retorts that Spielvogel should have asked his permission before revealing confidential information; the difference between a novelist who because he writes fiction does not ask permission and a psychoanalyst who writes a scientific article is serious and significant: "It's in the nature of being a novelist to make private life public—that's a part of what a novelist is up to. But certainly it is not what I thought *you* were up to when I came here" (*MLAM*, 250).

The impasse they reach leads Spielvogel to propose ending treatment, but Tarnopol is still too dependent upon his therapist. In the course of the episode he reveals something important about the nature of fiction, specifically the writing of novels, that bears directly on what Roth is doing in *My Life as a Man*: "his *self*," Tarnopol says, "is to many a novelist what his own physiognomy is to a painter of portraits: the closest subject at hand demanding scrutiny, a problem for his art to solve—given the enormous obstacles to truthfulness, *the* artistic problem." Neither the novelist nor the portrait painter is a narcissist, because success depends on powers of detachment, on "*de*-narcissizing" oneself. "That's where the excitement comes in," Tarnopol says. "That hard *conscious* work that makes it *art!*" (*MLAM*, 240).

Many novelists and critics will object to Tarnopol's formulation of the novelist's task here, whether or not it helps distinguish a novelist from a poet, as Tarnopol argues. Novelists may include themselves in their work, as William Styron does, for example, in *Sophie's Choice*, or they may not, as Singer does not in *The Slave*. They have that choice. But as much of Roth's writing shows, *for what he himself does in his fiction*, the passage is highly relevant. His own experience—for example, as a boy in Hebrew school ("The Conversion of the Jews"), as a page in the Newark Public Library ("Goodbye, Columbus"), or as a graduate student and teacher at a midwestern university (*Letting Go*)—has been the source of much of his fiction. But in every instance, as in *My Life as a Man*, Roth takes liberties with "facts" to write "truth," to tackle what Tarnopol calls "*the* artistic problem."

Regarding the "truth" of fiction, it matters little whether or not Roth's therapist (he had one at the time) wrote an article such as Spielvogel's. What does matter is that the article, real or imagined, provides Roth with an opportunity to raise questions about creativity and narcissism and about the relation between the two. Through Tarnopol Roth presents the strongest possible arguments a character like Peter can conceive. At the same time he presents powerful counterarguments through the character of Spielvogel. The "truth" will emerge not necessarily in the arguments of one or the other but partly through the dialectic that develops and partly through the evidence the rest of the novel presents.

The fact is that, despite Tarnopol's vehement refusal to accept Spielvogel's diagnosis of his narcissism, much in his behavior confirms the diagnosis. That is an essential aspect of Roth's comedy. Tarnopol may be justly upset about Spielvogel's article: the psychiatrist had no right to present information about his patient that could easily reveal his identity to a knowledgeable reader. But Tarnopol errs in vigorously denying a basic element of his character, his inordinate preoccupation with himself. By his own admission that quality was fostered in him from his earliest years; then it was violently challenged by Maureen, a competitor for his attention—the most demanding one he has ever known. Her jealousy is the obverse of his narcissism, resulting in their basic incompatibility. Matters then worsen when she begins to fancy herself a competitor as a writer of fiction to boot.

Roth knows that the artistic problem involves getting the proper distance, or detachment, from his subject, particularly when his subject is himself. That is not only where the "excitement comes in" but also where the fun begins.[5] And it has led Roth, as it will later lead Zuckerman (in *Zuckerman Unbound,* for example), into problems of trying to disentangle himself from his fiction. *Portnoy's Complaint* borrowed from Roth's boyhood to present certain aspects of Newark during the war years and of middle-class Jewish home life; as a result, many readers wrongly began to make wholesale one-to-one equivalencies regarding Alexander Portnoy and Philip Roth. In *My Life as a Man* Roth fictionalizes his marital experience and attempts, through the device of the "Useful Fictions," to forewarn the reader against similar equivalencies. To the extent that the reader observes and registers the point, Roth is successful. Nevertheless, readers can be notoriously unobservant, and a vulgar curiosity for gossip can become overwhelming, especially when offered such tantalizing bait as this novel offers.[6]

Again, it matters little whether or not the real-life counterpart for Susan Seabury McCall, whom Roth dubs "May Aldridge" in *The Facts,* attempted suicide.[7] In the context of the novel it is an important "truth," first in developing the character and second in reaffirming Tarnopol's narcissism. Moreover, as Zuckerman says in the postscript to *The Facts*, Roth is apt to be much more honest in fiction than in autobiography: "You don't appear to have the heart—the gall, the guts—to do in autobiography what you consider absolutely essential in a novel" (*TF*, 183). Susan is just the kind of woman who, abandoned by her lover and puzzled by his action, would desperately turn to suicide to get back her man. And her strategy almost works (*MLAM*, 138–50).

For, as Spielvogel points out, Peter is just the kind of man who would interpret Susan's action as his responsibility rather than her own. Peter had earlier interpreted Maureen's suicide attempt the same way, much to her derision (*MLAM*, 127). A confirmed narcissist, he naturally sees events the only way he can, and against the available contrary evidence, such as that which Spielvogel brings to bear. Susan knew that her cleaning woman was expected early the next morning and had a key to let herself in; thus, she would be found in a few hours. She did what she did to get what she wanted, to get Peter to come running. And Spielvogel reminds Tarnopol, "You did come running. And you are running yet. Maybe only in circles, but that for her is still better than out of her life completely. It is you, you see, who is blowing this up out of all proportion. Your narcissism again, if I may say so. Much too much overestimation of—well, practically everything" (*MLAM*, 222). Nevertheless, Tarnopol uses this incident, coupled with that involving the "Creativity" article earlier, to break off therapy and go into isolation again.

And that is where the novel ends, with Maureen dead, Susan convalescing at home with her mother, and Peter alone at Quahsay writing his stories. He is "Free" at last, as the final chapter is called. Free to become a man? Free to write the novel he has been trying to write for years? Free to confront his past and struggle toward a future? "This me who is me being me and none other"—the final words in the novel—carry all these implications and a host of others.[8] It is the artist scrutinizing his *self*, with all the wonder, fear, and amazement that object holds.

## Chapter Ten

# What Happens When "Looking at Kafka":

### *The Professor of Desire* and *The Breast*

Written after *The Breast* and in some ways its sequel, *The Professor of Desire* presents its protagonist, David Kepesh, from his earliest years until a year before his transformation occurs. It is, of course, that transformation, so reminiscent of "The Metamorphosis," that directly links Roth with Franz Kafka. But as noted, the links between Roth and Kafka were forged much earlier, if not directly or consciously, then indirectly and intuitively. Clearly Roth is Kafka's literary and spiritual descendant, as Morton Levitt says,[1] but more connects them than Levitt indicates. Let us look at Roth looking at Kafka, as he does in a piece entitled "'I Always Wanted You to Admire My Fasting'; or, Looking at Kafka" (*RMAO,* 247–70).

## A Counterlife for Kafka

Written in 1973, soon after teaching Kafka's fiction at the University of Pennsylvania, Roth dedicated the piece to his students. It begins with Roth studying a picture of Kafka at age 40—Roth's own age at the time of writing—and thus the identification begins. The last year of his life, Kafka's forty-first was "as sweet and hopeful a year as he may ever have known as a man" (*RMAO,* 247). Kafka seemed finally to have broken free from his family, particularly his father's hold upon him, and after moving to Berlin he formed a new relationship with a young woman half his age. Dora Dymant was lovely, warm, and firmly devoted to him. At last here was someone, unlike his previous fiancées or his lover, Milena, with whom Kafka could imagine a life together; accordingly, he wrote Dora's Orthodox Jewish father for her hand in marriage.

Does it matter that his request was refused? The two went on living together anyway. Does it matter whether they consummated the relationship? Roth suggests that despite the erotic fantasies conveyed in "The Burrow," the story he was writing about "life in a hole," Kafka remained celibate: "Certainly a dreamer like Kafka need never have entered the young girl's body for her tender presence to kindle in him a fantasy of a hidden orifice that promises 'satisfied desire' . . . but that, once penetrated and in one's possession, arouses the most terrifying and heartbreaking fears of retribution and loss" (*RMAO,* 257). Sound familiar? Recall the ending of *Portnoy's Complaint,* or Gabe Wallach's fate in *Letting Go,* or Peter Tarnopol's in *My Life as a Man.* This is Roth's comic paradigm, used once again, with significant variations, in *The Professor of Desire.*

In "Looking at Kafka" Roth goes on to imagine Kafka escaping death and, like Karl Rossmann, arriving in America, where he becomes a teacher in Roth's Hebrew school.[2] The story of the poor, lonely refugee, nicknamed Dr. Kishka by his irreverent pupils, is both funny and touching, less didactic and terrifying than "The Conversion of the Jews" but drawn from the same milieu. Young Roth, a great mimic even then, delights his friends with imitations of their teacher's "precise and finicky professorial manner, his German accent, his cough, his gloom" (*RMAO,* 258). Later, overcome by shame and sadness, Philip tells his family that his teacher lives in "a room" and is astonished when his mother responds by inviting the man to Friday-night dinner.

Events rapidly get complicated, as Philip's father invites his stylish but spinsterish sister-in-law to dinner also, and the matchmaking begins. It concludes after the couple go to Atlantic City for a weekend, and whatever happened, happened. All young Philip can learn is what his older brother conveys through the single word "Sex!" (*RMAO,* 268). Years later at college, Philip reads Kafka's obituary, as sad as it is brief: not only no one but nothing survives him—no stories, no books, no diaries. This is Roth's vision of Kafka's counterlife—mundane, yes, but surely more "true to life." Or, as Roth says with telling irony, "No, it simply is not in the cards for Kafka ever to become *the* Kafka—why, that would be stranger even than a man turning into an insect. No one would believe it, Kafka least of all" (*RMAO,* 270).

## Young David Kepesh

Nor would anyone believe in a man turning into an oversize breast, which is what later happens to David Alan Kepesh, the professor in *The Professor of Desire.* But before examining Roth's extraordinary novel, written in 1972 and revised in 1980 after *The Professor of Desire* appeared, let us consider the story of David Kepesh's earlier life.[3] The comic paradigm of desire-attainment-loss, or fear of loss, is exemplified par excellence in this story of a young academic who in temperament and circumstances resembles Gabe Wallach in *Letting Go,* but, like all good writers, Roth does not repeat himself, however closely the underlying comic structures of his work are related.

Some connections with *My Life as a Man* are patent: both Peter Tarnopol and David Kepesh are bright young Jewish males who early in life fall into disastrous marriages, painfully extricate themselves, and then find placid, somewhat voluptuous lovers who provide peace and contentment and apparently everything a man can possibly want. But both novels end with presentiments of dissatisfaction, of ebbing passion—a sense in each protagonist that the enormous fulfillment he has experienced is somehow not fulfilling enough. It is not simply a craving for more, although more excitement, more adventure, more *something* lies near the heart of the matter. Perhaps it is a quixotic longing after a wholeness, a completeness that is not quite attainable in this world, or at least in the world Roth's characters inhabit. Striving for what they can neither have nor even imagine but nonetheless avidly desire is their comic predicament.

David Kepesh grows up in the Catskills, the son of hardworking parents such as we have seen, mutatis mutandis, in other novels. Abe and Belle Kepesh, thoroughly devoted to each other and to their only son, run a small mountain resort, the Hungarian Royale Hotel ("Dietary Laws Strictly Observed"), which brings them a small but decent income from a small but decent clientele (*POD,* 14). Never mind that during the season "A-owitz" and "B-owitz" and "C-owitz" drive the proprietors, the staff, and one another crazy with their kibitzing and complaining and pretentiousness. During the long winter evenings letters flow back and forth, cementing lifelong relationships. In this snug cocoon David grows up, enters Syracuse University, and then embarks on his own life.

The first phase of David's postadolescence, if it can be called that, is a Fulbright year abroad to study literature at the University of London. Before long he meets the Scandinavians Elisabeth and Birgitta, and establishes a ménage à trois with them, until Elisabeth, desperately in love with him and unable to take their sex games any longer, attempts suicide. Recovering, she returns home, while David and Birgitta continue their sexual adventure, which ends only after David too feels he must go home. When he tells Birgitta his decision, that he must resume his "serious education" as a graduate student at Stanford (*POD,* 49), she does not argue; she simply gets dressed and leaves, saying, "Why did I like you so much? You are such a boy" (*POD,* 50).

David is indeed "such a boy," dazzled at first by his wildest, most lascivious dreams come true through Elisabeth and Birgitta, mostly Birgitta. He cannot understand his decision, only that he must make it. When Birgitta accepts it without demur, he contemplates her actions and his own with a questioning that characterizes much of his later behavior. "My God, she is bolder even than I imagined!" he says to himself. "She dares to do everything, and yet she is as sane as I am. Sane, clever, courageous, self-possessed—and wildly lascivious! Just what I've always wanted. Why am I running away, then?" he wonders. Is it from his own nature? To Birgitta he has admitted his nature is that of a whoremaster, a polygamist, a rapist even, and she says he can't "change his mind" about what is essentially himself. If he has second thoughts about that, she has none (*POD,* 49–50).

David's relationship with Birgitta recalls Alexander Portnoy's with The Monkey, Mary Jane Reed. The reasons the relationships end are also similar—and comic: an attempt to resolve the by-now-familiar conflict in Roth's protagonists between two imperatives, sexual and moral, or, in Freudian terms, the pleasure principle and the reality principle.[4] What Kepesh is running away from, comically enough, are the pleasures that he has been taught are unhealthy, forbidden, immoral. Maturing, he feels he must give up such pleasures for "real" life, serious study, and a responsible position in the world. Or so he believes.

## Marriage with Helen Baird

A few years later, as he is completing a doctorate in comparative literature at Stanford, David meets Helen Baird, whom he eventually marries. She is another exotic—a stunningly handsome woman who at 18 ran off to Hong Kong with a married man twice her age and who for the next eight years enjoyed a life filled with multiple and varied pleasures such as she could never have known had she remained at the University of Southern California, finished her degree, and settled into the kind of middle-class existence her WASP parents represent. Under David's interrogation she reveals that she gave everything up after her lover offered to have his wife killed if she would marry him. Despite her apparent amorality, Helen could not consent to the crime. All it would have taken, she says, was the single word *yes*; nevertheless, for perhaps the only time in her life Helen allows a moral impulse to oversway her. And now she is back, ready to start life anew. But first she has "to figure out some way to stop crying" (*POD,* 55).

Enter her rescuer, her knight in shining armor, her David, who, despite some skepticism about her adventures, finds her "enthralling and full of fascination" (POD, 57). In a way, she too is, or tries to be, David's rescuer—from his life of study to the thing itself. As their affair commences and she confesses her detestation of libraries, books, and schools—everything, in short, Kepesh has dedicated himself to—she astutely comments that he really hates what he is doing. It has turned him into "something slightly other, slightly . . . wrong," she says. "You're misusing yourself, David. You're hopelessly intent on being what you're not. I get the sense that you may be riding for a very bad fall" (POD, 60). David is indeed riding for a very bad fall, and the fall is marrying Helen Baird, though at first neither of them realizes it.

Why does David marry Helen? Like Gabe Wallach with Martha Regenhart or Peter Tarnopol with Maureen Johnson, Kepesh finds in Helen Baird a woman who has "lived." That is not quite how he puts it, but certainly it underlies her fascination for him. Her "fearlessness" draws her to him, "that determined abandon with which she will give herself to whatever strongly beckons, and regardless of how likely it is to bring in the end as much pain as pleasure" (POD, 61). Her "capacity for pain-filled renunciation," coupled with her gift for sensual abandon, makes her irresistible (POD, 64). Allowing his skepticism and suspiciousness to subside, Kepesh acquiesces in the relationship despite the continued fencing and parrying that goes on between them and that presages an uneasy and finally catastrophic union.

Their marriage is not simply a replay of Peter Tarnapol's to Maureen Johnson or Gabe Wallach's liaison with Martha Regenhart. Helen is a far more accomplished woman, and the pain she inflicts is far more exquisite than either Martha or Maureen is capable of. And Kepesh is apparently far more subservient, becoming more and more Helen's servant and less and less her husband or lover. Only after she finally runs off to Hong Kong in a vain attempt to recover her former lover does David accept the inevitable.

## Kepesh Recuperates

Soon after their divorce Kepesh winds up teaching comparative literature in New York and having his marriage "demythologized" by Dr. Frederick Klinger, a psychiatrist whose patient he has become. Apart from having become depressed and impotent, Kepesh insistently defends Helen against Dr. Klinger, who insistently defends David against himself. By this time David has been teaching Chekhov's short stories, on which he based his doctoral dissertation, and Chekhov's influence becomes the principal influence in the novel, as it is on David's life. Not that Kafka disappears altogether. Far from from it: he makes an important reappearance later in the novel, and the comic paradigm, described earlier, remains in effect. But by lending the novel its peculiarly elegiac tone, Chekhov's influence tempers Kafka's, especially in the last two sections (Rodgers, 166–69).

While Kepesh slowly recuperates, several new characters enter his life and several important events occur. During a visit from his parents, David learns that his mother is dying of cancer. The poignancy of the visit is not lost on him. He smiles at his mother's horror when, as she unloads the food she has prepared and frozen for her son, she opens his nearly empty refrigerator and sees a lemon that looks, she says, older than she is. After his parents have gone to bed, David ponders his life, the errors he has made, the futility of his efforts to make a success of his marriage. And the questioning recurs: "Instead of being enemies, why couldn't Helen and I have put that effort into satisfying each other, into steady, dedicated living? Would that have been so hard for two such strong-willed people?" He thinks how sweet, how welcoming Elisabeth would have been to his widowed father. "But without an Elisabeth, what can I do for him?" he asks himself. "How ever will he survive up there on his own? Oh, why must it be Helen and Birgitta at one extreme or life with a lemon at the other?" (*POD*, 109).

It does not have to be, of course, as David discovers when he meets and falls in love with Claire Ovington. But before that he experiences a long winter of discontent, punctuated by a falling-out with Arthur and Debbie Schonbrunn, the couple who befriended him at Stanford during his troubles and who are now in New York, where Arthur is David's chairman (earlier Arthur had been David's dissertation supervisor). The winter is also punctuated by outings with a new friend, the poet Ralph Baumgarten, whose outrageous behavior and poetry antagonize Debbie Schonbrunn. Meanwhile Belle Kepesh dies and Abe goes to live, temporarily at first, with his brother in Cedarhurst. He then sells the Hungarian Royale but, unlike Gabe Wallach's father, does not burden his son with pleas for company and companionship, heavily though he weighs on David's conscience.

## In Love with Claire

Into this dreary existence Claire enters. At first and last glance she appears wonderfully appealing: serene, well educated, sexually alluring, intelligent, giving, and undemanding. She immediately reminds one of

Susan Seabury McCall, except that she is not a widow, is not as rich, and, unlike Susan, comes from an unhappy home life. Claire's parents, alcoholics both, constantly battle with each other, providing Claire and her sister Olivia with bitter memories and a need for order in their lives. Just as Susan succors Tarnopol, so Claire provides a refuge—not from the depredations of a scheming wife but from the loneliness, impotence, and disorderliness that have afflicted Kepesh since leaving Helen. Theirs is as close to an ideal relationship as one can imagine; they share similar interests, mutual respect, good sex, and real caring. "My, how easy life is when it's easy," Kepesh remarks a year later, "and how hard when it's hard!" (POD, 155).

In this newfound contentment David returns to his work on Chekhov, abandoned amid the turmoil two years earlier. His interest is rekindled by such short stories as "Man in a Shell," "Gooseberries," and "The Duel." He observes how Chekhov reveals "the humiliations and failures—worst of all, the destructive power—of those who seek a way *out* of the shell of restrictions and convention, out of the pervasive boredom and the stifling despair, out of the painful marital situations and the endemic social falsity, into what they take to be a vibrant and desirable life" (POD, 156). If "license and restraint" have alternately characterized Kepesh's own life until now, it is this insight that doubtless motivates him to complete a 40,000-word essay on their prevalence in Chekhov's world (POD, 157).

Claire is to "steadiness," David tells Dr. Klinger, concluding two years of therapy, what Birgitta was to "impetuosity." Feeling triumphant, he nevertheless questions his success: "*Can* it be that I've come through? Just like that? Just because of Claire?" he asks. "What if I awaken tomorrow once again a man with a crater instead of a heart, once again without a man's capacity and appetite and strength and judgment, without the least bit of mastery over my flesh or my intelligence or my feelings. . . ." (POD, 158). The questioning persists as, during a trip to Europe the following summer, David contemplates his good fortune: "I ask myself again if this serenity truly exists, if this contentment, this wonderful accord is real. *Is* the worst over? Have I no more terrible mistakes to make? And no more to pay on those behind me? Was all that only so much Getting Started, a longish and misguided youth out of which I have finally aged?" (POD, 159–60). These are apt questions, for the memory of Birgitta soon haunts David, and the nagging sense of dissatisfaction with Claire begins.

Throughout the trip, which includes visits to Italy, Vienna, Belgium, and Czechoslovakia, Kepesh controls his incipient discontent, exorcising more or less successfully Birgitta's ghost. But repeatedly Claire's picture taking irritates him, knowing that the album of photographs will be placed at the foot of her bed where other volumes are stored, and that he will be "stored" along with them. Although at one point he recognizes he is being "sealed up into something wonderful" (*POD*, 164), sealing up is what troubles him, vaguely at first but increasingly as time goes on.

## Prague

The high point in their trip is Prague, home to Franz Kafka, whose attraction—notwithstanding Chekhov's ameliorating influence—remains strong, for David if not for Claire. There they meet Professor Soska, a sometime political dissident and forcibly retired teacher of literature, now reduced to making a useless translation of *Moby-Dick*. Soska's wry comments on the absurdity of his life—indeed, of everyone's life in Communist Czechoslovakia—strike a resonant chord in David. To the professor's account of political totalitarianism and consequent despair Kepesh draws an analogy of sexual totalitarianism and despair. He speaks of "vows of chastity that seem somehow to have been taken behind my back, and which I lived with against my will. Either I turned against my flesh, or it turned against me" (*POD*, 171).

Kepesh pursues the analogy to his reading of Kafka, specifically *The Castle*. "You think poor K. is clever—you should have heard me trying to outfox impotence," he tells Soska (*POD*, 172). Although Kepesh admits that for him "the worst is over," he cautions (himself more than Soska), "*May* be over. At least is over for *now*" (*POD*, 171). His nagging doubts persist. If earlier he had equated Birgitta with "more" and claimed that he no longer needed her or what she represents, that Claire was "enough" (*POD*, 164–65), his vacillations continue, as they will to the end of the novel. This is Kepesh's comic predicament, recalling the predicaments of Kafka's fictional heroes (whose names also begin with $K$) as well as Chekhov's.[5]

Before David and Claire leave Prague, two other notable events occur. The first concerns the draft of an opening lecture Kepesh writes for a course in comparative literature he plans to give in the fall. Inspired by Kafka's "Report to an Academy" (delivered by an ape addressing a scientific meeting), it introduces the subject of erotic desire around which Kepesh intends to organize the course (hence, the title of this novel). He starts writing the lecture while seated in the hotel's café two tables away from a couple of pretty, young prostitutes, for whom he orders cognac. Kepesh is exuberant, for the moment anyway, about his "happy new life" (*POD,* 181), which prompts him to write about "the most intimate facts" of his personal experience. First, though, he must present his rationale; the personal revelations will arrive in due time (in this novel). Despite his conservative appearance and demeanor, Kepesh means to demonstrate that he, like his students, is actual "flesh and blood." Moreover, he hopes to turn them away from the jargon of contemporary literary criticism and, through books like *Madame Bovary, Anna Karenina,* and "Death in Venice," help them learn "something of value about life in one of its most puzzling and maddening aspects" (*POD,* 184). Finally, he confesses that though he is never happier than when he is in the classroom, with his books and his notes, "nothing lives in me like my life" (*POD,* 185). His life will therefore be the first "text" in the course.

The draft ends there, and since the novel ends before classes start, we never learn whether Kepesh goes through with his plan. Nevertheless, the draft provides a kind of apologia for Kepesh, for the novel Roth is writing as well as the teaching he has presumably done. If Kepesh rejects his colleagues' conviction that literature is "fundamentally nonreferential," Roth too wants the import of his fiction to be meaningful, as Kafka's is to him and others. The conflicts his protagonist struggles with are real conflicts, Roth implies, not simply fictional constructs, no matter how comical they may seem. As such, they relate to our experience, real or imagined, just as Kepesh insists on connecting the novels his students will read with what they know of life.

The other incident concerns a dream Kepesh has the night before leaving Prague. Feeling "absolutely triumphant" over his happiness with Claire (*POD,* 186), he dreams of being introduced to Kafka's whore, who tells him about her experience with Franz when she was 25 and he 33. Kepesh's reluctance to view, let alone touch, Eva's vagina elicits from her an indecent remark that his intermediary refuses to translate, but he is finally persuaded to pay for the sight by several satiric arguments (*POD,* 192). The dream finally suggests that Kepesh's sexual anxieties are merely repressed, not vanquished (Rodgers, 163).

## Playing House in the Catskills

The novel's concluding episodes make the point clear. Returning home in early summer, David and Claire rent a small house in the Catskills 20 miles from where David grew up. The occasion is momentous for Kepesh, who has not lived in daily proximity with a woman since his marriage.

Although his anxieties reassert themselves, the summer proves to be idyllic. Together David and Claire spend the days reading, writing, swimming, hiking, gardening—growing fit physically and spiritually—until David comes to feel that he is "living at last in accordance with my true spirit, that, indeed, I am 'home'" (*POD,* 196).

Two intrusions, however, disturb the peace he has found. Just as David seems reconciled to life with Claire, his ebbing passion notwithstanding, Helen stops by with her new husband, Les Lowery, en route to Vermont to visit his family. Her sudden appearance causes a slight strain between David and Claire, forcing Claire to confront the future of their relationship. Helen wants to see David because she feels he is the only friend she has. She is two months pregnant and needs advice about whether to have the baby or not. She confesses she can no longer stand her husband, who, like Claire, is "bright and pretty and good" (*POD,* 216). But then, she admits, she finds she can't much stand anyone (*POD,* 218).

Kepesh offers no advice beyond saying that perhaps Helen will love her baby. "That happens sometimes," he sardonically remarks (219). After the Lowerys leave, he joins Claire at their swimming hole and finds she has been crying. Not only the visit but other things have upset her. She then tells Kepesh about the abortion she has secretly had because she did not want to force him into marriage. Although she feels privileged to love David, who has become her whole life, Helen's visit has made her wonder whether she can make him happy after all. If she cannot, she wants him to let her know so that they can break off before he is "absolutely in every breath" she draws (*POD,* 223). Unlike Susan McCall, Claire is not suicidal but, like Susan, she wants a family—not immediately, not soon, but somewhere down the road she wants one that will be different from all those she has known that never "made the least bit of sense" (*POD,* 224).

Claire's statement is not an ultimatum, she says, only a "clarification." She does not want reassurances or any other response from David, unless there is something he thinks she should know. Despite the irony of what Helen has just told him, he says there isn't, and so they go home. But his silence, which ends this episode, speaks volumes. It indicates David's own uncertainty about the future, specifically the kind of future Claire has in mind. His thoughts about that are exacerbated by the second eventful intrusion—his father's visit over Labor Day weekend with his friend, Mr. Barbatnik, a Holocaust survivor.

Even before they arrive Abe Kepesh is anxious that Claire and his son should settle down together permanently. "Claire," he says on the telephone, "does he know enough by now to appreciate what he's got?" (*POD,* 228). After all the trouble in his life, at last David seems to have found "somebody worthwhile." No matter that she is not Jewish—the issue of intermarriage never arises. Even though Abe has become an ardent fund-raiser for the United Jewish Appeal, his only concern is that his son marry a decent woman and raise a family.

His father's anxieties trigger David's, as they all spend a frantic day opening presents, driving to the old Hungarian Royale, and listening to Abe talk almost nonstop. The son's anxieties are compounded by worry over the father's health: "What if he should drop dead from all this fervor in his heart? And before I have married the devoted girl, bought the cozy house, raised the handsome children. . . . Then what am I waiting for?" he asks. "If later, why not now, so he too can be happy and count his life a success? What am I waiting for?" (*POD*, 241).

The questions persist. At dinner, as the four of them are seated around the table enjoying Claire's cooking, David gazes at Claire's face and finds more questions, along with answers that are themselves questions. If Claire's face seems more than ever "so apple-smooth, apple-small, apple-shiny, apple-plain, apple-fresh," he asks "to what am I willfully blinding myself that in time must set us apart?" But then: "Is there not something a little dubious and dreamy about all this gentle, tender adoration? What will happen when the *rest* of Claire obtrudes? What happens if no 'rest of her' is there!" The thought troubles him: "How much longer before I've had a bellyful of wholesome innocence—how long before the lovely blandness of a life with Claire begins to cloy, to pall, and I am out there once again, mourning what I've lost and looking for my way!" (*POD*, 251).

His suppressed doubts thus forcefully released, Kepesh feels as if he has been run through with a spike, and the novel ends with his conflict unresolved. Fearing that within a year his passion will be dead, that he (like Paul Herz in *Letting Go*) will be unable to touch Claire unless duty, not desire, makes him do so, he compares himself with the character in Gogol's story whose nose disappears, making him "the butt of a ridiculous, vicious, inexplicable joke!" (*POD*, 262). But for David, as for Alexander Portnoy, his predicament is no joke, comic though it must appear.

## The Breast

Despairing over his situation, David Kepesh at the end of *The Professor of Desire* awakens early the next morning to find everything is as it was. The house has not burned down, Claire is still with him, and his father and his friend lie sleeping in the spare room, "each in his freshly made bed." He presses himself against Claire's sleeping body, raises her nightdress, and sucks "in desperate frenzy" at her breast "until the pale, velvety, childlike areolae erupt in tiny granules" around her nipples "and her moan begins" (*POD*, 263). Roth thus prepares us for Kepesh's transformation into a huge breast a year later. In fact, several indications throughout the novel anticipate the event,[6] which was recorded in *The Breast* several years before *The Professor of Desire* was written.[7]

In a sense, just as Gregor Samsa's transformation into a beetle or cockroach in Kafka's "The Metamorphosis" is retribution for the life he has lived—or failed to live—Kepesh's transformation is retribution for his failures. For a year his passion for Claire has been fading to nearly nothing. No longer the lover he once was, Kepesh is about to resume therapy with Dr. Klinger when he suddenly finds renewed interest, real passion in their lovemaking. Well, if not passion—"'passion' is the wrong word," he admits,[8] then certainly physical delight. But this experience lasts only a few weeks and is the harbinger to catastrophe—transformation into a 155-pound, six-foot breast.

Roth takes pains to make the transformation as credible as possible, incredible as it must appear. Of course, making the incredible credible has been one of Roth's major interests, as *The Great American Novel* and *Our Gang*—to cite the most obvious examples—reveal. Not surprisingly, all three novels were written in the same period, while Roth was struggling to fictionalize his incredible marriage in *My Life as a Man*. In *The Breast* he imitates the language of anatomy and medicine to describe the phenomenon: Kepesh's transformation is variously explained as "a massive hormonal influx," "an endocrinopathic catastrophe," and "a hermaphroditic explosion of chromosomes" (*TB*, 13). The terminology, sounding technical, is pure nonsense but in context serves its purpose. A full description of the condition follows, explaining how Kepesh can still speak and hear, though he cannot see, taste, smell, or move (*TB*, 13–16). He can feel; in fact, his tactile sensibility is vastly increased—for example, when his nurse bathes him or later when Claire stimulates him. He retains rudimentary or "irregular" respiratory, cardiovascular, and excretory systems within the massive adipose tissue that now composes his overall form, culminating in a five-inch, highly sensitive nipple that provides immense tactile pleasure.

It almost sounds plausible, the way Roth presents it, especially as it is admittedly "like nothing *anyone* has ever known" (*TB*, 12). Making it still more convincing is Kepesh's long and persistent struggle to compre-

hend his fate. This is the real heart of the story, as it is in Gogol's "The
Nose," which at one point Kepesh, still the professor of literature, recalls
along with Kafka's "The Metamorphosis." If what has happened to David
is "beyond understanding, beyond compassion, beyond comedy" (*TB*,
12), it does not stop others—including himself—from trying to understand it scientifically, or express sympathy, or laugh out loud, as even
staid Arthur Schonbrunn does when he comes to visit his erstwhile colleague. But until then Kepesh allows only Claire, his father (who, in
reciting the latest news, tries to act as if nothing has happened), and Dr.
Klinger to visit him. Otherwise he sways in his hammock in a private
hospital room, cared for by his nurse and supported by intravenous feeding and any number of other tubes and devices that help keep him alive,
if not kicking.

Two crises occur during the 15-month period of the narration. The
first is Kepesh's growing need, or desire, for erotic stimulation beyond
that which Claire provides by stroking his skin or sucking his nipple.
Afraid to ask her to go further, to let him penetrate her with his nipple,
he propositions his spinsterish, 56-year-old nurse instead—whereupon a
male nurse takes her place and other steps are taken to keep him calm.
The second crisis occurs when Kepesh convinces himself that he has gone
mad, that what has happened has not actually happened, that it is all a
dream. Although he argues with Dr. Klinger that he is the victim of an
illusion, engendered in part by his reading of Kafka and Gogol, Klinger
repeatedly rejects the hypothesis. Nevertheless, Kepesh insists that everything is the result of a "post-analytic collapse" (*TB*, 70). What precipitated the collapse—the trauma Kepesh has been looking for (and what
returns *The Breast* to the comic predicament of *The Professor of Desire* and
other fictions)—was "success," "a happy life." He theorizes that he
couldn't take "Rewards—instead of punishment! Wholeness! Comfort!
Pleasure! A gratifying way of life, a life *without*—" (*TB*, 71–72). But here
Klinger cuts him off, insisting that Kepesh could take happiness "with
the best of them."

Klinger is wrong, but so is Kepesh. Happiness, comfort, and rewards
are precisely what Kepesh cannot take, as *The Professor of Desire* shows and
as Roth's other protagonists reveal, even as their most longed-for wishes
are fulfilled. "Wholeness" seems unreal, illusory, radically incomplete, or
(what amounts to the same thing) ultimately unattainable. But Kepesh
is wrong too. He *is* a breast. Roth leaves no doubt about that, physiologi-
cally, biologically, and anatomically "impossible" though it may seem
(*TB*, 54). Kepesh thinks he has "out- Kafkaed Kafka," become the victim

of his own imagination and his love of the extreme in literature. Whereas Gogol, Kafka, and Swift could only envision the incredible, Kepesh "took the leap. Made the word flesh" (*TB*, 82). But these "delusions of grandeur" don't persuade Klinger either.

If not delusions of grandeur, then what about abasement, Kepesh says, as he contemplates escaping from the hospital to make a lot of money as a freak, a sideshow. He will get his colleague and friend (the poet Baumgarten in *The Professor of Desire*) to help. Klinger rejects this alternative as well, reminding his patient of "our friend with the beard who sits on the throne." "Mr. Reality," as Kepesh rightly names him. "And his principle," Klinger adds (*TB*, 88). People will not take Kepesh on his own terms. To them he will still be a joke, nothing more, and besides, they are busy with their own troubles.

Kepesh concludes his hour-long lecture,[9] in which he tells his story for the first time, with Rilke's poem "Archaic Torso of Apollo." He hopes what he has said will help illuminate the great lines that meditate on a headless torso and end with the famous admonition "You must / change your life." From Kepesh's present perspective the admonition may not seem so "elevated" a sentiment after all, he warns. Nevertheless, he advises his audience to "proceed with our education, one and all" (*TB*, 88). Professor Kepesh is Professor Kepesh yet.

In an interview with Alan Lelchuk Roth discussed the potential for comedy in *The Breast* and explains why he resisted making the story more comic or more grotesque, or both: "Since the joke was there before I even began, perhaps the best thing was to stand it on its head by *refusing* to take it as a joke." He admits to a reluctance to do what is supposed to be his "number": "In all, it seemed to me that if I was going to come up with anything new . . . it might best be done by taking this potentially hilarious situation and treating it perfectly *seriously*. I think there are still funny moments in the story, but that's okay with me too" (*RMAO*, 74). Roth accomplished what he set out to do. The many funny moments occur especially toward the beginning, when the surprise and the enormity of Kepesh's transformation are most acutely felt, by Kepesh above all, for as usual Roth endows his protagonist with a keen sense of irony and wit. This attribute manifests itself, for example, when Kepesh recognizes that no sort of "retaliatory raid" by his "anti-mammogenic hormones" will undo his condition. "I suspect it's a little late for that," he says, "and so it is not with this hope springing eternally in the human breast that the human breast continues to want to be. Human I insist I am, but not that human" (*TB*, 24). Later the jokes and wit shade into a deeper sense of irony as Kepesh struggles with his fate, particularly in the chapters in which he tries to deny it, claiming madness. Here Kepesh's plight passes into real agony—a tribute to Roth's mastery of comedy, which, like tragedy, can encompass many diverse elements, including its opposite.

## Chapter Eleven

# Comic *Bildungsroman:*

## Zuckerman Bound

"Not everything has to be a book," Nathan Zuckerman says to himself near the end of *The Anatomy Lesson,* the third novel of the trilogy *Zuckerman Bound.* In the hospital recovering from a variety of illnesses, he thinks further: "The burden isn't that everything has to be a book. It's that everything *can* be a book. And doesn't count as life until it is."[1] And so it can, so it does. If a disastrous marriage gave Roth *My Life as a Man,* the success of *Portnoy's Complaint* gave him *Zuckerman Bound.*

## The Ghost Writer

As young Zuckerman goes to visit the esteemed writer E. I. Lonoff in *The Ghost Writer,* the first novel in the trilogy, he is already contemplating his own "massive" *Bildungsroman.*[2] That was 20 years ago. Much has happened since, as much had happened to Roth. But note the second word in the German compound: *roman,* meaning "novel." Though partly based on autobiography, *Zuckerman Bound* is not autobiography, no more than *My Life as a Man* is. It is a *Bildungsroman,* a development, or portrait, novel—a comic one, for all its indebtedness (acknowledged or not) to James Joyce, Marcel Proust, and others who have essayed the genre.

Appropriately, *The Ghost Writer* expresses the exuberance of youth.[3] Nathan, previously encountered in Peter Tarnopol's "Useful Fictions,"[4] is full of himself, his expectations, and his anxieties as "the great man" greets him. Incongruities multiply fast. From inside his clapboard farmhouse in the Berkshires, Lonoff emerges dressed in a gabardine suit, a knitted blue tie clipped to a white shirt by a silver clasp, and "ministerial" black shoes (*GW,* 3–4). A ceremonious greeting bespeaks the distinguished figure, but the black shoes remind Nathan of someone "stepping down from a shoeshine stand rather than from the high altar of art." Everything in their meeting surprises Nathan, who thinks Lonoff "looks more like the local superintendent of schools than the region's most original storyteller since Melville and Hawthorne" (*GW,* 4).

Other surprises await Zuckerman, visiting from Quahsay, a nearby artists' colony. For example, Lonoff's quiet and demure wife, Hope, explodes more than once during the brief visit. A "smallish woman with gentle gray eyes and soft white hair," her features and "timorous manner" suggest a "frontier survivor" rather than the wife of a writer like Lonoff (*GW,* 31). But living with Lonoff for 30 years, as he turns his sentences around and around, perfecting his style, apparently has taken its toll; in addition, her husband's self-effacing attitude, stoicism, and moral courage have worn her down. Suddenly during a discussion at dinner, she erupts. Throwing a wineglass against the wall, she shouts, "Chuck me out. . . . Don't tell me you can't, because you must! I want you to! I'll finish the dishes, then chuck me out, tonight! I beg of you—I'd rather live and die alone, I'd rather endure that than another moment of your bravery!" (*GW,* 41–2).

Because Hope Lonoff regards herself as her husband's "jailer," she urges him to get rid of her in favor of young Amy Bellette—a former student at the local college where Lonoff teaches—who is obviously infatuated with him. "Take her, Manny," she cries, "and then you won't be so miserable, and everything in the world won't be so bleak" (*GW,* 43). Distraught, Hope proposes this action out of a despair Nathan only begins to perceive. The ending of his own recent love affair, juxtaposed against this and also accompanied with shattering kitchenware, lightens the scene somewhat, along with Nathan's astonishment and the reader's. The event, otherwise heartrending and dreadful, thus appears slightly ludicrous.

Another juxtaposition immediately afterward enhances the comic effect. As Lonoff and Zuckerman sit talking together in the living room after dinner, "each sipping with admirable temperance at the tablespoon of cognac [Lonoff] had divided between two large snifters," Hope goes into the kitchen and dutifully does the dishes (*GW,* 44). "We talked about literature and I was in heaven," Nathan recalls; he was also "in a sweat" from the spotlight Lonoff was giving him to bask in. "The effect of his concentrated attention," Nathan says, "was to make me heap insight onto precocious insight, and then to hang upon his every sigh and grimace, investing what was only a little bout of after-dinner dyspepsia with the direst implications about my taste and my intelligence" (*GW,* 46). They talk of Kafka, Isaac Babel, and other great writers. Inevitably,

Nathan compares them with Lonoff, "the Jew who got away"—from Russia, from New York, but not from Jewishness, or, rather, from Jews, who constantly people his stories. This is the puzzle Zuckerman can't and Lonoff won't explain (*GW*, 50–51). It is also a paradox of Roth's fiction.[5]

The conversation turns to a discussion of Felix Abravanel, another contemporary Jewish-American author and a striking contrast to Lonoff. (A parallel contrast between Bernard Malamud and Saul Bellow is tempting but not essential for the comedy.)[6] Flamboyant, frequently married and divorced, well traveled and admired, indefatigable in every possible pursuit, Abravanel is at the opposite pole, personally, from Lonoff. Nevertheless, as a writer he has Lonoff's esteem: "Like him? No. But impressed, oh yes. Absolutely. It's no picnic up there in the egosphere" (*GW*, 53). Because Abravanel's ego is monumental, his books contain "gigantic types." They "*have* to be that big to give him something to think about to rival himself," Lonoff remarks (*GW*, 53). Meanwhile it is still snowing outside, and Nathan begins to mutter something about catching the last bus back.

Of course, Nathan does not really want to leave. Besides, he wants to see Amy Bellette again, the young woman he had glimpsed that afternoon helping Lonoff sort some papers. She is expected back later, and Hope's demand that Lonoff exchange her for Amy is not baseless. A refugee brought up in England and educated at the nearby college, Amy is something of a protégée and would like to be more. But Lonoff, as severe with himself as with others, refuses. This Nathan learns during the night he spends there and the next morning before he leaves.

The visit to Lonoff forms part of Nathan's education as a writer and as a man; as such, it is appropriate to this comic *Bildungsroman*. But it is much more. It provides the opportunity for many revelations about Zuckerman's own life, from his experience selling magazines to New Jersey housewives, to his relations with his family and his tumultuous affair with Betsy. These stand in comic contrast to the life of his "Maestro." Given the vast differences between them, why, then, does Nathan choose to submit himself "for candidacy as nothing less than E. I. Lonoff's spiritual son" (*GW*, 9)? He would seem to have much more in common with Felix Abravanel, whom he met while at college and who apparently liked Nathan's apprentice fiction. But Nathan senses that Abravanel, accompanied by a voluptuous-looking woman, had "other things" to think about than Nathan's stories and "was clearly not in the market for a

twenty-three-year-old son" (*GW*, 66). That is why, Nathan says, he
mailed his four published stories to Lonoff and has come over from
Quahsay to visit him. He thinks too that Lonoff is the kind of writer he
would like to be and that his life is the kind of life he would like to lead.
He could not be more wrong,[7] as Lonoff realizes and tries to suggest, and
as Nathan later in life discovers for himself.

## Lonoff's Fantasy

Apart from Lonoff's asceticism and Nathan's libidinousness, their attitude toward illusion, or fantasy, is one of many other differences between
them. Both of them indulge in fantasy, Nathan more than Lonoff, colorful and engaging fantasies at that. For example, when Nathan asks Lonoff
how he would prefer to live, the older man describes life in a villa outside
Florence, Italy, with a 35-year-old woman "who would make life beautiful for me" (*GW*, 69). He goes on for a few moments in this vein,
encouraged by his interlocutor, who thinks it would not be so hard to
arrange. But Lonoff demurs: "Like the fat lady said about the polka-dot
dress, 'It's nice, but it's not Lonoff'" (*GW*, 70). "Why not?" Nathan
asks; if that's what he wants, why shouldn't he have it? "Not a good
enough reason," comes the reply; "you don't chuck a woman out after
thirty-five years because you'd prefer to see a new face over your fruit
juice" (*GW*, 71). Beyond that, Lonoff knows his limitations and those of
his fantasies, which are quite different from his published fiction, into
which not even his wife or any of his three children had been allowed to
enter. "In his seven volumes of short stories," Nathan recalls, "I could
not think of a single hero who was not a bachelor, a widower, an orphan,
a foundling, or a reluctant fiancé" (*GW*, 71).

A villa outside Florence with a charming woman to drive him to San
Gimignano or the Uffizi is not exactly the kind of fantasy Nathan indulges in. As he wanders around Lonoff's study, where he spends the
night on a daybed, his imagination is otherwise fired, kindled by a conversation he overhears between Lonoff and Amy when she returns to the
house. But before that happens he examines Lonoff's library and mulls
over the praise he has received. At dinner Lonoff had toasted Nathan as
"a wonderful new writer" (*GW*, 29) and earlier had told his wife that
"Zuckerman has the most compelling voice I've encountered in years"
(*GW*, 72). These are comments Nathan wants someone else to know
too—the "first" of his fathers, Dr. Zuckerman, the chiropodist in Newark, where Nathan was born and grew up.

### "Higher Education"

Like Alexander Portnoy, Nathan has an impassioned love-hate relationship with his parents, especially his father. Although raised as the family's pride and joy, during adolescence he began quarreling with his parents over such issues as the hours he kept, his fashions in footwear, and his "alleged but ceaselessly disavowed penchant for having the last word" (*GW*, 80). Nevertheless, they remained a very close-knit family. Recently, however, a more serious and continuing schism had developed between them regarding "Higher Education," the draft of a story Nathan has drawn directly from family incidents. Whereas Nathan admits he naively anticipated only praise such as he usually received, his father is outraged by what he regards as "the most shameful and disreputable transgressions of family decency and trust" (*GW*, 81).

It is, of course, a classical case of generational conflict and misunderstanding, and of the antagonism between art and philistinism—not for nothing is this section titled "Nathan Dedalus."[8] Thus early in his life, as in Roth's, the problems of the artist surface to plague the writer, and Nathan is perplexed, angry, and defensive—to little avail where his family and others are concerned. For his father, "Higher Education" is simply "about kikes. Kikes and their love of money" (*GW*, 94). Nothing Nathan is able to say can dissuade him from the conviction that his son is doing a signal disservice not only to the family but to Jews everywhere. And nothing Dr. Zuckerman says can dissuade his son from the conviction that what he has written is a libel against neither the family nor the Jewish people but is simply art.

Dr. Zuckerman's recourse to Judge Leopold Wapter results in one of the funniest and most satiric episodes in all of Roth's fiction. Along with Meyer Ellenstein, Newark's first Jewish mayor, and Rabbi Joachim Prinz, Judge Wapter is among the most respected Jews in Newark. Seven years earlier he had agreed to write a letter of recommendation in behalf of Nathan's application to the University of Chicago. Nathan's interview—his initial encounter with Wapter's pomposity and self-importance—is an hilarious episode in this comic *Bildungsroman*. But what Zuckerman experienced then pales before what he is subjected to now, as once again his father appeals to the judge. During his second week at Quahsay, Nathan receives a letter from Wapter that is utterly outrageous in its condescension and impertinence. Had it been calculated to stiffen Nathan's resolve or further inflame his ardor, it could not have succeeded better.

The patronizing tone of the letter is exceeded only by the effrontery of the questionnaire appended to it. Although Wapter nods benignly toward the "unique contributions" that artists make to mankind and against the intolerance that the Greeks showed to Socrates, he comes down firmly on the artist's "responsibility to his fellow man, to the society in which he lives, and to the cause of truth and justice" (*GW*, 101). That is the sole criterion, he says, on which to judge Nathan's story for publication. He then proceeds to the questionnaire, adding a postscript recommending the current Broadway production of *The Diary of Anne Frank*. (Although Zuckerman has only read the book, both it and the play later become important in the novel.)

Wapter's questionnaire begins, "1. If you had been living in Nazi Germany in the thirties, would you have written such a story?" and proceeds to still more irrelevant, inflammatory, and unconscionable inquisition. For example, he questions the credentials Nathan has that qualify him to write about Jewish life in national magazines. He asks why physical intimacy "between a married Jewish man and an unmarried Christian woman" should be portrayed. And he asks, "Why in a story with a Jewish background must there be (a) adultery; (b) incessant fighting within a family over money; (c) warped human behavior in general?" His tenth and last question is: "Can you honestly say that there is anything in your short story that would not warm the heart of a Julius Streicher or a Joseph Goebbels?" (*GW*, 102–4).

The essays in *Reading Myself and Others* address many of the issues Wapter raises, preeminently the irrelevance of question 9, how Nathan's story might benefit his family or the Jewish people (meaning "Is it good for the Jews?"). In *The Ghost Writer* Roth reinvents and recasts his experiences, to brilliantly comic effect. After Wapter's letter, nothing can bring Nathan to reconcile with his father. He feels he owes no explanations, and those he might offer would not be acceptable anyway. He is truly on his own (*GW*, 109).

Infuriated anew by his recollection of Wapter's letter and frustrated in his efforts now to write his father, Nathan hears Amy's little Renault come up the driveway. Although he sees and hears scarcely anything as she enters the house, Nathan is erotically aroused and masturbates "on the daybed in E. I. Lonoff's study" (*GW*, 112). Shades of Alexander Portnoy! Feeling shabby, Nathan then takes "the high road" and reads James's story, "The Middle Years," from which Lonoff had extracted a passage about "the madness of art" and pinned it on a bulletin board beside his desk (*GW*, 113). As he contemplates events in the story, along with Lonoff's annotations—particularly the passage including the sentence "The thing is to have made somebody care" (*GW*, 115)—he hears muffled voices from the room above. Shamelessly he climbs onto Lonoff's desk, raising himself on the volume of James's stories to hear better. Hopelessly in love with the maestro, Amy begs him to run away with her to Florence. Lonoff steadfastly refuses but allows her to sit on his lap while he sings one of his funny songs. His loyalty to Hope is absolute; rejecting Amy's appeal to kiss her bare breasts and ordering her to cover up, he leaves her room.

The scene ends with not only Amy but also Nathan in despair, though of different kinds. "Oh, if only I could have imagained the scene I'd overheard!" Nathan muses. "If only I could invent as presumptuously as real life! If one day I could just *approach* the originality and excitement of what actually goes on!" (*GW*, 121). He can, and he does, as the next section, "Femme Fatale," shows.

## "Femme Fatale"

Nathan imagines that Amy Bellette is really Anne Frank, miraculously saved from death in the concentration camps and eventually brought to America, where she meets and studies with E. I. Lonoff at Athene College. Fantastic as the story seems, it begins in a deliberately understated and credible fashion: "It was only a year earlier that Amy had told Lonoff her whole story" (*GW*, 122). Weeping hysterically, she had telephoned Lonoff from a New York hotel room after seeing a matinee performance of *The Diary of Anne Frank*. What follows is a highly detailed narrative, culled partly from *The Diary* for the Amsterdam episodes, but mostly invented—for example, Anne's recovery in a British field hospital at the end of the war, her experience of English foster homes, and her discovery years later while browsing through old copy of *Time* magazine that her diary had been published and her father was alive. As if to forestall disbelief, several aspects of the narrative are explicitly recognized as improbable, especially Amy's behavior after her discovery of the magazine article, but invariably Zuckerman finds credible explanations. For example, of her failure to travel to Switzerland, where the family members were to meet if any survived, he asks if it is likely that a weak, 16-year-old girl would take a journey "requiring money, visas—requiring hope—only to learn at the other end that she was as lost and alone as she feared" (*GW*, 129). As for her failure to call *Time* and announce her survival, the powerful effect of *The Diary* depended on her remaining dead, a victim of the

Holocaust and Nazi anti-Semitism. As the "incarnation of the millions of
unlived years robbed from the murdered Jews," Amy feels it is too late
for her to be alive now. "I am a saint," she tells a disbelieving Lonoff,
and she must remain one (*GW*, 150).

The point of Amy's confession to Lonoff, her "consuming delusion"
(*GW*, 152), concludes with her fervent wish to go off with him and live
together in Florence: this is how Nathan's fantasy connects with the overheard conversation. Roth's point, however, is different and might be
misconstrued. Of course, its comic function is clear: Nathan falls in love
with Amy and wants to marry her, thereby showing his father, Judge
Wapter, and everyone else that he is a good Jew after all—the best! But
his fantasy is punctured the next morning when he finds not a single trace
of a concentration camp number on Amy's forearm (*GW*, 167–68). To
some critics, even sympathetic ones, the episode thus seems like a cheap-
ening of the Anne Frank story, "a lapse of taste, a failure of aesthetic
judgment."[9] To others it appears as "one of the most sensitive and powerfully written contributions to Holocaust literature."[10] Certainly, the
impassioned critique of *The Diary,* the imagined re-creation of its composition, and the vivid representation of what *might* have been are extraordinary.

## Lonoff vs. Zuckerman

All that notwithstanding, Roth has other points to make concerning
the art of fiction, the structure of the novel, the nature of his protagonist,
and the composition of a comic *Bildungsroman.* The fantasy underscores
an important contrast between Zuckerman and Lonoff, the writer whom
Nathan admires but whose talents are vastly different from his. Although
the point is made earlier, when Lonoff praises the "turbulence" of Zuckerman's fiction (*GW*, 33), it is repeated at the very end, after another of
Hope's explosions. Lonoff rightly suspects everything will become grist
to the young writer's mill. "I'll be curious to see how we all come out
someday," he says. "It could be an interesting story. You're not so nice
and polite in your fiction. . . . You're a different person." "Am I?"
Nathan asks. "I should hope so," comes the instant reply (*GW*, 180).

Whereas the older man spends his solitary days turning sentences
around, creating his version of "fantasy" (*GW*, 17–18, 30), Zuckerman's
"unruly" personal life, Lonoff says, will probably serve him better and
should be nourished (*GW*, 33). Nathan's fiction, or "fantasy," has more
of real life—of liveliness—in it. So it does, as the "Femme Fatale" epi-

sode, his controversial story "Higher Education," and the *Bildungsroman* itself indicate. In a book about writers lit. wit naturally abounds, and the shades of many famous writers haunt the novel, providing significant contrasts and parallels—none more so than the allusion to Isaac Babel's description of the Jewish writer as "a man with autumn in his heart and spectacles on his nose." The description fits Lonoff exactly; however, when Zuckerman is inspired to add, "and blood in his penis," he incorporates a vision of himself, as well he understands: "I . . . then recorded the words like a challenge—a flaming Dedalian formula to ignite *my* soul's smithy" (*GW,* 49). Thus, a connection between Nathan Zuckerman and the premier *Bildungsroman* author of this century, or between Joyce and Roth, is forged—with every bit of comic potential included.

## Zuckerman Unbound

"Blood in his penis" brings Zuckerman problems as well as fame and fortune years later. The second volume of the trilogy, *Zuckerman Unbound,* records events that follow from the publication of four novels, especially the highly successful and highly controversial *Carnovsky.* Here Roth, using Zuckerman as his surrogate, recounts the experience of publishing a work outrageously and explicitly sexual and—what is worse, where the Jewish community is concerned—mainly about Jews. If Judge Wapter and others were concerned about the composition of "Higher Education," that was nothing compared to what came later. Now a celebrity, Zuckerman is scarcely able to ride a bus or walk down the street without being recognized. For many, even those who have only heard or read *about* the book, Zuckerman *is* Carnovsky, the infamous hero, and his mother and father are Carnovsky's parents. Alas for Zuckerman, they "had mistaken impersonation for confession" (*ZU,* 190), and he must suffer the consequences.

As Roth suffered for *Portnoy's Complaint!* If years ago Zuckerman had difficulty arguing about the autonomy of fiction, now he has both hands full. Not that he wasn't warned. The book's epigraph comes from E. I. Lonoff's conversation with his wife, as they sit at breakfast with Nathan and Amy opening the day's mail in *The Ghost Writer:* "Let Nathan see what it is to be lifted from obscurity. Let him not come hammering at our door to tell us he wasn't warned" (*ZU,* 162). It is 13 years and four books later, the spring of 1969. Zuckerman has been through a lot, including three marriages, and now lives alone in Manhattan trying to cope with success. It is not easy.

## Zuckerman vs. Pepler

For one thing, he has to deal with would-be hangers-on, such as Alvin Pepler, the Jewish ex-marine and quiz-show wonder who in the scandalously fixed programs of the 1950s was bumped from "Smart Money" to make way for the WASPish Hewlett Lincoln (shades of Charles Van Doren). A Newark native also, Pepler claims more than kinship with his *landsmann*: he wants advice and help. Besides having a phenomenal memory Pepler has an extremely inventive imagination. He has written an autobiography, and, he claims, an important Broadway producer, Marty Paté, is going to make a musical based on it. At the moment, while Paté is in Israel, Pepler is staying at the producer's apartment with Paté's aged father, Mr. Perlmutter. Also living at the apartment is a movie star, Gayle Gibralter, and Pepler tells Zuckerman about her various adventures, such as jumping from an airplane for UNESCO (*ZU,* 211). Although the story about the U.S. Marines and the quiz show is true, as Zuckerman later learns, Pepler's obvious paranoia causes problems. Convinced he is the victim of Jewish anti-Semitism (all the producers of "Smart Money" were Jewish), he desperately wants to clear his name, and he wants Nathan to help.

Eventually Zuckerman is able to lose Pepler, only to encounter him again the next day, when Pepler astonishes him with his memory of "Hit Parade" songs going back to the 1940s. But just as Zuckerman starts enjoying the bravado performance Pepler turns to another subject—his work as a literary critic and a review of *Carnovsky* he has drafted. Put off by Pepler's pretentiousness, Zuckerman gently but pointedly criticizes the essay, whereupon Pepler turns nasty, claims Zuckerman has plagiarized his life story for *Carnovsky,* and forces the writer to shake him once more. These episodes present a rival imagination[11] against which Roth juxtaposes his invention of Zuckerman's experience, such as the date with Caesara O'Shea, the Irish film star. If Pepler's account of Gayle Gibralter is in every sense fantastic, Roth presents Zuckerman's fling with Caesara O'Shea, however fantastic seeming, as real. As well it might have been, given the notoriety of each character, the circumstances of their meeting, and their mutual attraction. Throughout the trilogy, fantasy versus reality is a major theme, the one competing with the other for credibility, often for comic effect, as in *The Ghost Writer.* In subsequent novels Roth develops the theme still further. His *Bildungsroman* is essentially a portrait of the artist's imagination, not only Zuckerman's but Roth's too.[12] The invention of Alvin Pepler, the Jewish ex-marine, is a triumph of the comic imagination, though not the only one in *Zuckerman Unbound*. Rochelle, who provides Zuckerman's answering service; Mary Schevitz, his agent's wife; the telephone extortionist who threatens to kidnap Zuckerman's mother; Cousin Essie; and above all Caesara O'Shea, the witty and seductive film star,[13] testify to the fecundity of Roth's creative powers.

In some ways many of Roth's novels—for example, *Portnoy's Complaint, My Life as a Man,* and *The Professor of Desire*—are also portrait novels. They depend less on plot than character, and particularly the contemplation of character within situations rather than the situations themselves. This aspect becomes increasingly apparent in *Zuckerman Unbound,* which treats mainly the comedy of Zuckerman's predicament caused by the success of *Carnovsky.* Various episodes, such as the encounters with Alvin Pepler and the recent breakup of Zuckerman's marriage to Laura, do not substantially contribute to a linear plot, or narrative; instead, like *The Ghost Writer* and Roth's other *Bildungsromanen, Zuckerman Bound* moves freely around in time and space, often juxtaposing characters or events for comic effect while still retaining the focus on its protagonist.

Caesara O'Shea's note from Havana, for example, reminds Zuckerman of the way he and she had met at a Shevitzes' dinner party. Caesara had expressly asked to meet the author of *Carnovsky,* and the Shevitzes urge Nathan to come. Mary describes the actress as "a very unassuming, gentle, and intelligent woman," not merely a sex symbol, a woman who has had "terrible luck with men." She then comments on Nathan and his three marriages, the last one to "a certified public saint": "Frankly, how you picked that Mother Superior I'll never know. But then there's a little Mother Superior in you too, isn't there? Or maybe that's part of the act. Keeping the Kike at Bay. More Goyish than the Puritan Fathers" (*ZU,* 257).

Mary's acute analysis hits home, as Nathan recognizes, but it also sets up a glorious interlude that has little to do with narrative development. More important, it brings into sharper focus two aspects of Zuckerman's character only partly revealed in *The Ghost Writer,* in which he was a mere lad of 23 and as yet unmarried, though not inexperienced with women. A powerful dualism lies deeply rooted in Zuckerman's nature: his "Mother Superior" attitude conflicts with the "blood in his penis," just as the scandalous sexuality of *Carnovsky* and the caricatures of his parents conflict with his basically moral outlook and the genuine love he feels for his mother and father. It is this conflict, familiar by now in other Rothian heroes, that alternately fuels Zuckerman's creative energies or, as the third part of the trilogy shows, blocks them.[14]

Although he complains that he hasn't worked in months (*ZU,* 345), Zuckerman is not completely blocked—yet. He actively takes notes and transcribes incidents, such as Pepler's monologues and the extortionist's telephone conversations, thinking of his next novel. Intent on resolving a major part of his conflict, Zuckerman decides to attempt a reconciliation with Laura (Mary's "Mother Superior"). He has been lonely and miserable, and thinks he was foolish to leave her in the first place. En route to the Bank Street apartment where she still lives, he imagines an argument between them during which, against Nathan's strong protestations, she freely admits how boring she was for the three years of their marriage. But the discussion, continuing in Nathan's imagination, never takes place. Laura is not home; she is off at Allentown Prison visiting Father Douglas Muller, one of the war resisters that she, a lawyer devoted to noble causes, has made it her business to defend. Zuckerman talks instead with Rosemary, a neighbor, who tells him how *Carnovsky* has damaged Laura too.[15]

## Family Problems

Calling his answering service from the apartment, Zuckerman discovers a message from Cousin Essie: "*Urgent. Call me in Miami Beach at once*" (*ZU,* 353). Immediately he fantasizes his mother's kidnapping and feels an enormous guilt. But the fantasy is mistaken and the guilt misplaced: not his mother but his father is in trouble, as he learns when he stops recollecting childhood incidents that fuel his fantasy. Suffering from the effects of a stroke, his father has now had a serious coronary.

The alarming news ushers in the last section of the novel, "Look Homeward, Angel," centering on Zuckerman's relations with his family before and after *Carnovsky.* Another variation on a familiar theme, the father-son conflict is still powerful, still affecting, and the deathbed episode exceptionally moving. Far from maudlin, the scene incorporates the right blend of wit, humor, and devotion to a deeply loved but frequently antagonistic parent. While Cousin Essie recalls the old days when their grandmother baked mandel bread, Nathan tells his father the latest theories on the creation of the universe, from a paperback he bought on the flight down. The mandel bread was a much better idea, Nathan admits, more to the point of his father's "real life." If the mandel bread oration was "Essie being Essie," Nathan's reading from the paperback was "himself being himself": "Last chance to tell the man what he still doesn't know. Last chance ever to make him see it all another way. You'll change him yet" (*ZU*, 367). Of course, he doesn't; he can't and never could change old Doc Zuckerman, he realizes: "Enough for now of what is and isn't so. Enough science, enough art, enough of fathers and sons" (*ZU*, 372). But Nathan's farewell, his "unbinding," is illusory. And it is not Roth's, for whom "fathers and sons" remains a favorite theme.

It continues in the antagonism between the two brothers, Nathan and Henry, at the end and carries forward into the third part of the trilogy—and later into one of Roth's best novels, *The Counterlife*. At first only a shadowy figure, Henry comes into his own in the last 50 pages of *Zuckerman Unbound*. Before boarding the flight to Miami with him, Nathan worries about having to look after his "emotionally more fragile" kid brother. But Henry, a successful dentist, arrives at the airport looking self-assured and professional. "And so Zuckerman, a little let down at not having to buck him up, and a little amused at feeling a little let down" (*ZU*, 365), reads his book on cosmology during the trip. But Henry is not as fully composed as he looks; during the funeral and at times afterward he breaks down in tears and needs comforting—comforting he is unable to reciprocate when Nathan needs it.

The crisis between the brothers occurs after their return to Newark. Old Dr. Zuckerman's last utterance was apparently the single word *bastard*. Though spoken directly "into the eyes of the apostate son" (*ZU*, 373), it is barely audible and leaves Nathan unsure who is meant—Lyndon Johnson? Hubert Humphrey? Richard Nixon? God? Or had he mistaken the word (*ZU*, 379–80)? Finally Nathan asks Henry, who during the flight at first evades the issue, saying the word was probably "Batter," as in "Batter up!" Listening to Cousin Essie talk about mandel bread, their father must have been recalling his boyhood (*ZU*, 388). A few moments later Henry suddenly turns the conversation to his marriage with Carol and the inane reasons that led him into it. His tongue loosened by unaccustomed drinking, he unloads to his brother who, picking up his assumed cue exhorts Henry to abandon his long-held role as an obedient son and a dutiful husband (*ZU*, 392–95).

But the admonition to change his life backfires, far more disastrously than the advice young Nathan had presumed to give Lonoff in *The Ghost Writer* did. After arriving at Newark Airport, Nathan offers his brother a place to sleep if he needs one, whereupon Henry suddenly turns on him. Apparently he has been seething ever since their earlier conversation: "He did say 'Bastard,' Nathan. He called you a bastard," he begins, and through tears and anger delivers a furious diatribe against Nathan's heartlessness, irresponsibility, and betrayals: "Love, marriage, children, what the hell do you care? To you it's all fun and games. . . . You killed him, Nathan. Nobody will tell you—they're too frightened of you to say it. . . . But you killed him, Nathan. With that book. *Of course* he said 'Bastard.' He'd seen it! He'd seen what you had done to him and Mother in that book!" (*ZU,* 397). Continuing to excoriate his brother, Henry ends: "Oh, you miserable bastard, don't you tell me about fathers and sons! I *have* a son! I know what it is to love a son, and you don't, you selfish bastard, and you never will!" (*ZU,* 399).

With these words Henry leaves, and Nathan drives through their old Newark neighborhood in a limousine with an armed driver, the "only way, according to Pepler, to enter this city anymore" (*ZU,* 401). The derelict building that once was home, the converted schools and shops, the absence of stores where one could buy a loaf of bread or a pound of meat—everything fills him with a sense of loss. It is all over, he thinks: "Over. Over. Over. Over. Over. I've served my time" (*ZU,* 403). The feeling he once had for Newark had all gone into *Carnovsky,* and there was no longer any other place for it. Another valediction, completing still others, it culminates in Nathan's answer to a young black man who asks, "Who you supposed to be?": "'No one,' replied Zuckerman, and that was the end of that. You are no longer any man's son, you are no longer some good woman's husband, you are no longer your brother's brother, and you don't come from anywhere anymore, either" (*ZU,* 404–5).

## The Anatomy Lesson

No wonder that Zuckerman is fully blocked and in pain—serious pain—several years later, as *The Anatomy Lesson* opens. Before it ends, Nathan tries, out of despair and frustration, to change his life, with little success. He learns something about himself, about real pain and loss, and about caring. The novel begins, however, with the familiar theme of excess: "When he is sick, every man wants his mother; if she's not around, other women must do. Zuckerman was making do with four other women. He'd never had so many women at one time, or so many doctors, or drunk so much vodka, or done so little work, or known despair of such wild proportions. Yet he didn't seem to have a disease that anybody could take seriously" (*AL,* 409). That is the novel in a nutshell, another version of Zuckerman's predicament. No doctor can diagnose, let alone success- fully treat, his pain. Yet it is both real and acute: hence, his dependence on drink, and on drugs too; hence, his dependence on four women who tend to his needs, his sexual needs especially.

## Zuckerman's Attendants

They are all different, his women. There is Jenny, independent Jenny, a painter who comes down from Vermont occasionally to feed and comfort him and to encourage him to change his life by living with her in the mountains. Tempting as her proposition is, Zuckerman knows better: "Choose like a patient in need of a nurse? A wife as Band-Aid? In a fix like this, the only choice is not to choose" (*AL,* 430). Then there is Diana, a student at nearby Finch College who works sometimes as his secretary and who already has had a long, unhappy experience with men. Lit. wit abounds in their conversation and in Zuckerman's reflections. For example, after their first hour together Nathan felt "as if Temple Drake had hitched up from Memphis to talk about Popeye with Nathaniel Hawthorne" (*AL,* 496). Gloria Galanter, the wife of Zuckerman's financial adviser, is another member of the quartet. Although Zuckerman feels guilty cuckolding his friend Marvin, his wife's breasts are irresistible: "Of the four women in the harem, it was with Gloria that his helplessness hit bottom—while Gloria herself seemed the happiest, in a strange and delightful way seemed the most playfully independent, tethered though she was to his wretched needs. She distracted him with her breasts and delivered his food" (*AL,* 525). She is also the most sexually adept and imaginative, carrying various accoutrements in her purse, such as nippleless bras, crotchless panties, and a length of braided rope. "A child is sick," she says, "you bring toys" (*AL,* 526).

Finally there is Jaga, the Polish émigré whom Zuckerman meets at a trichological clinic. She treats him for falling hair (yes, he also suffers from that affliction) and entertains him in his apartment. Her mordant humor and inconsistent behavior amuse Zuckerman as much as her endless monologues while she straddles his penis. The "best woman in the world for falling in love with the wrong man," she holds the record in Communist countries. Of her lovers she says: "Either they are married, or they are murderers, or they are like you, men finished with love. Gentle, sympathetic, kind with money and wine, but interested in you mainly as a subject. Warm ice. I know writers" (*AL,* 538).

How Jaga came to know writers Zuckerman does not ask, but he believes she is right about them: "Monstrous that all the world's suffering is good to me inasmuch as it's grist to my mill—that all I can do, when confronted with anyone's story, is to wish to turn it into *material,* but if that's the way one is possessed, that is the way one is possessed" (*AL,* 539). This nagging concern, along with his writer's block, ultimately moves Zuckerman to think of doing something else with his life. The death of his father and the transformation of Newark have left him without a subject: "No longer a son, no longer a writer. Everything that had galvanized him had been extinguished" (*AL,* 446).

## Zuckerman Blocked

A year after his father's death, his mother had died of a brain tumor. A quiet woman devoted to nurturing her family, one who left politics and current Jewish history to her husband, her last word baffles Zuckerman more than his father's had done. On a slip of paper where the neurologist had asked her to write her name she had instead written "Holocaust" (*AL,* 447).[16] Her death does nothing to reconcile the two brothers, Henry and Nathan, who after her funeral are as estranged as ever. Henry lets his wife, Carol, settle with Nathan on the disposition of their mother's things and uses his funeral eulogy to set the historical record straight—that is, to remove from the minds of her Florida friends the libelous portrait in *Carnovsky.* Life and art are distinct and nothing could be clearer, Nathan believes. "Yet the distinction is wholly elusive. That writing is an act of imagination seems to perplex and infuriate everyone" (*AL,* 450).

But Zuckerman's occupation is gone. In relentless pain, he cannot write. He takes no comfort from his comforters, who try to persuade him that the pain is self-inflicted punishment for writing *Carnovsky,* that he needs to relax, that he needs another worthy wife to release him from loneliness, also a cause of pain. Suffering, they claim, is what Zuckerman is good at: "he was always finding new ways to be unhappy and didn't know how to enjoy himself unless he was suffering" (*AL,* 439–40). But none of this convinces him, including the argument that his unconscious was "suppressing his talent for fear of what it'd do next." His unconscious is his friend, Zuckerman feels; for him as a writer, it was his best friend, an ally he could count on: "If anything, it was tougher and smarter than he was, probably what *protected* him against the envy of rivals, or the contempt of mandarins, or the outrage of Jews." If the pain originated there, he thinks, then the message had to be other than "Don't ever write that stuff again" (*AL,* 441). Zuckerman is most likely wrong; something unconscious is blocking him and inflicting pain, which neither he nor anyone else can figure out. As for the "contempt of mandarins" and "the outrage of Jews," Zuckerman explodes when, in the midst of everything, the critic Milton Appel wants him to write an op-ed article for the *Times* in behalf of Israel.

## Milton Appel

As Irving Howe had done in *Commentary* after *Portnoy's Complaint* appeared, Milton Appel had criticized *Carnovsky* and "reappraised" Zuckerman's fiction in *Inquiry*. He who had called Zuckerman's stories "fresh, authoritative, exact" now found them "tendentious junk" and unleashed an attack "that made Macduff's assault upon Macbeth look almost lackadaisical" (*AL*, 474–45). Worse, he had done so in the same Jewish magazine that had published Zuckerman's early stories. Worse still, Zuckerman, like his friends at the University of Chicago, had once "cherished" Appel's essays in *The Partisan Review* and looked up to them—and him—with near idolatry. Now this.

A further irony is that Appel had fought early and hard against his own Jewish upbringing. He had written vividly about "the gulf between the coarse-grained Jewish fathers whose values had developed in an embattled American immigrant milieu and their bookish, nervous American sons" (*AL*, 477). If anything, Appel's conflict with his father was far worse than Zuckerman's; he made it sound like the inner turmoil of "a convict on a Mississippi chain gang" rather than the predicament of a second-generation Jewish intellectual. Significantly, Zuckerman wonders if "there might be more comedy in the conflict than Appel was willing to admit" (*AL*, 478)—the kind of comedy that Roth dramatized in *Portnoy's Complaint* and presumably Zuckerman had done in *Carnovsky*.

Zuckerman plumbs deeper and darker ironies: in attacking him, Appel had given aid and comfort to the middle-class, suburbanite Jews whose tastes in everything—entertainment, politics, literature—Appel thoroughly despised. That was "the real joke," Zuckerman thinks (*AL*, 483–84). Whereas he had been raised in that class and knew them well as family and friends, nothing Zuckerman had ever written equaled the profound disgust Appel felt for them: "The comedy is that the real visceral haters of the bourgeois Jews, with the *real* contempt for their everyday lives, are these complex intellectual giants" (*AL*, 504). Some comedy.

Roth is obviously having a good time at Howe's expense, but the best/worst is yet to come. Diana refuses to type the letter Zuckerman has drafted in response to Appel's request and argues with him about it. But Zuckerman insists on attacking Appel. Then, in a sudden about-face, Zuckerman concedes that Appel's criticism of his books just might be right. Now Diana springs to Zuckerman's defense: "But he *exaggerates*. . . . He doesn't see the good things. He won't even acknowledge that you're funny" (*AL,* 507). Zuckerman perseveres in his self- doubt, however, and ends by announcing that he's going to medical school.

Before leaving for the University of Chicago, where he plans to go back to school, Zuckerman telephones Appel at Harvard to vent his anger, since Diana still refuses to type the letter. In an argument with himself while waiting for Appel to come on the line, Zuckerman shows he has not entirely lost his sense of humor. He makes puns. He makes jokes about himself (*"To be 'understood' is no longer necessary once you seriously begin losing your hair"*; *AL,* 564). He tries—however vainly—to get things into perspective (*"You two are a perfect mismatch. You draw stories from your vices, dream up doubles for your demons—he finds criticism a voice for virtue, the pulpit to berate us for our failings"*; *AL,* 566–67). But the humor soon grows mordant (*"you are acting out indefensible desires by spurious pseudo-literary means, committing the culture crime of desublimation. There's the quarrel, as banal as that: you shouldn't make a Jewish comedy out of genital life. Leave the spurting hard-on to goyim like Genet. Sublimate, my child, sublimate, like the physicists who gave us the atomic bomb"*; *AL,* 567). In the event, Nathan's fury, though he scores points, is no match against Appel's dignity. Zuckerman thus resorts to other tactics, equally ineffectual if personally satisfying, to act out his revenge.[17]

On the plane to Chicago Zuckerman begins impersonating Appel as the infamous publisher of *Lickety Split,* a pornographic magazine that makes *Playboy* look tame. Claiming he is going to see Hugh Hefner about national distribution, he thoroughly discomfits the businessman seated next to him with his outrageous chatter: *"Lickety Split . . .* doesn't have Jean-Paul Sartre in it to make it kosher for a guy like you to buy at a newsstand and go home and jerk off to the tits" (*AL,* 579). In the private limousine he takes from the airport Zuckerman continues his act. His driver is a competent young woman dressed in chauffeur's livery, whom he tries hard to antagonize with his streaming, indecent fantasy implicating not only Appel but "Mortimer Horowitz" (read: Norman Podhoretz). He describes how his wife took Horowitz as a lover, "the first in her life," and he felt "destroyed" (*AL,* 599). He goes on and on, inventing a seven-year-old son and further regaling his driver, Ricky, with stories about "Milton's Millenium" (his club), Supercarnal Productions, and his porno philosophy.

Throughout this wild discourse Ricky keeps her cool, until the next day, when she is again driving him around Chicago and he goes too far, comparing himself with Jesus, the Man of Sorrows, "Appel Dolorosus" (*AL,* 647). She then starts telling him off, he calls her a God damn

feminist, and that really gets her going. "No, I don't find you unaccept-
able because I'm a God damn feminist," she says. "It's because I'm a
human being. You don't just debase women. . . . You debase everything. Your life is filth. On every level. And you make it all the worse
because you won't shut up" (*AL,* 650). As Appel, Zuckerman won't shut
up. Roth lets him have the last word, or rather page (actually, three
pages' worth), of argument, defending men against women and claiming
that he is "setting this country free!" (*AL,* 653). A tour de force, doubtless, and brilliant as the fantasies in *Our Gang* and *The Great American
Novel* were brilliant. So much for Roth's revenge against Irving Howe.[18]

## Chicago

Zuckerman's meeting at University hospital with his classmate Bobby
Freytag, an established anesthesiologist, begins cordially enough. Before
long, though, Bobby tries to talk his old friend out of what he (like
Diana) considers a harebrained idea—entering medical school at age 40.
Zuckerman insists he wants "a second life" (*AL,* 601). He waxes eloquent; he waxes earnest; he means everything he says. "Look, it's simple:
I'm sick of raiding my memory and feeding on the past," he says. "I want
an active connection to life and I want it now. I want an active connection
to *myself.* I'm sick of channeling everything into writing. I want the real
thing, the thing *in the raw,* and not for the writing but for itself" (*AL,*
610). But Freytag doesn't buy the argument. He says the problems that
plague his friend as a writer will plague him as a doctor: "You can grow
sick and tired of the real thing too. . . . You can get just as tired of
malignant tumors as you can of anything else" (*AL,* 611). Moreover,
Zuckerman will still be Zuckerman, whether at the typewriter or in the
consulting room: "Your temperament's your temperament, and it'll still
be yourself you're telling to say 'Ahhh'" (*AL,* 612).

During their talk Bobby's father calls. A recent widower, he fills his
son with "infinite tenderness and infinite exasperation." Their roles have
become reversed: "The mother dies, the old father becomes the son's son"
(*AL,* 619). Zuckerman remembers Mr. Freytag and offers to take him to
the cemetery the next day to visit his wife's grave, since neither Bobby
nor his scapegrace 18-year-old adopted son is able to. It is there that the
final disaster strikes.

Since arriving in Chicago Zuckerman has hidden from Bobby and everyone else his pain and his drug addiction. En route to pick up Mr.
Freytag in the limousine with Ricky, he takes too much Percodan and

drinks too much vodka, so that by the time they reach the cemetery he is in no shape to deal with the old man's Jewish sanctimoniousness and sentimentalism. Mr. Freytag's invective against Gregory, Bobby's ungrateful and disrespectful son, finally snaps something in Zuckerman. He lunges at the old man and tries to strangle him—a son attempting to kill a father, a Jew attacking another for his Jewish pride. What Henry had accused him of doing with *Carnovsky* Zuckerman now acts out against Mr. Freytag. Shocked by his behavior, Mr. Freytag escapes and calls Ricky to help. Meanwhile Zuckerman, in pursuit slipping and sliding on the snow-laden ground, intones a blasphemous decalogue: "Honor thy Finklestein! Do not commit Kaufman! Make no idols in the form of Levine! Thou shalt not take in vain the name of Katz!" (*AL,* 668). When Ricky comes up to him he tries to knock her down, falls on a tombstone, and fractures his jaw.

The rest of the novel takes place in the hospital. There Bobby looks after his friend and cures him of his addiction while his jaw, wired shut, mends. Zuckerman now learns what real pain is. To endure it, to get "from one minute to the next," he again invokes fantasy, imagining, for example, that he is in a courtroom, being sentenced (with poetic justice) by a judge for his attack on poor Mr. Freytag. "You have opened the wrong windows," the judge proclaims, "closed the wrong doors, you have granted jurisdiction over your conscience to the wrong court" (*AL,* 682). In hiding all his life and "a son far too long," Zuckerman has been "the most improbable slave to embarrassment and shame," yet nothing comes close to his stupidity in chasing across a cemetery, through a snowstorm, the retired old handbag salesman: "To fix all that pain and repression and exhaustion upon this Katzenjammer Karamazov, this bush-league Pontifex, to smash him, like some false divinity, into smithereens." Clearly Zuckerman has lost his way and is not worthy of Thomas Mann's imagined charge that he become a great man. The judge therefore sentences him to "a mouth clamped shut" (*AL,* 682–83). Later, when he receives a conciliatory note from Mr. Freytag, Zuckerman muses with further lit. wit on how in this day and democracy a father—"and not even a father of learning or eminence or demonstrable power—could still assume the stature of a father in a Kafka story" (*AL,* 686).

In the hospital Zuckerman meets other doctors, other patients. Among them is Gordon Walsh, the emergency room doctor whom Zuckerman pumps for information, still thinking of becoming a physician himself. Although Dr. Walsh is also recovering from drug addiction, induced by family and professional pressures, he represents a model Zuckerman wants to follow. Letting his beard grow out, white as it is, Zuckerman wanders the wards, helping postoperative patients learn to walk again. He befriends a restaurateur, who dies six days later from a hemorrhage. He sits and waits in the lounge with the families of surgical patients. He visits the emergency room and accompanies the interns on their rounds: "In every bed the fear was different. What the doctor wanted to know the patient told him. Nobody's secret a scandal or a disgrace—everything revealed and everything at stake. And always the enemy was wicked and real" (*AL*, 696).

"What a job!" Zuckerman reflects. "The paternal bond to those in duress, the urgent, immediate human exchange! All this indispensable work to be done, all this digging away at disease—and he'd given his fanatical devotion to sitting with a typewriter alone in a room!" (*AL*, 697). As his drug addiction recedes under Bobby Freytag's care, Zuckerman says little about his pain: in the context of what he experiences it apparently now seems insignificant even to him. Intent on serving others, he deludes himself that he "could unchain himself from a future as a man apart and escape the corpus that was his" (*AL*, 697).

## Epilogue: The Prague Orgy

With a pun on the word *corpus*, *The Anatomy Lesson* appropriately ends. Zuckerman cannot escape either himself or his profession, as the epilogue to the trilogy shows. Derived "from Zuckerman's notebooks," *Epilogue: The Prague Orgy* resumes a first-person narrative and places in perspective everything that has gone before. As a famous writer, Zuckerman (again, like Roth) is admired and respected by Czech writers, notably Zdenek Sisovsky, an exile who visits him in New York with his mistress, a once-famous Chekhovian actress. Persecuted for different reasons, they have left Prague after Sisovky's work was banned and Eva was fired from the National Theater. Although poor émigrés, they have not come for charity. They have come, rather, to ask Zuckerman's aid in recovering from Sisovsky's estranged wife the manuscript stories his father wrote in Yiddish before the Nazis killed him.

Like Caesara O'Shea, Eva Kalinova has also played Anne Frank on the stage with great success. But her success, coupled with the abandonment of her husband for a Jew, has contributed to her downfall. Sisovsky's "scandal," which led to his work being banned, involved a small satiric book, published when he was only 25. It hardly deserves comparison with the scandal caused by *Carnovsky,* but Sisovsky, like Zuckerman, has since been plagued with doubt. He does not know if his work is any good or if it was worth leaving Czechoslovakia for a country where he is a writer, but *"only* a writer." He is *"totally* in doubt."[19]

Their histories, fraught with bitterness, irony, and paradox, are the prelude to Zuckerman's arrival in Prague a few weeks later on 4 February 1976. There Zuckerman meets Bolotka, formerly an impresario and now a janitor in a museum, who interprets for him and introduces him to Olga Sisovsky. Olga is well known in Czechoslovakia, her husband said, "for her writing, for her drinking, and for showing everybody her cunt" (*PO,* 721). Zuckerman meets her at Klenek's, famous in Prague for orgies, intrigues, and sexual spying, "the final stage of the revolution," as Bolotka describes it. But Zuckerman has been warned not to sleep with Olga too soon, if he wants to get the stories.

Not that he is interested in sleeping with her, willing though she may be—and she is. Her wildly comic despair invariably expresses itself this way, as well as in drink. At Klenek's the first night and in Olga's garret room the next day Zuckerman and she resemble David Kepesh and Kafka's whore in *The Professor of Desire.* Repeatedly Olga presses Zuckerman to marry her and take her to America. Despite her resentment of her husband and his mistress and despite Zuckerman's failure to accept her proposals, she turns over the stories to him. Fifteen minutes after Zuckerman enters his hotel room, however, the police arrive, confiscate the manuscripts, and expel him from Czechoslovakia. So much for the comic plot of *The Prague Orgy.*

But *The Prague Orgy,* like the novels that precede it, is about much more than Zuckerman's misadventure, which is merely the vehicle for further observations on a writer's life, the absurdity of contemporary existence, and the evils of totalitarianism. For example, by contrast with stories Jews tell—"wild with lament and rippling with amusement"—in Prague "stories aren't simply stories," Zuckerman learns; "it's what they have instead of life. Here they have become their stories, in lieu of being permitted to be anything else" (*PO,* 761–62). Storytelling is a form of resistance against the powers that be. Spying is ubiquitous, and the police are like literary critics, Bolotka says: "of what little they see, they get most wrong anyway" (*PO,* 763). Remember, this is Kafka's city.

As always, Zuckerman is excessively given to introspection and self-mockery. En route to Olga's garret to get the manuscripts, he questions his motives: *"Why am I forcing the issue? What's the motive here? Is this a passionate struggle for those marvelous stories or a renewal of the struggle toward self-caricature? Still the son, still the child, in strenuous pursuit of the father's loving response? (Even when the father is Sisovsky's?)" (PO,* 766). A few moments later he recalls the parables about spiritual life, in which the hero searches for *"a kind of holiness, or holy object, or transcendence."* His quest becomes *"the mockery of that parable, that parable the idealization of this farce. The soul sinking into ridiculousness even while it strives to be saved. Enter Zuckerman, a serious person" (PO,* 766–67).

Even "serious" persons become involved in ridiculousness; farce partly depends on them. Certainly Zuckerman from the outset has been serious about the pursuit of high art, if nothing else, as *The Ghost Writer* showed. Throughout his *Bildungsroman* Roth develops the comedy inherent in this pursuit. Eventually Zuckerman himself comes to question whether *Carnovsky* was high art, however highly it is esteemed by Alvin Pepler, Diana Rutherford, or Zdenek Sisovsky. And his doubts persist. Escorted to the airport with Novak, the Kulturminister, he reflects on how farcical his efforts have been and consequently how irrelevant he now feels: "Another assault upon a world of significance degenerating into a personal fiasco, and this time in a record forty-eight hours!" *(PO,* 782). But as he listens to Novak's story of his own father's "patriotism" (that is, political expediency), he wonders if this isn't "yet another fabricated father manufactured to serve the purposes of a storytelling son," and he comes to some important insights about himself. They connect with the ending of *The Anatomy Lesson* and look forward to *The Counterlife* and *Deception*: "No, one's story isn't a skin to be shed—it's inescapable, one's body and blood. You go on pumping it out till you die, the story veined with the themes of your life, the ever-recurring story that's at once your invention and the invention of you. To be transformed into a cultural eminence elevated by the literary deeds he performs would not seem to be my fate. A forty-minute valedictory from the Minister of Culture on artistic deviance and filial respect is all I have been given to carry home. They must have seen me coming" *(PO,* 782–83). Probably they did see Zuckerman coming, in Roth's vision of Zuckerman. Against this fiction is juxtaposed the reality of Roth's own visits to Prague. Whether or not we consider him a "literary eminence," Roth carried home much more than a "forty-minute valedictory" from the minister of culture or anyone else. To this not only his work, imbued with scenes of the city and transmutations of persons and events encountered there, but also the series he edits on "Writers from the Other Europe" abundantly testify. The *Bildungsroman* that is *Zuckerman Bound* is not, after all, Roth's autobiography; "his novels

place autobiography wholly at the disposal of myth and the imagination"
(Shechner, 234)—the *comic* imagination, I would emphasize. For autobiography, Roth offers *The Facts,* together with Zuckerman's commentary
on "the facts." They highlight the importance each comic writer has for
the other.

## Chapter Twelve

# The Comedy of Counterlives:

### *The Counterlife* and *Deception*

In *The Facts* Zuckerman responds to Roth's letter by saying, "Your medium for the really merciless self-evisceration, your medium for genuine self-confrontation, is me" (*TF*, 185). In *The Counterlife* Roth mercilessly eviscerates both Zuckerman and Zuckerman's brother, Henry. In so doing he confronts himself and his preoccupations as a novelist, a human being, and a Jew. The result is a profound comedy of counterselves, or counterlives, such as Roth had never attempted before, not even in *My Life as a Man*, in which he first introduced Nathan Zuckerman as Peter Tarnopol's "counterself."

### *The Counterlife*

The novel is full of surprises. Deliberately, Roth withholds from the reader anything resembling such devices as the introductory stories in *My Life as a Man*. Each chapter represents a fresh beginning, or almost one; we don't quite start over from where we were at the outset, since we cannot put entirely out of our minds what has gone before, and should not. The point of much of the comedy lies in juxtaposing a new story, a new version of reality, against what preceded it—a different way of imagining what might have happened, did happen, or should have happened to the principal characters. This is the basic technique of *The Counterlife*: imagining counterlives, or counterexperiences; constructing alternative fates as an *idea*.[1]

### Henry's Dilemma: "Basel"

The first section centers on Henry Zuckerman's dilemma: at 39 he suffers from a serious heart ailment, but the beta-blocker he takes to alleviate the condition renders him impotent. It is a cruelly comic dilemma, worse even than Jake Barnes's predicament in *The Sun Also Rises*, because Henry does have an alternative that Jake does not: he can risk undergoing bypass surgery, which, if it succeeds, can free him from having to use the drug. But the risk is serious: he could die. In the 1970s, when these events occur, the operation was still new, and Henry's wife, Carol, is fiercely opposed to it. Their marriage after many years has settled into a comfortable routine, she feels, and sex has long since ceased to matter much to either of them; they can do without it. The main thing is for Henry, a successful dentist, to keep on living and supporting her and their three young children, who depend on him for financial subsistence and a great deal more: their whole way of life.

That's not quite how Henry sees it. What Carol doesn't know—and what upsets Henry to the point of distraction—is that the drug therapy deprives him of the erstwhile sexual gratification provided daily by his adoring dental assistant, Wendy Casselman. Their encounters, he feels, had become essential to his well-being, to his mental and emotional stability. Try as she will—and she is indefatigable and ingenious in her attempts to arouse him—Wendy can no longer bring him the satisfaction of an erection. Their frustration is maddening; it is more than Henry can bear; hence, he determines to go through with the operation.

It does not work, and Henry dies. Before his decision to have the surgery, Henry confides in his brother, Nathan, from whom he has been estranged for nearly a decade, ever since their father's death. He tells him the real reason for undergoing surgery and confesses that Wendy is not his first adultery. There have been others, especially Maria, the exquisite Swiss, a patient with whom Henry fell in love 10 years earlier. In *Zuckerman Unbound* Henry had explained his feelings about Carol, though he had not gone so far as to confess anything about Maria.[2] Now the pressures building up had become too great; consequently, he telephoned Nathan, "his last remaining consolation," and went to see him.[3]

At Henry's funeral Nathan is unable to deliver the three-thousand-word eulogy Carol had requested; therefore, she eulogizes her husband herself, providing the "officially authorized version" of Henry's life as her husband and the father of their children. Roth sandwiches her eloquent and candid words ("Henry died to recover the fullness and richness of married love"; *C,* 26) between Nathan's recollections of Henry's adulteries with Maria and Wendy. And so the day goes on, through the rest of the ceremony, the private interment in the cemetery, the gathering at home afterward. Though the ironies deepen, they are not funny. "Harmless Henry" turns out to be a character worth sympathy after all, as Nathan's conversations with the children reveal. But Zuckerman is first of all a novelist; it is his novelist's affliction, as he regards it, that has prevented him from writing or, rather, delivering the eulogy on his brother: "The trouble was that words that were morally inappropriate for a funeral were just the sort of words that engaged him." A narrative had begun to form in Nathan's mind immediately after his brother's death, and he was having a tough time getting through the day "without seeing everything that happened as *more*, a continuation not of life but of his work or work-to-be" (*C*, 13).

Nathan hangs around waiting to see if Wendy will show up, wondering how she'd behave with Carol, or how she differed from the snapshot Henry had shown him. Disappointed in those expectations, he imagines as he says goodbye to Carol that he hears her say she knows all about Henry's affairs, has known all along, and even confronted him about the first one. But when Henry went "berserk," had "a hysterical fit," and wept for days afterwards, she knew she had to keep silent thereafter, and did (*C*, 47): what mattered was that he remain a good father to his children and a decent husband to her. That is not what Nathan hears, however; that is his version of Carol's "counterlife." What he hears is simply her gratitude to him for being there. But Carol's counterlife is irresistible to Zuckerman, who keeps on imagining a conversation different from, and counterpointed to, the one they actually have.

## Henry's Counterlife: "Judea"

"Basel" is the title of the first section because of Henry's fantasy of running away to Switzerland with Maria and becoming an expatriate dentist. The second section, "Judea," involves another fantasy, though fantastic only in a single sense. This is Henry's lived "counterlife," wherein he survives the operation but experiences a prolonged depression following the surgery. Desperately trying to help her husband, Carol persuades him eight months later to go with her and three others on a snorkeling trip to Israel. Nathan's persuasion reinforces Carol's, and Henry reluctantly agrees. During the trip, however, Henry breaks away from the rest and, while wandering around Mea She'arim, the Orthodox quarter in Jerusalem, undergoes a kind of ethnic conversion. Outside the classroom of a religious school, listening to children intone their lessons, he suddenly realizes that "at the root of my life, the very *root* of it, *I was them*. I always *had* been them" (*C*, 60). While the others go off to Crete, Henry stays in Israel, ending up eventually under the influence of Mordecai Lippman, the extreme right-wing leader of Agor, a settlement on the West Bank.

It is Henry's defection—from his family, his country, his life as he has previously lived it—that brings Nathan to Israel for the first time since his initial visit 20 years earlier. At that time Nathan had made friends with a liberal journalist, Shuki Elchanan, and Elchanan's father. Nathan's recollection of a lunch with them at the Knesset (Israel's parliament) opens "Judea." It also opens a whole series of counterpositions on Judaism and Israel, in which Nathan as well as others participates. These enliven the chapter and the book, and through Zuckerman they provide insights into Roth's understandings, feelings, and attitudes.

Like many an American Jew visiting Israel for the first time, Nathan earlier was challenged by the elder Elchanan to settle in the Jewish homeland. A committed Zionist, Elchanan cannot comprehend why any Jew would wish to live elsewhere. Under Shuki's prompting Nathan debates with the older man, explaining why Israel does not attract him the same way:

To be the Jew that I was . . . , which was neither more nor less than the Jew I wished to be, I didn't need to live in a Jewish nation any more than he, from what I understood, felt obliged to pray in a synagogue three times a day. My landscape wasn't the Negev wilderness, or the Galilean hills, or the coastal plain of ancient Philistia; it was industrial, immigrant America—Newark where I'd been raised, Chicago where I'd been educated, and New York where I was living in a basement apartment on a Lower East Side street among poor Ukrainians and Puerto Ricans. My sacred text wasn't the Bible but novels translated from Russian, German, and French into the language in which I was beginning to write and publish my own fiction—not the semantic range of classical Hebrew but the jumpy beat of American English was what excited me. (C, 53)

Zuckerman goes on to explain that he was not a survivor of the Holocaust, or a Jewish socialist, or a Jewish nationalist, or a religious Jew, or any of the other kinds that might make Israel his natural habitat. As the American-born grandson of simple Galician merchants who fled Christian-dominated Europe to save their own Jewish skins and not the whole Jewish people, he understood their brand of Zionism, "which meant taking upon oneself, rather than leaving to others, responsibility for one's survival as a Jew" (C, 53). Moreover, as he saw it America did not boil down to "Jew and Gentile"; nor were anti-Semites the American Jew's biggest problem. America had "institutionalized" tolerance to a level never achieved by any previous society and had placed pluralism "smack at the center of its publicly advertised dream of itself" (C, 54). If he was somewhat idealistic about his country, he had found no reason to alter his view.

That was then; this is now. That was after *Higher Education* but before *Carnovsky*. That was before his three marriages, all to admirable shiksas; this is after his fourth marriage recently to Maria, a divorced English-woman who is pregnant with his first child and with whom he now lives in London.[4] That was seven years before the Six-Day War; this is five years after the Yom Kippur War. Much has happened, and Shuki asks Zuck-erman why he still pretends to be so detached from his Jewish feelings, when all his books seem to focus on "What is a Jew?" When Nathan explains why he is in Israel, Shuki is again surprised: "You're making this up. Carnovsky's brother on the West Bank? This is another of your hi-larious ideas" (*C,* 74).

It is, as other self-reflexive aspects of the novel reveal. But for the moment it is real and made to seem real. Nathan's trip to Agor to visit his brother contains all the heat and grit of an Israeli journey into the desert, and the characters he encounters en route have all the toughness and arrogance of zealots, native-born or otherwise. But they scarcely rival Lippman, whose diatribe at the Sabbath dinner in his home Nathan is compelled to endure. Shuki, whose liberal views diametrically oppose Lippman's, has tried to prepare Nathan. In a way, so have Nathan's experiences in Jerusalem the night before, when he had wandered around the Old City, visited the Wailing Wall, and met several colorful charac-ters. Finding Henry at last and hearing his newly formulated Zionist attitudes and explanations have also somewhat prepared him. Somewhat, but not totally. Nothing could quite prepare Nathan, or the reader, for the vigor and, given his premises, the cogency of Lippman's arguments.

## Lippman's Nationalism

Backed up by others present at dinner, such as Lippman's wife, Ronit (originally from Pelham, New York); his friends Buki and Daphna; and silently even by Henry (now called Hanoch), Lippman launches into a sturdy defense of Israeli nationalism. He opposes everything Shuki Elcha-nan stands for, deriding his views as those of the "niceys and goodies" of Tel Aviv who want to be "humane," who are "embarrassed by the necessi-ties of survival in a jungle" (*C,* 116). For Lippman survival in Israel, not only in West Bank settlements, is tantamount to living in a jungle with wild beasts all around. He scorns Jewish weakness masquerading as Jewish morality, the philosophy of "losing"—and not only losing but

losing "the right way," so as not to offend the goy. In its place he advocates strong Jewish resistance to those he calls "Hellenized Jews" and to
Arabs, whose basic goal has always been to obliterate Israel (*C,* 117).

For Lippman nothing is impossible. All Jews have to do is decide what
they want, and they can achieve it. What Lippman and his followers want
is to live in Israel, at peace, if possible, with their Arab neighbors, but
in any event to *live.* Moreover, they are not afraid to rule, to be masters,
if survival depends on it. "We do not wish to crush the Arab—we simply
will not allow him to crush *us,*" he says. He can live alongside Arabs and
even speak to them in their own tongue, but he will meet violence *with*
violence, not the "fantasy" of violence in a novel or a Hollywood movie.
"I am not an American-Jewish novelist who steps back and from a
distance appropriates the reality for his literary purposes," he tells
Nathan, and he does not worry about "the approval of *Time* magazine"
(*C,* 127–28).

Powerful words, these, and Lippman is by no means finished. The
argument goes on throughout dinner. Lippman is all for coexistence but
adamantly opposed to Arab statehood within present Israeli borders. If
Arabs yearn for statehood, he says, they have 15 Arab states to choose
from: "The Arab homeland is vast, it is enormous, while the State of
Israel is no more than a speck on the map of the world. You can put the
State of Israel *seven times* into the state of Illinois, but it is the only place
on this entire planet where a *Jew* can have the experience of statehood,
and that is why *we do not give ground!*" (*C,* 129).

Zuckerman barely responds to all this, remaining essentially mute.
Well enough acquainted with disputation in his career as a writer, he feels
in Lippman's "seminar" that language was no longer his domain: "never
in my life had I felt so enclosed by a world so contentious, where the
argument is so enormous and constant and everything turns out to be pro
or con, positions taken, positions argued, and everything italicized by
indignation and rage" (*C,* 130). Although he may have given the impression to others that he was "saving himself up like some noble silent
person," the simple truth is that he felt "outclassed."

## The Brothers Zuckerman

As the Zuckerman brothers leave Lippman's house, Nathan speculates
on Henry's silence and the feelings and attitudes underlying it. Perhaps
Henry really wanted to leave Israel now but was afraid to risk humiliation
by admitting it. Or perhaps what kept him here was not the discovery of
his roots in Mea She'arim but the opportunity to become *uprooted,* to

defect from the life he had known and no longer found bearable: "Israel instead of Jersey, Zionism instead of Wendy, assuring that he'd never again be bound to the actual in the old, suffocating, self-strangulating way" (*C*, 132). Or perhaps his flight was from "the folly of sex" that in restoring his potency his surgery had again made possible. Nathan did not know whether these reasons or others motivated Henry, whose present "incarnation" was the most provocative, if not the most convincing, from a novelist's viewpoint. Moreover, Zuckerman confesses that as a novelist, looking to exploit character and situation, his motives too must be taken into account (*C*, 133).

At last Nathan breaks their silence, and within moments a vigorous quarrel ensues. Henry becomes defensive and rejects Nathan's attempt to psychoanalyze, and thus trivialize, everything he tries to do. As the argument approaches violence, Henry suddenly appeals to his brother for better understanding of what he has done, which he says has little to do with "motives," or the "Freudian lock" Nathan puts on life. "All you see is escaping Momma, escaping Poppa—why don't you see what I have escaped *into?*" he cries. As opposed to Jews who revel in "intellectual games," who have only their "hilarious inner landscape" to go on, Israeli Jews have something more, "an *outer* landscape, a nation, a world!" Israelis are *making* history, not trying to escape from it, like their grandparents did. "This isn't some exercise for the brain divorced from reality! This isn't writing a novel, Nathan!" he argues. Here people don't constantly worry "about what's going on inside their heads and whether they should see their psychiatrists—here you fight, you struggle, here you worry about what's going on in *Damascus*! What matters isn't Momma and Poppa and the kitchen table, it isn't *any* of that crap you write about—*it's who runs Judea!*" (*C*, 140).

Furious, Henry leaves, giving his brother no opportunity to talk him into going home. His speech, like Lippman's, highlights important elements of *The Counterlife,* not only a man's fierce commitment to changing his life but a critique of fantasy as against reality, or the novelist's version of reality versus the reality of history, of lived life. The latter is an opposition of which Zuckerman himself is entirely conscious, as he reveals from time to time, and subsequent sections of the novel show how far Roth is willing to take that opposition and play with it.

## Conflicts "Aloft"

In "Aloft," for example, he continues the dialectic, although this section of the novel is basically an interlude, a fantasy of Nathan's return from Tel Aviv aboard El Al flight 315. Uncomfortable with having left Henry and Agor as he did, Nathan writes to his brother, trying to show that despite serious misgivings he can and does see things from the other's point of view. In the process Nathan makes several observations on imagination and reality that are directly pertinent to the novel and perhaps to all novels. Writing of his concern that Henry's identity was being formed by "an imagination richer with reality" than his own (that is, Lippman's), he says: "The treacherous imagination is everybody's maker—we are all the invention of each other, everybody a conjuration conjuring up everyone else. We are all each other's authors" (C, 145). Or later, on the development of Zionism: "The construction of a counterlife that is one's own anti-myth was at its very core. It was a species of fabulous utopianism, a manifesto for human transformation as extreme—and, at the outset, as implausible—as any ever conceived. A Jew could be a new person if he wanted to" (C, 147). Nevertheless, though he concedes everything, or almost everything, to Henry's viewpoint, Nathan does not completely submerge his doubts: "*If* it's true that you were enduring intolerable limitations and living in agonizing opposition to yourself, then for all I know you have used your strength wisely and everything I say is irrelevant. *Maybe* it's appropriate that you've wound up there; it *may be* what you've needed all your life—a combative métier where you feel guilt-free" (C, 148; emphasis added). But later, as he puts the letter into his briefcase, he wonders if he hasn't been writing mainly for his own elucidation, making Henry more interesting and vital than he really was, investing his escape with some "heightened meaning" that it did not necessarily have (C, 155).[5]

Another letter, one from Shuki Elchanan, provides a further dimension of the dialectic. Shuki knows Nathan well (as Zuckerman/Roth's invention, why shouldn't he?); he is therefore concerned that what Zuckerman has seen and heard at Agor he will turn into a novel with unfortunate effects on American support for Israel. He is particularly concerned that Lippman, a "vivid" Jew, will inordinately appeal to Nathan's imagination, delighted by "Jewish self-exaggeration and the hypnotic appeal of a Jew unrestrained," as opposed to Zuckerman's "relative indifference as a novelist to our gentle, rational thinkers, our Jewish models of sweetness and light." "The people you actually like and admire," Shuki continues, "you find least fascinating, while everything cautious in your own typically ironic and tightly self-disciplined Jewish nature is disproportionately engaged by the spectacle of what morally repels you, of your antithesis, the unimpeded and excessive Jew whose life is anything but a guarded, defended masquerade of clever self-concealment and whose talent runs not towards dialectics like yours but to apocalypse" (*C,* 157). Just as in *The Facts* Zuckerman comments on Roth, so Shuki criticizes Zuckerman, noting his "strong proclivity for exploring serious, even grave, subjects through their comical possibilities" (*C,* 157–158).

In fairness to Zuckerman and Roth, the comedy of Lippman already witnessed is neither in the figure he cut nor in the arguments he and his cohorts waged in the preceding chapter but their impact on Nathan, rendering him all but speechless for perhaps the only time in his life. The real comedy of *The Counterlife,* however, comes later, in the next section, when Henry reads drafts of the preceding chapters after experiencing neither a fatal heart operation nor an escape from family and profession to the desert outpost of Agor. But meanwhile Roth, for whatever reasons (and one can imagine many), felt impelled to include his friend's vigorous counterattack against Lippman's views, which Shuki says seriously pervert the humane principles on which the State of Israel was founded. As cogent as Lippman's and as well anchored in solid premises, Shuki's points continue to be argued just as vehemently by liberals today as the other side is by the extreme right wing. This is the gravity of the situation. The comedy, as Shuki sees it, is that of "Shuki the Patriot and P.R. man" calling for Jewish solidarity and responsibility when in fact he is a highly critical, even somewhat disaffected Israeli himself (*C,* 161).

As Nathan begins his response to Shuki, reassuring him that anything he might write would hardly influence the American people, let alone the Congress of the United States, he is interrupted by the man sitting next to him, who seems to be having a heart attack or seizure. But no, it is only Jimmy Ben-Joseph (born Lustig) of West Orange, New Jersey, whom Nathan had met at the Wailing Wall. Here disguised as a rabbi, Ben-Joseph blurts out, "How ya' doin', Nathan?" (*C,* 163). He is planning to hijack the airplane—with Zuckerman's help—because he wants Israel to give up the memorial to the Holocaust, Yad Vashem; to "Forget Remembering"; and to eliminate masochism from the Jewish soul. In calling for an end to Jewish suffering Jimmy Ben-Joseph's platform parodies Lippman's. All Zuckerman's attempts to talk him out of his plan fail, as Jimmy shows him the pistol and hand grenade he has smuggled aboard, and Nathan grimly contemplates the scene: "Farce is the genre, climaxing in blood" (*C,* 171).

What follows is both hilarious and disturbing. Unable to dissuade the young man from his harebrained scheme, Zuckerman becomes implicated in it, as security guards jump both men and carry them off to the first-class compartment. There searches and interrogations begin, along with further roughing up. Blood flows, as Nathan predicted, and the tough security men, caricatures of Israeli heroes, work their victims over. The deadly farce concludes with another but different parody of Lippmanism, a long lecture to Jimmy and Zuckerman on anti-Semitism and its roots, illustrated from the poetry of T. S. Eliot ("Burbank with a Baedeker: Bleistein with a Cigar"), the aftermath of the Six-Day War, and gentile attitudes toward the Jewish id—what the goy really despises and wishes to eradicate, not the Jewish superego. In this fashion naked and shackled to his seat, a helpless figure in a farce he has unwittingly helped to construct, Zuckerman is returned to the Promised Land.

## Nathan's Counterlife: "Gloucestershire"

"Gloucestershire," the next section, offers yet another "counterlife." Now Nathan, not Henry, suffers from a serious heart ailment, and Maria, not Carol, opposes the surgery—Maria, the wife of his upstairs neighbor. Nathan has fallen in love with her and wants to marry her and have children. Already the mother of one-year-old Phoebe, Maria resists Nathan's pleas, content with their rather one-sided affair (Nathan is on the beta-blocker now) and unwilling to deprive her child of her father, or him of her. Like Shuki, she knows Nathan: "You have a defiant intelligence: you like turning resistance to your own advantage. Opposition determines your direction. You would probably never have written those books about Jews if Jews hadn't insisted on telling you not to. You only want a child now because you can't" (C, 188).

"Gloucestershire" (the English county of Maria's origins) is full of oppositions, contrasts, counterlives. Maria's husband, an English diplomat, is a suitable husband for Maria in the world's eye but is withdrawn, abusive, and unappreciative of her as a woman, wife, or mother. He nonetheless lusts after her and has intercourse with her almost nightly. Nathan is totally different. He adores Maria, has long conversations with her, admires her beauty and everything else about her. Impotent, he wonders why she stays in the relationship, but she tells him that "without the physical commitment somehow a woman like me feels stronger" (C, 197). Her conventional upbringing and attitudes, she insists, would make her a highly unsuitable wife for Nathan, but he feels strongly otherwise. Their age difference—she is 27, he 45—is an attraction, not a liability—on that much they agree. A writer too, she calls herself a "hackette" who writes "fluent clichés and fluffy ephemera for silly magazines" (C, 189), unlike the virile, explosive fiction Zuckerman composes. Still, when she shows Nathan one of her stories, he thinks she writes better than he does (*C*, 194). Afraid Nathan will use her in one of his books, Maria asks him not to write about her. She knows he has "an easily excited imagination" and feels he is already turning her into somebody else, "inventing a woman who doesn't exist" (*C*, 191). He is and he isn't, as subsequent events reveal.

Characteristically questioning his motives and feelings, Zuckerman nevertheless convinces himself that he must undergo surgery to restore his health and his potency. Although he tells his cardiologist that he wants to marry and have a child, he knows there is more to his decision than that. "*If I can have this wonderfully bruised, supercivilized woman, I can be recovered from my affliction fully,*" he thinks.[6] Fiercely Maria argues, "Oh, this *is* awful. An ordinary afternoon soap opera and we've magnified it into *Tristan und Isolde*! *That's* the farce" (*C*, 204). But finally she submits. Whether she recognizes it or not, he is caught up entirely in a "purely mythic endeavor, a defiant, dreamlike quest for the self-emancipating act, possessed by an intractable idea of how my existence is to be fulfilled" (*C*, 205). It is to be fulfilled by leading "a calm, conventionally placid, conventionally satisfying life" (*C*, 203). It is, and it isn't.

Nathan dies in surgery—at least here he does. And now it is Henry's turn to find himself unable to deliver a eulogy at his brother's funeral. Instead, a young editor delivers it, concentrating almost exclusively on *Carnovsky* and praising exactly those "exploitative" aspects of the novel which Henry could never forgive. What Henry later learns, after sitting through the agonizing account of the book, is that Nathan himself had composed the eulogy, extolling *Carnovsky* as "a classic of irresponsible exaggeration, reckless comedy on a strangely human scale, animated by the impudence of a writer exaggerating his faults and proposing for himself the most hilarious sense of wrongdoing—conjecture run wild" (*C*, 211). The words haunt Henry, antagonizing him even more when he finds out who wrote them.

He finds out by getting into Nathan's apartment after the funeral and looking through his manuscripts. There he also discovers Nathan's notebooks and several chapters of the book that is *The Counterlife*, here simply called "Draft #2." Turning back on itself, the novel becomes highly comic as Henry reads first the notebook entries about him and the affair with *his* Maria and then the drafts of "Basel" and "Judea." He can't stand it. "Of all the classics of irresponsible exaggeration," he thinks, "this was the filthiest, most recklessly irresponsible of all" (*C*, 226). Nathan was writing not about Henry but about himself, using his brother "to conceal himself while simultaneously disguising himself *as* himself, as *responsible*, as *sane,* disguising himself as a reasonable man while I am revealed as the absolute dope. The son of a bitch seemingly abandons the disguise *at the very moment he's lying most!"* (*C,* 226–27).

No wonder Henry absconds with more than 250 pages of the manuscript, leaving only part of "Aloft" and most of another section called "Christendom" to be found by Maria, who later enters the apartment surreptitiously and reads what her dead lover has written. Henry's comments on "Christendom" and Maria's anticipate the chapter that follows "Gloucestershire" (a section apparently not in "Draft #2"); the novel thus comments on itself both retrospectively and prospectively, and in each instance establishes the point that Zuckerman (read: Roth) altered, falsified, exaggerated, *fictionalized* everything and everyone in his novels. To Henry "Christendom" was Nathan's "dream of escape" from everything in Newark—"a pure magical dream of flight—from the father, the fatherland, the disease, flight from the pathetically uninhabited world of his inescapable character" (*C,* 228).

For Maria too "Christendom" was fantasy, though she takes a more charitable view of it than Henry. What touched her so much was Nathan's "longing just to shed it all and have another life, his longing to be a father and a husband, things the poor man never was" (*C,* 242). Although he changed everything but people's names in the draft, he presented Phoebe as she was, "just a child, a little girl." Certain aspects of the fiction repel Maria, however, such as the caricature of Sarah, her sister, whom Nathan makes a superior, anti-Semitic person, unlike the "real" Sarah.

All this and more Maria says in response to questions from Nathan's ghost, his imagined ghost, *her* fantasy. But unlike Henry, she does not destroy the manuscript, the fruit of Nathan's "unconsumed potency as a man"—their imagined life together, their only "offspring" (*C,* 245). If it is published with everyone's name intact, she says, she will lie her way out of whatever difficulty she finds herself in with her husband, claiming it is all made up; she'll be lying but she'll also be telling the truth. And to the extent that their life together, chronicled in "Judea" and "Aloft" as well as in "Christendom," is imaginary, Maria is right. But then Maria is imaginary too, as she herself recognizes near the end of the novel (*C,* 312). And real, with the reality that a good novelist creates.

## More Counterlives: "Christendom"

Thus, the novel doubles back upon itself, once, twice, three times, providing counterlives to counterlives, countereulogies to countereulogies (not only Henry after the funeral but others in effect recite them). "Christendom," the final section, begins where "Judea" ends; "Aloft" is thus imaginary in a double sense, though the strategic position of the letters makes it important and useful. If the last section is, as Henry regards it, "a pure magical dream" of escape (*C*, 228), it appears, like the earlier chapters, nonetheless solid and real. That is the quality of Zuckerman/Roth's fiction. Or, as the eulogist (again, Zuckerman/Roth) indicated in the preceding chapter, "fiction is for [the superior artist] at once playful hypothesis and serious supposition, an imaginative form of inquiry—everything that exhibitionism is not" (*C*, 210).

As both "playful hypothesis and serious supposition," then, "Christendom" presents Henry and Maria now married, living in England, and expecting their first child, while their newly purchased house in Chiswick is being remodeled. As Maria warned in "Gloucestershire," Nathan has reinvented her family, transforming her mother—an ordinary woman who watches television and never sets pen to paper—into a cold but scrupulously "correct" matron, one who is an author in her own right and who, at least according to Sarah, has more than a touch of anti-Semitism about her, as do all her clan and class. Of course, Sarah too has been reinvented; the "lovingly articulated hymn of hate" (*C*, 282) she recites to Nathan is fashioned from whole cloth. But besides anti-Zionist sentiments Maria has felt obliged to counter at a London dinner party, incidents of English anti-Semitism turn up again in Roth's next novel, *Deception*. One wonders, therefore, just how much has been "reinvented"—or reported.

English anti-Semitism becomes the focus of a nasty scene in a London restaurant, where Nathan has taken Maria to celebrate her twenty-eighth birthday after the carol service. (In "Gloucestershire" Maria says that Nathan reinvents the scene from an incident he experienced with one of his previous wives.) The scene in turn becomes the occasion for a quarrel between Nathan and Maria, seriously threatening to dissolve their recently formed marriage. Surprised by Nathan's unexpected reaction to the bigoted Englishwoman in the restaurant and to her sister, and provoked first into discussing her family's attitudes and others' toward Jews and then into describing her own feelings about them, Maria concludes with a long, anguished monologue in which she says that Nathan is no better than Mordecai Lippman, that he *is* Mordecai Lippman, and that she is thoroughly fed up with him, his hypersensitivity, and his antagonisms. Things were bad enough in her first marriage; she hadn't counted on this with him.

Nathan leaves the apartment where they are staying and, though it is midnight, goes to the unfinished house in Chiswick to think things over, to imagine how things will be. *Imagine* is in fact the word that begins his contemplations (*C,* 306). He is, as ever, the self-conscious author and at one point cautions himself against "overwriting" his scene by stumbling around in the dark and breaking his neck (*C,* 309). What has upset and surprised *him* most is neither Maria's tolerance toward her mother's anti-Semitism nor her naive belief that she could avoid disaster by pretending to Nathan "that there wasn't that kind of poison around." No; the "unpredictable development" was that it all made him furious (*C,* 307). Usually it was the Semites, not the anti-Semites, who attacked him for being the kind of Jew he was; hence, he was totally unprepared for what happened in England, especially since he had never experienced anything of that sort in America. Jewishness, Nathan's Jewishness in particular, a recurrent theme in the novel, now becomes the focus and the center of his existence as well as of his marriage in ways he had not thought conceivable. That is the high comedy of the situation he finds himself in, although the ironies Zuckerman recognizes do not seem to him funny at all.

## Zuckerman's Jewishness and Maria's Letter

Searching his soul, Nathan wonders if he wasn't being "a paranoid Jew attaching false significance to a manageable problem requiring no more than common sense to defuse," if he wasn't "overimagining everything; . . . *wanting* the anti-Semitism to be there, and in a big way" (*C,* 307). Given his gift for exaggeration, he probably is, but only to an extent. He is building from *something,* after all, as he also realizes. But then he imagines the consequences: what if Maria is not there when he goes home? What if he is forced back into his old afflictions—the life within the skull, "the isolating unnaturalness of self-battling" (*C,* 311) that have been his lot up to now, until his marriage to Maria? His agony seems and is real. And then he imagines the letter Maria has left. It begins: "Dear Nathan, I'm leaving. I've left. I'm leaving you and I'm leaving the book" (*C,* 312).

Maria's letter, the action of a character rebelling against the author, puts the novel in yet another comic perspective. Like Henry, she complains that Nathan "overdoes" things: "I recognize that to be born, to live, and to die is to change form," she says, "but you overdo it. It was not fair to put me through your illness and the operation and your death. 'Wake up, wake up, Maria—it was all only a dream!' But that gets wearing after a while. I can't take a lifetime of never knowing if you're fooling. I can't be toyed with forever" (*C*, 312–13). She is afraid, moreover, of what may happen to her daughter. If Nathan could kill Henry, kill himself, and invent the hijacking episode, he could do as much with Phoebe for the sake of making her "interesting." "When I think about literary surgery being performed experimentally upon those I love, I understand what drives antivivisectionists nuts," Maria says (*C*, 313). She complains about the bent of Nathan's imagination (what Edgar Allan Poe would call "the imp of the perverse"): why can't he imagine them being happy? Why did he have to spoil their evening out with that scene in the restaurant? "Why this preoccupation with irresolvable conflict?" she asks. "Don't you want a new mental life?" (*C*, 313).

Of course, Nathan does—that is the point of *The Counterlife*, in both theme and structure. Maria recognizes the role she was supposed to play in his new life, in which Zuckerman would "rise in exuberant rebellion" against *his* author and strike out happily on a new course, remaking his life. But then she, or rather he, discovered that Jews were right at his "irreducible core," and she cannot fathom why. It seems "boring and regressive and crazy" for Nathan to dwell on a connection to a group into which he "simply happened to have been born, and a very long time ago at that." She asks, "Hasn't the man who has led your life been a loyal child long enough?" (*C*, 314).

A question to be asked, and Roth's next novel provides some answers. Meanwhile Maria brings up the question of circumcision, should their unborn child be a boy, and imagines her reaction as well as Nathan's. Throughout her letter she maintains her sense of humor, her sense of perspective, and her sense of character—her sense of a character in a fiction. Doing so, she pens a highly perceptive critique of Zuckerman, or Roth, and *The Counterlife*. But then Roth has always been a pretty good critic of himself and his work, maintaining exactly those virtues with which he endows Maria, one of the most spirited and intellectually attractive women in his novels. She knows, as Roth does, that a peaceful, tranquil life, which she wants and enjoys, is not for him. Cozy and strifeless contentment makes for "bad art." "The pastoral is not your genre," she says. "Your chosen fate, as you see it, is to be innocent of innocence at all costs, certainly not to let me, with my pastoral origins, cunningly transform you into a pastoralized Jew" (*C*, 317–18).

Imagining Maria's letter, Zuckerman imagines his response, in which he totally discounts the concept of an irreducible self. He claims that "one is acutely a performer"; a person enacts many roles, impersonates many selves, "and after a while impersonates best the self that best gets one through" (*C,* 320). He therefore refuses to perpetrate on himself "the joke of a self," realizing that he has instead "a variety of impersonations . . . a troupe of players" that he has "internalized" (*C,* 321).[7] He therefore also invites Maria to return to the life that is "as close to life as you, and I, and our child can ever hope to come" (*C,* 324). As for pastoralism and circumcision, he agrees with her that the former is definitely not his genre, though paradoxically it may be Lippman's and the Agor Jews'. He then links circumcision to pastoralism in an unusual but illuminating way: circumcision is the means Jews have found to show the child that he is born into the world and out of the womb, or the primordial pastoral environment. The act is startling, but that is what Jews may have had in mind in the first place, what makes it seem "quintessentially Jewish and the mark of their reality." For Zuckerman " [c]ircumcision is everything that the pastoral is not and . . . reinforces what the world is about, which isn't strifeless unity" (*C,* 323). No, it isn't, but it *is* the world to which he asks Maria to return. As we know from page 243 of *The Counterlife* and from the end of Zuckerman's letter in *The Facts,* Maria does return, fully realizing that their lives will be "tremendously difficult." They will be full lives and doubtless "interesting," though Roth's "Zuckerman Domesticus" has yet to appear.

## Deception

"What people envy in the novelist," the eulogist said at Nathan's funeral, "aren't the things that the novelists think are so enviable but the performing selves that the author indulges, the slipping irresponsibly in and out of his skin, the reveling not in 'I' but in escaping 'I'. . . . What's envied is the gift for theatrical self-transformation, the way they are able to loosen and make ambiguous their connection to a real life through the imposition of talent. . . . Isn't it true that, contrary to the general belief, it is the *distance* between the writer's life and his novel that is the most intriguing aspect of his imagination?" (*C,* 210). We have seen "performing selves" aplenty in *The Counterlife,* as in Roth's other novels, and the distance between fictitious Zuckerman and real Roth is without question intriguing, even tantalizing. In *Deception,* also set in London, the distance becomes still more intriguing, for here Roth drops Zuckerman and identifies his central character as Philip Roth.

His strategy is deliberately subtle or, like everything else in the novel, deceptive. Not until midway through the book does the reader get more and more hints about the central character's identity. He is a novelist whose first name is Philip, who writes about Zuckerman, lives in England, visits Czechoslovakia, and so on. Near the end, in a quarrel with his "wife" over what is real and what is imaginary, Philip refuses to alter his name to "Nathan." His wife complains that his readers and critics will not know any more than she does that his book is "just a little story of an imagination in love." To which he responds, acutely: "They generally don't, so what difference does that make? I write fiction and I'm told it's autobiography, I write autobiography and I'm told it's fiction, so since I'm so dim and they're so smart, let *them* decide what it is or it isn't" (*D,* 190). Therein lies much, though by no means all, of the comedy in *Deception.*[8]

In a novel that eschews exposition, being written almost entirely in dialogue (which provides such exposition as is needed), Roth takes on his readers, his critics, his friends, and his lovers, past and present. He plays games of deception and betrayal, "impersonates" himself, "ventriloquizes" himself, and has a thoroughly good time experimenting with what for him is also a new form of fiction.[9] He enjoys implicating himself, he says, "because it is not enough just to be present. . . . What heats things up is compromising me. It kind of makes the indictment juicier, besmirching myself" (*D,* 183–84). Juicier it is; delicious by any test. But these desserts come later, near the end of the meal. The starters, the entrées, the salads—are all tasty too.

The novel consists mainly of dialogues between two lovers, "Philip" and a married Englishwoman. Philip later identifies her as a model for Maria in *The Counterlife,* wherein she was combined with other lovers, particularly "Rosalie Nichols," who lived with her husband upstairs from him on Eighty-first Street in New York years ago, just as Maria did in "Gloucestershire." Rosalie too makes an appearance in one of the sections interspliced between the dialogues with Maria, as I shall call her, though she remains unnamed here. In fact, all of the sections between Philip and Maria are interspersed with dialogues Philip has with others—ex-patriot Czechs, former lovers, a Polish woman interested in politics. Counterpointing, heightening, and sometimes mirroring the dialogues with Maria, they are on sex, infidelity, family and work, psychotherapy, sleeplessness, divorce lawyers, English anti-Semitism, and other subjects.

One of the mirroring episodes is the fourth section, which includes a conversation with a Czech girl Roth had met years before in Prague. In the immediately preceding dialogue Maria had remarked to Philip that theirs "isn't a love story, really—it's a cultural story," directly alluding to Philip's interest in her as an Englishwoman (*D,* 50). She calls him "the Albert Schweitzer of cross-cultural fucking" (*D,* 51). In the next section the Czech girl describes what happened to her after the Russian tanks arrived in Prague in 1968. An émigré, she has had a colorful and varied history, including work as a call girl. Although it is not clear whether Philip ever slept with her, he remains very interested in her and her adventures.

After the next dialogue with Maria, Philip again re-creates a dialogue on "cross-cultural fucking," this time with Ivan, whose wife, Olina, has run away with a big American black. In his consternation Ivan accuses Philip of also having an affair with his wife and goes on to denigrate his fiction. Ivan says he slept with his wife for her stories. [10] If other men listen patiently as part of the strategy of sexual seduction, Philip gets women in bed to talk with them. Olina had complained, "Why does he keep asking these irritating questions? It is not emotionally conventional to ask so many questions. Do all Americans do this?" (*D,* 93). Philip denies everything, but Ivan persists: "You are a treacherous bastard who cannot resist a narrative even from the wife of his refugee friend. The stronger the narrative impulse in her, the more captivated you are" (*D,* 93). Philip defends himself and his fiction, claiming that in this instance Ivan and Olina are the ones who are making things up. Ivan is not assuaged. As the scene ends, he threatens to get a shotgun and shoot Philip, not into his trousers but into his ears (*D,* 96).

The comedy is redoubled later when Philip insists to his wife that though the lunch occurred and Olina did leave her husband, he—Philip—never slept with her, and Ivan never accused him of doing so. Nor did he ever criticize his work as a "rotten fictionalizing" of the reality that Olina and other women have lived. Mrs. Roth remains skeptical as before, but as he storms out of the house alone Philip sees that in one important respect his wife has paid his writing a high compliment.

As if to give the lie to Zuckerman in *The Facts,* that he requires him as his medium for "merciless self-evisceration," Roth introduces apparently very self-incriminating episodes. One of the intercalary sections consists of a dialogue with an unnamed former lover, now devastated by drugs and men, with whom Philip had an affair while she was his student. He remembers now, many years later, how brilliant and articulate she was, and he is shocked by her transformation. As a 19-year-old she had impressed him as "[i]ntellectually stubborn and . . . boldly aloof for a kid" (*D,* 124). In a course on Kafka she had bowled him and her classmates over by remarking how "Metamorphosis" and *The Trial* derived not from Kafka's relationship with his father but the other way around. "By the time a novelist worth his salt is thirty-six," she said, "he's no longer translating experience into fable—he's imposing his fable onto experience" (*D*, 125). The episode suggests that Roth was not pristine pure as a professor of English at the University of Pennsylvania— though he may have been, for all we know, and in understanding *Deception* the point is of little consequence. More significantly, the episode refers to Roth's fiction as well as Kafka's. Again, as in *Zuckerman Bound* and elsewhere, Roth is doing precisely what his student claimed for Kafka.[11]

## "Reality Shifts"

One of the funny and intriguing games Philip and Maria play in *Deception* is called "reality shift," a phrase mentioned in passing in *The Counterlife* but more fully and consciously developed here. In one episode Philip persuades his lover to play the role of Nathan Zuckerman's biographer, a young man who has written a biography of E. I. Lonoff and now wants to write a quick one of Zuckerman, who has died at age 44 after writing four novels. Philip will play himself, he says, and Maria will interview him for information about Zuckerman. Puzzled by how Philip will do this, Maria is told to leave that to him, though she questions the advisability of writing a book with both him *and* Zuckerman in it (*D*, 101).

In the event, Maria does brilliantly, acting the role with verve and imagination, much to Philip's delight and the reader's. As the dialogue evolves, it is Philip who soon begins interviewing the interviewer on the difficulties experienced in writing about Lonoff, especially concerning the reticences, timidity, and scrupulousness of the Lonoff family. In an aside Maria confesses that her sympathies are all with the Lonoffs, not with the biographer pumping them for information, but Philip urges her to continue: "You're on fire! You're dazzling! Go on, go on" (*D*, 103). At the end, in tribute to her dazzling performance, he says she should be the writer, not he. But she demurs: she is "Not a bad enough fellow. Insufficiently aggressive. Insufficiently ruthless. Insufficiently capricious, venomous, childish, *et cetera*" (*D*, 105). (More Roth self-evisceration, although the immediate reference is to writers like Dostoyevski.) Philip then quotes back to her a line she had quoted from *The Ghost Writer* during the "reality shift": "But maybe you're not as nice as you look either." She retorts: "I'm afraid I am. It's grotesque. I'm English. I'm even nicer" (*D*, 105).

In another episode of the same section Roth exposes himself to feminist critics who have attacked his writing as misogynist. Abandoning preliminaries, the dialogue at once enters "reality shift," Maria playing a prosecutor in a court of law, Philip playing himself in the dock as the accused. Again Maria is brilliant, witty, and clever, fending off Philip's defensive arguments and pressing the attack:

> "Why did you portray Mrs. Portnoy as a hysteric? Why did you portray Lucy Nelson as a psychopath? Why did you portray Maureen Tarnopol as a liar and a cheat? Does this not defame and denigrate women? Why do you depict women as shrews, if not to malign them?
>
> "Why did Shakespeare? You refer to women as though every woman is a person to be extolled."
>
> "You dare to compare yourself to Shakespeare?"
>
> "I am only—"
>
> "Next you will be comparing yourself to Margaret Atwood and Alice Walker!" (D, 114–15)

The dialogue becomes increasingly energetic and comic, overwhelming Philip with admiration and desire for Maria, who jokingly continues protesting his behavior to the magistrate, even as her lover moves toward her with single-minded intention.

## British Anti-Semitism Again

Deception also reintroduces the question of anti-Semitism, a vexing issue in the final chapter of The Counterlife. Philip recounts an incident he experienced while walking in Chelsea with his friend Aharon Appelfeld, the Israeli novelist, and his son Itzak—an incident similar to the restaurant scene with Maria in The Counterlife. Philip repeats the complaint voiced then by Maria: "Oh, why do you Jews make such a fuss about being Jewish?" and asks if she believes it is true that they do. Seeing that he is "boiling," she abruptly ends the conversation (D, 110), but it is taken up at once in the following dialogue, where she tries to explain that British "distaste" for Jews is, in her opinion, merely "snobbery" (D, 110). She says it is not felt about Jews who are part of the aristocratic establishment or the upper-middle-class establishment, who have become "part of British culture," but about those who are not. Try as she will to give a rational and in a way "anthropological" explanation of phenomena that interest, even obsess, her lover, she senses that he is growing increasingly resentful, and again abruptly ends their talk.

The conflict between them or, rather, between Philip and the British milieu is resolved—if it can be called that—when he leaves England for good and returns to New York. It is not the first of the separations between him and Maria, but it sounds like the final one. The concluding dialogue in the novel is a transatlantic telephone conversation between them. Among other topics they discuss, such as Maria's second child (a surprise), the intermingling of imagination and reality, and reactions to his latest novel (obviously *The Counterlife*), the subject of Jews reemerges. Philip admits that by returning to New York and walking around the city he discovered what he missed so much while living in England—Jews:

> Jews with force. . . . Jews with appetite. Jews without shame. Complaining Jews who get under your skin. Brash Jews who eat with their elbows on the table. Unaccommodating Jews, full of anger, insult, argument, and impudence. . . .
> So England *was* too Christian for you.
> Tel Aviv's too Christian compared to this place. After London even Ed Koch looks good. (*D*, 204)

Who says you can't go home again? Philip Roth—both the imagined one here and the real one with an address in Connecticut—has returned home. He has returned not to Jewish Newark, which no longer exists, perhaps not even in his imagination, but to New York, the cultural center of the United States, if not the world, for born-and-bred easterners like him.[12] There he feels himself "centered," even comfortable, among the Jews he has described. They may no longer attack him as they once did,[13] but they can still provide the kind of inspiration, humor, and *haimischness* (comfortable familiarity) he could not find abroad, where he evidently felt like one of the displaced persons in his novels, such as the unfortunate Czech girl in *Deception*. Perhaps this is the ultimate comedy of Philip Roth, a kind of joke on himself, one he and his readers can both enjoy. Just as Zuckerman needs him, Roth needs his Jews. Or so "Philip" says.

## Conclusion:
# Roth's Firmament

In August 1987 *Esquire* published its second "Guide to the Literary Universe." Everyone's favorite authors, publishers, and editors were presented on a three-page, fold-out spread. In the middle is a fiery ball, the "Red Hot Center," where Saul Bellow heads a list that includes John Updike and Norman Mailer among its few authors (the rest are editors, publishers, and agents). Close to the center are the "planets": Random House; Farrar, Straus & Giroux; Simon & Schuster; Alfred A. Knopf; and others. Further out "The Critics" inhabit their own sphere and divide into "Those with Influence" and "Also Known to Sell a Book or Two." Much further out, or "Lost in Space," are Poetry, Anatole Broyard, Truman Capote's *Answered Prayers,* and—topping the list—Academic Criticism. There are Rising Stars and Falling Stars; Media Showers; Star Trekkers; Heavenly Bodies; and Space Invaders (British or Commonwealth authors like Ian McEwan and Nadine Gordimer). In a "Black Hole," of course, is Hollywood.

Where in all this galaxy is Philip Roth? A little to the left of the center and somewhat below is a small constellation called "Star of David." That's Philip Roth. He also appears among the "Comets" ("Writers whose work, whenever—if ever—it comes around, always attracts a crowd"), which include Saul Bellow (again), E. L. Doctorow, Thomas Pynchon, Alice Walker, and other notables. You can also find him, now anachronistically, near the "Red-Hot Center" among the Farrar, Straus & Giroux list of writers, along with Isaac Bashevis Singer, Leonard Michaels, and a number of others, not all of them Jewish.

Although the distinctions this literary map makes may be debatable, if not misleading (authors and others have argued fiercely about them), *Esquire*'s editor thinks that the important thing is to be *on* the map, not in a particular location (he does not discuss the phenomenon of being simultaneously in two or more locations). Roth's primary position as "Star of David" has its own sort of justice—and irony: *Esquire*'s joke, perhaps, on the American writer who more than any other today is a source as well as an object of much Jewish-American humor. People still have not stopped laughing—and raging—over *Portnoy's Complaint*. Despite some forays into a gentile world, as in *When She Was Good* and *The Great American Novel*, Roth's fiction has retained as its primary milieu Jewish-American life, Jewish-American family life in particular. That's where he began, and, as in *The Counterlife* and *Patrimony*, that's where he almost always returns.

Staying there, as he mostly does, does not mean Roth repeats himself. Among the many things said about Roth's fiction, one of the truest is that he is an avid experimenter. Again, *The Counterlife*, for all its affinities with *My Life as a Man*, shows this quality, but *Deception* does so even more. Roth experiments not only with technique but also with constantly shifting perspectives on his major subject. Some may say, with justice, that this subject is himself, variously disguised as Neil Klugman, Gabe Wallach, Alexander Portnoy, Nathan Zuckerman, Peter Tarnopol, or David Alan Kepesh[1]—all young, or youngish, American Jews brought up in or near Newark, New Jersey—many of them writers, teachers, and readers, like Roth himself. More generously as well as generally, however, others—myself included—would say that Roth's main subject is the moral issues, dilemmas, and conflicts in contemporary American life that sensitive, agonized (and agonizing) men experience who do not "happen to be" but *are* Jewish. And, being Jewish, they are strongly, sometimes fatally attracted to women who are not.

Being Jewish and writing about contemporary American Jews evidently make Roth an "American-Jewish" or "Jewish-American" writer. As Hana Wirth-Nesher has shown, definitions of Jewish-American literature abound, but none of them is really satisfactory.[2] Since straining for new definitions here would needlessly prolong the discussion, let us simply say, however tautologically, that Jewish-American writers are Jewish, American, and writers. More to the point, they are writers like Roth, who is preeminently serious but who usually takes as his fictional mode comedy—comedy in a variety of forms and techniques, as the foregoing chapters have demonstrated.

The context of Jewish-American family life and its many ramifications have provided Roth with the source for much (though by no means all) of his comedy, as we have seen. Involved early (age 26) in an unfortunate marriage that soon ended in separation, Roth remained a childless widower for years after his wife's death in 1968. Only in 1990 did he finally marry again. What, then, is this fascination with marriage and family? Was Roth so thoroughly traumatized by something in his childhood or in his first marriage that he is stuck on the subject? From the evidence of

*Portnoy's Complaint* and *My Life as a Man,* it looks that way. But the evidence of *Our Gang* and many essays points in another direction, and insofar as his later fiction treats Israeli politics, British anti-Semitism, and the postmodern novel, these ideas also interest him and provide new sources for his comedy, in both substance and form.

Whether or not his characters abandon Newark, New York, or Chicago to live with or marry gentile women abroad, as reincarnated Nathan Zuckerman does in *The Counterlife* or "Philip" does in *Deception,* Jewish subjects still fascinate Roth. For all that critics talk about "the autonomy of the imagination," writers are ill advised to abandon their roots or, more precisely, the ideas, attitudes, and emotions that are rooted in their consciousness. Being Jewish is very much rooted in Roth's consciousness—as why shouldn't it be? The end of *Deception* indicates that it is no good trying to escape from that consciousness, especially if it is the source of much good writing and good comedy. Besides, as the reaction to *Portnoy's Complaint* showed, Roth's detractors would not let him escape.

Roth found early in his career that Kafka—the wonderful "sit-down" comic—inspired much of his work. Kafka became, as Hana Wirth-Nesher says, one of the "fathers" that preoccupy Roth in his fiction. In the story "'I Always Wanted You to Admire My Fasting'; or, Looking at Kafka" Roth deals with his subject directly, both in historical fact and in a fictional re-creation of Kafka's life. In the juxtaposition of the two texts, Wirth-Nesher says, Roth "elegantly sets forth the moral and artistic quandary of the comic Jewish writer in America." The quandary involves striking a balance between the moral impulse to draw on the theme of Jewish suffering and the artist's insistence on creating "in his own terms, in this case his comic mode" (Wirth-Nesher, 24–25). That is where Roth excels. The Anne Frank episode in *The Anatomy Lesson* is but one of several examples, though the most obvious one, where he does this. But Alexander Portnoy also suffers, lest we forget; so do Peter Tarnopol and Nathan Zuckerman. Their suffering is not of the same order as Anne Frank's, to be sure. But that only makes Roth's subject more difficult, even as it affords greater scope for his comic genius.

Roth's constellation thus shines as brightly today as it did when it first rose above the horizon more than 30 years ago. If we count his novels as stars, then his is a growing and an expanding galaxy. And who knows what will appear next in it? Of only one thing can we feel confident: it will be new, and it will be brilliant.

# Notes and References

*Chapter One*

1. In *From Shtetl to Suburbia: The Family in Jewish Literary Imagination* ([Boston: Beacon Press, 1978]; hereafter cited in text) Sol Gittleman says the three "represent perhaps the most concentrated source of what has been termed Jewish-American fiction" (150). Compare Marvin Mudrick, *On Culture and Literature* (New York: Horizon Press, 1970): "Malamud, Bellow, and Roth have taken upon themselves the job of inventing the contemporary fictional Jew" (200).

2. On Roth's adaptation of the comic *spritz,* derived from stand-up comedians like Lenny Bruce and Henny Youngman, see Sheldon Grebstein, "The Comic Anatomy of *Portnoy's Complaint,*" in *Comic Relief: Humor in Contemporary American Literature,* ed. Sarah Blacher Cohen ([Urbana: University of Illinois Press, 1978]; hereafter cited in text), 154, and compare Roth's own comments in *Reading Myself and Others* ([New York: Farrar, Straus & Giroux, 1975]; hereafter cited in text as *RMAO*), 80–81.

3. On Bellow's humor, see Sarah Blacher Cohen, *Saul Bellow's Enigmatic Humor* (Urbana: University of Illinois Press, 1974); hereafter cited in text.

4. *Portnoy's Complaint* (New York: Random House, 1969), 37; hereafter cited in text as *PC.*

5. Allen Guttman, "Jewish Humor," in *The Comic Imagination in American Literature,* ed. Louis D. Rubin (New Brunswick, N.J.: Rutgers University Press, 1973), 329.

6. Adapted from William Novak and Moshe Waldoks, eds., *The Big Book of Jewish Humor* (New York: Harper & Row, 1981), 48.

7. Stephen J. Whitfield, "The Enchantment of Comedy," in *Voices of Jacob, Hands of Esau: Jews in American Life and Thought* (Hamden, Conn.: Archon Books, 1984), 122; hereafter cited in text.

8. Ruth Wisse, *The Schlemiel as Modern Hero* (Chicago: University of Chicago Press, 1971), 82; hereafter cited in text.

9. Roth excludes Lydia Ketterer in *My Life as a Man* from the Zuckerman trilogy. Even in the two "Useful Fictions" that serve as prologue to "My True Story" in that novel, Roth alters details of Zuckerman's life and family.

10. See, for example, Sarah Blacher Cohen, "Introduction: The Varieties of Jewish Humor," in *Jewish Wry,* ed. Sarah Blacher Cohen (Bloomington: Indiana University Press, 1987), 1–15.

11. Interview with Asher Z. Milbauer and Donald G. Watson in *Reading*

*Philip Roth,* ed. Asher Z. Milbauer and Donald G. Watson (New York: St. Martin's Press, 1988), 3.

12. Before *Our Gang* Roth wrote "Cambodia: A Modest Proposal," modeled on Swift's famous essay and collected in *Reading Myself and Others,* 185–90. For more recent satiric writing about politics, but without the fantasy, see "Roth's Complaint: My Problem with George Bush," *New Republic,* 26 September 1988, 12, 14.

13. See *The Facts: A Novelist's Autobiography* ([New York: Farrar, Straus & Giroux, 1988]; hereafter cited in text as *TF*), 130, and compare *Reading Myself and Others,* 78.

14. Mark Shechner, *After the Revolution: Studies in the Contemporary Jewish Imagination* (Bloomington: Indiana University Press, 1987), 225; hereafter cited in text.

15. *Zuckerman Unbound* (New York: Farrar, Straus & Giroux, 1981; reprinted in *Zuckerman Bound,* New York: Farrar, Straus & Giroux, 1985), 190; hereafter cited in text as *ZU,* with page numbers referring to the 1985 edition.

16. *Deception* (New York: Simon & Schuster, 1990), 190; hereafter cited in text as *D.*

17. *The Professor of Desire* (New York: Farrar, Straus & Giroux, 1977), 28; hereafter cited in text as *POD.*

18. *My Life as a Man* (New York: Farrar, Straus & Giroux, 1974), 55; hereafter cited in text as *MLAM.*

19. Lawrence E. Mitz, "Devil and Angel: Philip Roth's Humor," *Studies in American Jewish Literature* 8 (Fall 1989): 155.

*Chapter Two*

1. *Goodbye, Columbus and Five Stories* (Boston: Houghton Mifflin, 1959), 13; hereafter cited in text as *GC.*

2. They seem the prototypes for young Nathan Zuckerman and Sharon Shatzky in "Salad Days," one of Peter Tarnopol's "Useful Fictions" in *My Life as a Man.*

3. In his review of the book ("The Swamp of Prosperity," *Commentary,* July 1959, 77; hereafter cited in text) Saul Bellow says that Neil descends from the *schlemazel,* or unlucky fellow, in Jewish literary tradition, as well as from the poor clerk in Gogol's story "The Overcoat" and the (relatively) "pure youth" of Sherwood Anderson's "I'm a Fool." But to me Neil seems closer to the Jewish *schlemiel,* the archetypal fool, a loser and a victim. In any case the two types are closely related.

4. In his analysis of "Goodbye, Columbus" in *Philip Roth* ([Boston: Twayne Publishers, 1978]; hereafter cited in text), 34–46, Bernard F. Rodgers, Jr. sees Neil as both "a disapproving moralist" and "a libidinous slob." This dualism is at the heart of Neil's character, but Rodgers does not fully explore its comic implications.

5. See the discussion in chapter 6 and "Writing about Jews" in *Reading Myself and Others*, 157–67. Roth immediately earned the support of others, such as Saul Bellow, who urged him "to ignore all objections and to continue on his present course" (Bellow, "The Swamp of Prosperity," 79). He did.

6. Alfred Kazin, "Tough Minded Mr. Roth," in *Contemporaries* (Boston: Atlantic/Little, Brown, 1962), 262; hereafter cited in text. For some reason Kazin omitted this essay from the later edition of his book.

7. But see Guttmann, "Jewish Humor," in *The Comic Imagination*, ed. Rubin, 337–38, who says Roth rivals Saul Bellow "as a master of subtle irony" and uses this story as an example of his humor.

8. Sanford Pinsker, *The Comedy That "Hoits": An Essay on the Fiction of Philip Roth* (Columbia: University of Missouri Press, 1975), 4.

9. In *From Shtetl to Suburbia*, 156–61, Gittleman relates these stories to Roth's "Eli the Fanatic," which also treats the theme of Jewish identity.

10. Names here are significant. *Tsuref* sounds much like the Yiddish *tsurres* (sorrows, troubles); *Woodenton* suggests a stiff, "wooden" town; *Eli* recalls the priest in Israel who witnessed Hannah's distress (see 1 Samuel 1.1–28); and *Miriam* is the name of Aaron's sister, who led the women of Israel in rejoicing at the miracle of the Red Sea (Exodus 15.20–21).

11. In *Philip Roth* (London and New York: Methuen, 1982), 31, Hermione Lee compares Eli's "double" with Susskind, the character who makes Fidelman responsible for him in Malamud's story "Last Mohican."

12. Sol Liptzin, *The Jew in American Literature* (New York: Bloch, 1966), 228. Compare Pinsker, *The Comedy That "Hoits"*, 23, who cites Liptzin, and Rodgers, *Philip Roth*, 27–31, who analyzes the differences between Roth's Eli and the biblical Elijah he represents in the story.

13. Although Bellow quotes some of the dialogue between Eli and his friend Ted Heller to demonstrate the point, the speech of Artie Berg and Harry Shaw also demonstrates it; see *Goodbye, Columbus*, 270–73.

## Chapter Three

1. Compare Rodgers, *Philip Roth*, 47–59, in which he discusses Roth's motives in writing *Letting Go* and compares and contrasts James's *The Portrait of a Lady*, the novel Gabe Wallach talks about with Libby Herz. Irving Feldman draws further comparisons and contrasts with Flaubert's *A Sentimental Education* in "A Sentimental Education circa 1956," *Commentary*, September 1962, reprinted in *Critical Essays on Philip Roth*, ed. Sanford Pinsker (Boston: G. K. Hall, 1982), 32–36.

2. Compare Donald Kartiganer, "Fictions of Metamorphosis: From *Goodbye, Columbus* to *Portnoy's Complaint*," in *Reading Philip Roth*, ed. Milbauer and Watson, 88–89. In *The Facts* Roth admits that James's *The Portrait of a Lady* "had been a virtual handbook during the early drafts of *Letting Go*" (157).

3. John Gross overstates the case in his review of the novel in *New States-*

*man* (30 November 1962, 784, reprinted in *Critical Essays,* ed. Pinsker, 41): "Life in these pages is sour and soiled, full of small rancour. *Letting Go* is a book with a thousand wisecracks and scarcely a single joke."

4. See in *Reading Myself and Others,* "On *Portnoy's Complaint,*" 21–22, and "'I Always Wanted You to Admire My Fasting'; or, Looking at Kafka," 247–70.

5. Max Brod, *Franz Kafka: A Biography,* 3rd ed., trans. G. Humphrey Roberts and Richard Winston (New York: Schocken Books, 1961), 178, cited in Peter Mailloux, *A Hesitation before Birth* (Newark: University of Delaware Press, 1989), 328. In *Reading Myself and Others* Roth acknowledges he had read somewhere that Kafka giggled to himself while working, because "It was all so *funny,* this morbid preoccupation with punishment and guilt. Hideous, but funny" (22).

6. In "A Novelist of Great Promise" (*New Leader,* (11 June 1962, 23, reprinted in *Critical Essays,* ed. Pinsker, 39), Stanley Edgar Hyman also cites the two episodes mentioned here as extremely complex, "at once awful and uproarious."

7. *Letting Go* (New York: Random House, 1962), 2; hereafter cited in text as *LG.*

8. Compare the discussion of these terms in the notes to chapter 2, especially note 3.

9. Compare Lee, *Philip Roth,* 34–35.

## Chapter Four

1. Jonathan Baumbach, "What Hath Roth Got?" *Commonweal* 11 August 1967, 498.

2. *When She Was Good* (New York: Random House, 1967), 3; hereafter cited in text as *WSWG.*

3. Compare Pinsker, who cites this passage in *The Comedy That "Hoits":* "Roth's tone here is devastating, suggesting the sizable gap between what people hope to be and what they are" (49).

4. See Jay L. Halio, "The Way It Is—and Was," *Southern Review* 6, n.s. (Winter 1970): 256.

5. On the power struggles in the novel and their ironic outcomes, see Pinsker, *The Comedy That "Hoits,"* 52.

## Chapter Five

1. Compare *The Facts,* 157.

2. Grebstein, "The Comic Anatomy of *Portnoy's Complaint,*" in *Comic Relief,* ed. Cohen, 152–71; Pinsker, *The Comedy That "Hoits,"* 55–71; Patricia Meyer Spacks, "About Portnoy," *Yale Review* 58 (Summer 1969): 623–35—hereafter cited in text; and Lee, *Philip Roth,* 37–43.

3. Irving Howe, "Philip Roth Reconsidered," *Commentary,* December 1972, 74, reprinted in *Critical Essays,* ed. Pinsker, 239.

4. See *Reading Myself and Others,* 21–22.

5. See chapter 11 of this volume.

6. Compare Donald Kartiganer, "Fictions of Metamorphosis: From *Goodbye, Columbus* to *Portnoy's Complaint,*" in *Reading Philip Roth,* ed. Milbauer and Watson: "The novel twists and turns in an absolutely irreconcilable tension of id and superego, fleshed into life as the lustful and ethical selves of Alexander Portnoy. The tension becomes comic in the extravagance of each force—unbridled desire coexisting with moral outrage" (100). Also Grebstein, "The Comic Anatomy of *Portnoy's Complaint,*" in *Comic Relief,* ed. Cohen: "Past cannot be clearly separated from present; motive is subsumed by act; instinct is filtered through concept. All are inextricably and incongruously intertwined, especially in a highly educated, keenly intelligent, acutely sensitive Jew—for whom act and idea, event and feeling, are rarely separate. In fact, these confusions and juxtapositions are at the center, the root, so to speak, of Portnoy's problem. They also engender much of the novel's humor" (161).

7. See especially Melvin J. Friedman, "Jewish Mothers and Sons: The Expense of *Chuztpah,*" in *Contemporary American-Jewish Literature,* ed. Irving Malin (Bloomington: Indiana University Press, 1973), 156–74.

8. A problem other Rothian heroes confront—for example, Peter Tarnopol with Susan Seabury McCall in *My Life as a Man.*

9. Compare Northrop Frye, *Anatomy of Criticism* (Princeton, N.J.: Princeton University Press, 1957), 292, and Elmer Blisten, *Comedy in Action* (Durham, N.C.: Duke University Press, 1964), xi–xiv.

10. Bruno Bettelheim, "Portnoy Psychoanalyzed," *Midstream* 15 (July 1969): 3–10; hereafter cited in text.

11. In *The Facts* Roth says that this line "was intended not only to place a dubious seal of authority on the undecorous, un-Jamesian narrative liberties but to have a secondary, more personal irony for me as both hopeful instruction and congratulatory message" (157).

12. Chicken fat, or *schmalz,* was assiduously saved by Jewish families, who used it on bread in a meat meal (where butter was impermissible, since mixing milk and meat is forbidden) or in a snack between meals.

13. In Shakespeare's *Henry IV, Part 1,* act 2, scene 4.

14. Roth's later heroes—Peter Tarnopol, David Alan Kepesh, and Nathan Zuckerman especially—also have rich fantasy lives.

*Chapter Six*

1. Roth's bibliographer, Bernard F. Rodgers, Jr., records a movie scenario, "The Grimes Case," that Roth wrote in 1963 but never completed or published. See Bernard F. Rodgers, Jr., *Philip Roth: A Bibliography,* 2d ed. (Metuchen, N.J., and London: Scarecrow Press, 1984), 20, item A145.

2. That was decades ago, but a perennial problem. In the 1980s, for instance, who could have invented Oliver North? Jim and Tammy Faye Bakker? Nancy Reagan? Nancy Reagan's astrologer?

3. In *The Anatomy Lesson* Roth heavily satirizes Howe as the porn king Milton Appel; see chapter 11 of the present volume.

4. In "Some New Jewish Stereotypes," *Reading Myself and Others*, 137–47.

5. Actually, he never abandoned them. In an interview with Joyce Carol Oates ("After Eight Books," in *Reading Myself and Others*) Roth says that *My Life as a Man* was long and difficult to write and that he composed the others plus *The Breast* while it was "simmering away on the 'moral' back burner" (112).

6. Roth dedicates *Reading Myself and Others* "To Saul Bellow, the 'other' I have read from the beginning with the deepest pleasure and admiration." Bellow has read and written on Roth too: see, for example, "Some Notes on Recent American Fiction," *Encounter*, November 1963, 22–29, reprinted in *The American Novel since World War II*, ed. Marcus Klein (Greenwich, Conn.: Fawcett World Publications, 1969), 159–74. In "Are Many Modern Writers Merely Becoming Actors Who Behave like Writers?" (*Chicago Sun-Times Book Week*, 15 September 1968, 1) Bellow includes a reply to "Writing American Fiction," which he considers "a charming article"; see Rodgers, *Bibliography*, 265–66, items B845–47.

7. Compare Roth's fictionalized accounts of visits to Prague in *The Professor of Desire, Epilogue: The Prague Orgy*, and *Deception*.

8. Despite Zuckerman's disapproval (178–79), Roth insists on using this pseudonym for his wife and "May" for the lover he took after his separation.

9. Apparently he still does, as the conclusion of *Deception* strongly suggests. See chapter 12 in this volume.

10. Compare Robert Pinsky's review in the *New York Times Book Review* (6 January 1991, 30): "The self-portrait in this book is more rounded and less self-conscious than in Mr. Roth's previous autobiographical book, 'The Facts.'"

11. *Patrimony: A True Story* (New York: Simon & Schuster, 1991), 31; hereafter cited in text as *P*.

12. The comment is reminiscent of another father-son relationship, as Melvin J. Friedman reminds me (in conversation)—that of Hermann Kafka and his son Franz, whose work was (and apparently still is) a powerful influence on Philip Roth.

*Chapter Seven*

1. See "Writing American Fiction," in *Reading Myself and Others*, 120, and the discussion in chapter 6 of this volume.

2. "Imaginary Conversation with Our Leader" and "Imaginary Press Conference with Our Leader," *New York Review of Books*, 6 May 1971, 12, and 3 June 1971, 15–17, respectively.

3. Dwight MacDonald, "*Our Gang*," *New York Times*, 7 November 1971, reprinted in *Critical Essays*, ed. Pinsker, 61.

4. See Rodgers, *Philip Roth,* 107–8.
5. *Our Gang* (New York: Random House, 1971), 4; hereafter cited in text as *OG.*

*Chapter Eight*

1. The term is Stephen J. Whitfield's, from "In the Big Inning," in *Voices of Jacob, Hands of Esau,* 174.
2. Compare "After Eight Books," in *Reading Myself and Others*: "My Life as a Man . . . is a book I'd been writing, abandoning, and returning to ever since I published *Portnoy's Complaint.* Whenever I gave up on it I went to work on one of the 'playful' books—maybe my despair over the difficulties with the one book accounted for why I wanted to be so playful with the others" (112). In *The Comedy That "Hoits"* Pinsker sees this novel as partly "an attempt to give the whole notion of the G.A.N. (Great American Novel) the comic burial it deserves" and partly an attempt "to write that 'big book' his critics kept demanding" (85).
3. See Ben Siegel, "The Myths of Summer: Philip Roth's *The Great American Novel," Contemporary Literature* 17 (Spring 1976): 174–75; hereafter cited in text.
4. Donald G. Watson, "Fiction, Show Business, and the Land of Opportunity: Roth in the Early Seventies," in *Reading Philip Roth,* ed. Milbauer and Watson, 108; hereafter cited in text.
5. *The Great American Novel* (New York: Holt, Rinehart & Winston, 1973), 37; hereafter cited in text as *GAN.*
6. In his "Acknowledgements" Roth credits the tape-recorded recollections of professional baseball players at the Library of the Hall of Fame in Cooperstown, New York, and the quotations from them in Lawrence Ritter's *The Glory of Their Times* as a "source of inspiration" to him while he wrote this book.
7. See Rodgers, "The Great American Joke (*The Great American Novel*)," in *Philip Roth,* 109–22. Rodgers depends heavily on Walter Blair's *Native American Humor,* rev. ed. (1960), which Roth read in its earlier version while at the University of Chicago when he took courses from Blair (Rodgers, 78–79). For other specific sources and influences, see Siegel, "The Myths of Summer," 178, n. 23, and Shechner, *After the Revolution,* 111.
8. Walter Blair and Hamlin Hill, "*The Great American Novel,*" in *American Humor: From "Poor Richard" to "Doonesbury"* (New York: Oxford University Press, 1978), reprinted in *Critical Essays,* ed. Pinsker, 217–28; see especially 224.
9. As many have noticed, the name derives from Ruppert Stadium in Newark, New Jersey, where as a boy Roth watched minor league baseball.
10. The episode, actually a long digression in chapter 6, is highly comic. Fairsmith and his nephew, Billy, try to teach a tribe of cannibals baseball. The naked tribesmen love to slide; however, when Fairsmith refuses to allow them to slide into first base after getting a walk, he precipitates a crisis that nearly ends in his death and that of his nephew, who goes mad under the strain of events. The gloves and baseballs are all boiled and eaten, and young maidens are deflow-

ered in a ritualistic ceremony with baseball bats. Roth parodies Conrad's "Heart of Darkness"—for example, when Fairsmith cries out, "The horror! The horror!" in response to something Billy says (304), or when one of the native boys declares, after running around the bases clockwise, "Mistah Baseball—he dead" (305).

11. Like reviewers before him, Siegel ("The Myths of Summer," 185, n. 32) cites several other historical counterparts in the novel.

12. David Monaghan balances the novel's strengths against its weaknesses in "*The Great American Novel* and *My Life as a Man*: An Assessment of Philip Roth's Achievement," *International Fiction Review* 2 (1975): 113–20, reprinted in *Critical Essays,* ed. Pinsker, 68–77; see especially 72–75.

*Chapter Nine*

1. See, for example, Pinsker, *The Comedy That "Hoits,"* 103.
2. See *The Facts,* 152.
3. See chapter 6 of this volume and *The Facts,* 107, 111.
4. For a perceptive account of this episode and of Spielvogel's role in the novel, compare Shechner, *After the Revolution,* 218–22, to whom *My Life as a Man* is the first of several novels written "contra-*Portnoy,* a son's plea that it was Freudian doctrine or the Zeitgeist or the great books that led him astray, not his mother" (221).
5. Compare Rodgers, *Philip Roth,* 152: noting the many parallels between Roth's life and Tarnopol's, Rodgers says Roth "keeps the nature of the interpenetration of reality and fantasy before us constantly."
6. Compare Milan Kundera, "Some Notes on Roth's *My Life as a Man* and *The Professor of Desire,*" in *Reading Philip Roth,* ed. Milbauer and Watson, 163: Tarnopol is not a projection of Roth, but if he is, it is "a slaughtered, demolished, ridiculed Roth."
7. Roth's autobiography ends with a decision to leave "May," his lover for several years, and live on his own after *Portnoy's Complaint* appears. In *The Facts* he gives no indication of any suicide attempt, as his narrative stops at that point (159–60).
8. For Roth's own comments on the last line, see "After Eight Books," in *Reading Myself and Others,* 107–8.

*Chapter Ten*

1. Morton Levitt, "Roth and Kafka: Two Jews," in *Critical Essays,* ed. Pinsker, 245–54. See also Rodgers, *Philip Roth,* 154–66, and Alan Cooper, "The Jewish Sit-Down Comedy of Philip Roth," in *Jewish Wry,* ed. Cohen, 158–77.
2. Roth's fantasy anticipates a similar one involving Anne Frank in *The Ghost Writer,* discussed in the next chapter of this volume.
3. Here chronology of composition is important only to show how directly Roth's imagination was now influenced by his reading and teaching Kafka

and how vigorously it was at work in other directions while he was struggling with *My Life as a Man.*

4. Compare Rodgers, *Philip Roth,* 160: "The central conflict is, once again, between the disapproving moralist and the libidinous slob, the lawful and anarchic selves, the ego/superego and the id."

5. Roth cannot resist noting the irony of Kafka's fate. When Claire and David visit the Jewish cemetery, they see "a stout, elongated, whitish rock, tapering upward to its pointed glans, a tombstone phallus," marking the place where "the family-haunted son is buried forever—still—between the mother and the father who outlived him" (175).

6. See, for example, 152, where Kepesh describes his near obsession with Claire's breasts. Compare Frederick Crews, who comments on "Kepesh's fetishizing of Claire's breast" in "Uplift" (*New York Review of Books,* 16 November 1972, 18, reprinted in *Critical Essays,* ed. Pinsker, 66). Shechner, in *After the Revolution,* regards *The Breast* as a footnote to both *Portnoy's Complaint* and *My Life as a Man:* "Kepesh appears to be the disguised fulfillment of Alex's most primitive desire, to undo his ill-starred birth altogether in favor of a generational merger, to become, not just an infant, but his own mother in order to raise himself. Such merger permits him to hold on and let go at the same time, to *have* his mother without *having to deal* with her and to bring himself up according to his own laws" (215).

7. As Shechner notes in *After the Revolution* and as a cursory comparison reveals, the 1980 edition of *The Breast* is not very different from the earlier one. Some details are altered to conform with events in *The Professor of Desire;* for example, in the first edition Helen is married to an alcoholic and has become one herself (65), whereas in the revised edition the reasons for her unhappy life are left vague (66). This kind of authorial tinkering suggests that the novella must be a favorite of Roth's.

8. *The Breast* (New York: Holt, Rinehart & Winston, 1972; rev. ed., New York: Farrar, Straus & Giroux, 1980), 10; hereafter cited in text as *TB,* with page numbers referring to the 1980 edition.

9. Roth's device thus resembles the one he used in *Portnoy's Complaint.* But it can also be seen as the rest of Kepesh's lecture, begun while in Prague, to the students of his comparative literature class in *The Professor of Desire* or, rather, as the concluding lecture in a series that incorporates the chapters of that novel.

*Chapter Eleven*

1. *The Anatomy Lesson* (New York: Farrar, Straus & Giroux, 1981; reprinted in *Zuckerman Bound,* New York: Farrar, Straus & Giroux, 1985), 687; hereafter cited in text as *AL,* with page numbers referring to the 1985 edition.

2. *The Ghost Writer* (New York: Farrar, Straus & Giroux, 1979; reprinted in *Zuckerman Bound,* New York: Farrar, Straus & Giroux, 1985), 3; hereafter cited in text as *GW,* with page numbers referring to the 1985 edition.

3. As with *Goodbye, Columbus, Portnoy's Complaint,* and *My Life as a Man,* Roth uses the first person singular to help convey the exuberance, although he switches later, in *Zuckerman Unbound* and *The Anatomy Lesson,* whose humor is more somber, to third-person narrative.

4. As he did in "Courting Disaster," the second of the "Useful Fictions" in *My Life as a Man,* Roth again alters aspects of Zuckerman's life and background to offer still a different "legend of the self." In *Zuckerman Bound* Nathan was born and reared in Camden, New Jersey, not Newark; his father is a chiropodist, not a "shoedog"; he now has a younger brother, Henry, instead of an older brother, Sherman, or a sister, Sonia; he has attended the University of Chicago, not a small liberal arts college; he is a writer, not a teacher; and his three marriages, all ending in divorce, have been to exemplary women, as recalled (not dramatized) in *The Anatomy Lesson.* But Zuckerman is nonetheless recognizable as a character.

5. In "Forget Fathers" (*New Republic,* 19 December 1983, 32), Michael Wood notes how Roth's characters stumble into the irony of trying to escape their past but keep "getting entangled in someone else's present and past." The recurring comic form of this situation in Roth, he says, is marriage to a gentile.

6. As Jack Beatty, among others, points out in his review in the *New Republic,* 6 October 1979, 37.

7. Compare Zuckerman's aspirations in "Salad Days" in *My Life as a Man.*

8. As Beatty says, in his *New Republic* review, 39. The experience, however, is merely the prelude to what Nathan experiences later in *Zuckerman Unbound,* after the publication of his novel *Carnovsky.*

9. Beatty, in his *New Republic* review, 39. Compare Joseph Epstein, "Too Much Even of Kreplach," *Hudson Review* 33 (1980): 97–110; Rhoda Koenig, *Saturday Review,* December 1979, 58; John Leonard, "Fathers and Sons," *New York Review of Books,* 25 October 1979, 4–6; and Barbara K. Quart, "Fathers and Writers," *London Magazine,* March 1980, 87–90—all of these cited in Rodgers, *Bibliography.*

10. Robert A. Cohn, *St. Louis Jewish Light,* 12 September 1979, 7, cited in Rodgers, *Bibliography,* 199. Compare also Dan Isaac, "Philip Roth: His Art and Its Origins," *Midstream* (March 1981): 47–48; Christopher Lehmann-Haupt, *New York Times,* 4 September 1979, C10; Mark Shechner, "What Nathan Knew," *Nation,* 15 September 1979, 213–16—all cited in Rodgers, *Bibliography.* Although Roth's chapter is slight by comparison with William Styron's *Sophie's Choice,* the quality of the writing is as high.

11. Compare Jonathan Brent, who in "The Unspeakable Self: Philip Roth and the Imagination," in *Reading Philip Roth,* ed. Milbauer and Watson, regards Pepler as "a grotesquely caricatured anti-self of Zuckerman" and sees Zuckerman at the end of the trilogy as "weary and defeated, a caricature of himself: a Lonoff with a Pepler inside" (190). Shechner makes a similar point in *After the Revolution:* "Recalling Roth's myth of himself as a man torn between the measured and the

reckless, the civilized and the untamed, we might think of Lonoff and Pepler as bookends, examples of what can happen when either side takes full command" (229).

12. Among other self-reflexive comments, note Zuckerman's remarks on Pepler: "Oh, what a novel this guy would make! . . . He's glue, mental flypaper, can't forget a thing. . . . What a *novelist* this guy would make! Already is one! Paté, Gibralter, Perlmutter. . . ." (320). Later Zuckerman writes a note to himself: "P. as my pop self? Not far from how P. sees it. He who's made fantasy of others now fantasy of others" (339).

13. As a kind of in-joke, deriving from Zuckerman's infatuation with Amy Bellette, Caesara O'Shea says she rose to stardom at 19 when she portrayed Anne Frank at the Gate Theatre in Dublin (270). In *The Prague Orgy* Zuckerman meets another actress, Eva Kalinova, who also starred in the role.

14. Compare the comments by Brent and Shechner in note 11 of this chapter. On Roth's "blocked" Jewish heroes, see Lee, *Philip Roth,* 80–83.

15. Even Muller had got into *Carnovsky,* by telling Zuckerman about his "hapless struggle" with self-abuse as a high school student and his frequent visits to the confessional. A sympathetic Jesuit priest had finally refused to give him absolution more than once every 24 hours (*ZU,* 344).

16. Just as Zuckerman does not know what to do with the scrap of paper but cannot throw it away either, Roth cannot discard the Jewish tradition, which the word encapsulates. See Clive Sinclair, "With the Playmates on the Oedipal Playmat," (London) *Times Literary Supplement,* 24 February 1984, 183.

17. On Roth's contretemps with Howe, see Shechner, *After the Revolution,* 199–207. Of the "wild fantasy" that follows here, Shechner says neither Roth nor Zuckerman proposes it as "a proper answer." "It is simply a private release, a device for easing the pain while admitting defeat" (200).

18. Compare Sinclair, "With the Playmates," 183: "In Milton Appel, pornographer, Zuckerman creates his most successful literary impersonation for years, taking in all he meets."

19. *Epilogue: The Prague Orgy,* in *Zuckerman Bound,* 707; hereafter cited in text as *PO*.

## Chapter Twelve

1. See "After Eight Books," in *Reading Myself and Others,* 106, and compare Mark Shechner, "Zuckerman's Travels," in *The Conversion of the Jews and Other Essays* (New York: St. Martin's Press, 1990), 91: "An elegant novel, [*The Counterlife*] performs an elaborate counterpoint between the inertia of history and the agility of the imagination" and shows "that it is possible for a novel to contradict itself repeatedly and turn out all the more convincing for its contradictions."

2. The chronology is a bit tangled here. Apparently Henry had confided in Nathan about Maria 10 years earlier during his affair, and Nathan dutifully

recorded it in his notebooks (22, 48). But then the estrangement between the brothers occurred, and Henry ceased speaking to his brother altogether.

3. *The Counterlife* (New York: Farrar, Straus & Giroux, 1987), 12; hereafter cited in text as *C*.

4. *Note*: In New York City on 29 April 1990 Philip Roth married the English actress Claire Bloom, with whom he had been living for many years. It is his second marriage. Ms. Bloom, past childbearing, is not pregnant or likely to become so.

5. Compare Shechner, "Zuckerman's Travels," 97: While Roth steadfastly pursues "the formation and understanding of the self," he now operates under new ground rules, "the rules of *theater*, in which one exhibits oneself only in disguise, and the rules of *history*, in which the self appears as a resultant of [larger] forces." These ground rules directly conflict in the novel, but it is their collision that gives the novel its weight and its tension and makes it an "unsettling and absorbing" book.

6. *C*, 203. By his "affliction" Zuckerman refers not to his heart condition but to his tendency to self-absorption and "isolating unnaturalness" (*C*, 311), or what he bitterly complained of in *The Anatomy Lesson* and what drove him to try to become a doctor.

7. See *The Facts*, 162, where Zuckerman argues that Roth is essentially a "personficator."

8. Compare Hermione Lee's comments, in "Kiss and Tell" (*New Republic*, 30 April 1990, 39), on *betrayal*, a frequent term in the novel, and *deception*. Roth is not as intrigued by "adultery as sexual or social plot" as he is by "adultery as the occasion for authorial deception." "Betrayal is an act, deception is a craft," Lee says. "Betrayal is exposure, deception is concealment. This book isn't nearly so much about adultery as it is about writing."

9. The closest in *form* to *Deception* are the novels of Ivy Compton-Burnett, the Englishwoman whose fiction exists almost totally in dialogue. But in every other significant respect, Roth's novel is far different from any of hers.

10. Compare Jaga's comments to Zuckerman about writers as lovers in *The Anatomy Lesson*, 538, cited in chapter 11 of this volume.

11. Lee, in "Kiss and Tell," 42, says Roth has always done this and that is "why he matters so much."

12. Compare the experience of S. J. Perelman. As Whitfield reports in *Voices of Jacob, Hands of Esau*, 130, after leaving the United States to live in England, Perelman returned after several years because he found "too much couth" there.

13. See Roth's comments in the interview with Milbauer and Watson in *Reading Philip Roth*, ed. Milbauer and Watson, 3–5. For example: "After fifteen books I myself have become much less irritating than the Zuckerman I've depicted, largely because the Jewish generation that didn't go for me is by now less influential and the rest are no longer ashamed, if they ever were, of how Jews

behave in my fiction" (3). Roth's comments are perceptive and illuminating, not only about his fiction but about the current position of Jews in America. As Lee notes in "Kiss and Tell," 40, "[T]he butts of Roth's satiric rage have always been cant, hollow rhetoric, and fashions in lazy thinking," not Jews per se.

*Conclusion*

1. See, for example, Paul Gray, "A Surprising Mid-Life Striptease," *Time,* 19 September 1988, 94.

2. Hana Wirth-Nesher, "From Newark to Prague: Roth's Place in the American-Jewish Literary Tradition," in *Reading Philip Roth,* ed. Milbauer and Watson, 17–32; hereafter cited in text.

# Selected Bibliography

## PRIMARY SOURCES

*Books*

*The Anatomy Lesson.* New York: Farrar, Straus & Giroux, 1981.
*The Breast.* New York: Holt, Rinehart & Winston, 1972. Rev. Ed., New York: Farrar, Straus & Giroux, 1980.
*The Counterlife.* New York: Farrar, Straus & Giroux, 1987.
*Deception.* New York: Simon & Schuster, 1990.
*The Facts: A Novelist's Autobiography.* New York: Farrar, Straus & Giroux, 1988.
*The Ghost Writer.* New York: Farrar, Straus & Giroux, 1979.
*Goodbye, Columbus and Five Stories.* Boston: Houghton Mifflin, 1959.
*The Great American Novel.* New York: Holt, Rinehart & Winston, 1973.
*Letting Go.* New York: Random House, 1962.
*My Life as a Man.* New York: Farrar, Straus & Giroux, 1974.
*Our Gang.* New York: Random House, 1971.
*Patrimony: A True Story.* New York: Simon & Schuster, 1991.
*Portnoy's Complaint.* New York: Random House, 1969.
*The Professor of Desire.* New York: Farrar, Straus & Giroux, 1977.
*Reading Myself and Others.* New York: Farrar, Straus & Giroux, 1975.
*When She Was Good.* New York: Random House, 1967.
*Zuckerman Bound.* New York: Farrar, Straus & Giroux, 1985. Containing *The Ghost Writer, Zuckerman Unbound, The Anatomy Lesson,* and *Epilogue: The Prague Orgy.*
*Zuckerman Unbound.* New York: Farrar, Straus & Giroux, 1981.

## SECONDARY SOURCES

*Bibliographic Aids*

Leavey, Ann. "Philip Roth: A Bibliographic Essay (1984–1988)" *Studies in American Jewish Literature* 8 (Fall 1989): 212–18.
Rodgers, Bernard F., Jr. *Philip Roth: A Bibliography,* 2d ed. Metuchen, N.J.:

Scarecrow Press, 1984. Pages 10 through 23 list Roth's uncollected fiction, essays, interviews, and the like.

*Books about Roth*

Jones, J. P. and Nance, G. A. *Philip Roth.* New York: Frederick Ungar, 1981. An elementary study of Roth and his fiction.
McDaniel, John N. *The Fiction of Philip Roth.* Haddonfield, N.J.: Haddonfield House, 1974. An early study of Roth's fiction.
Lee, Hermione. *Philip Roth.* London and New York: Methuen, 1982. A concise and highly perceptive analysis of Roth's fiction.
Milbauer, Asher Z., and Donald G. Watson, eds. *Reading Philip Roth* (New York: St. Martin's Press, 1988). An excellent collection of essays by American, British, and other international scholars.
Pinsker, Sanford. *The Comedy That "Hoits": An Essay on the Fiction of Philip Roth.* Columbia: University of Missouri Press, 1975. An early study of Roth and one of the best, especially on the Jewish aspects of Roth's humor.
————, ed. *Critical Essays on Philip Roth.* Boston: G. K. Hall, 1982. Reprints a number of significant articles and reviews, along with several new essays on Roth noted in this bibliography.
Rodgers, Bernard F., Jr. *Philip Roth.* Boston: Twayne Publishers, 1978. An excellent early study, with a good deal on background sources.
Walden, Daniel, ed. *The Odyssey of a Writer: Rethinking Philip Roth.* Special issue of *Studies in American Jewish Literature* 8 (Fall 1989); on Roth, with eight new articles and a bibliographic essay.

*Articles and Chapters in Books*

Ardolino, Frank. "'Hit Sign, Win Suit': Abraham, Isaac, and the Schwabs Living over the Scoreboard in Roth's *The Great American Novel.*" *Studies in American Jewish Literature* 8 (Fall 1989): 219–23. "Onomastics" is a key to the novel; a family named Schwab once actually lived beneath the grandstand in New York's Polo Grounds, like the Ellises in Roth's novel.
Baumbach, Jonathan. "What Hath Roth Got?" *Commonweal,* 11 August 1967, 498. Review of *When She Was Good,* praising Roth's technique but noting the book's "thin" texture.
Beatty, Jack. "The Ghost Writer." *New Republic,* 6 October 1979, 36–40. Review of the novel as a "parable" about the relations between life and "the life of art."
Bellow, Saul. "The Swamp of Prosperity." *Commentary,* July 1959, 77–79. Review of "Goodbye, Columbus," recognizing Roth's as a new voice and urging him to ignore cries of anti-Semitism.
Blair, Walter, and Hill, Hamlin. "*The Great American Novel.*" In *America's Humor: From Poor Richard to Doonesbury,* 472–86. New York: Oxford Uni-

versity Press, 1978. reprinted in Sanford Pinsker, ed. *Critical Essays on Philip Roth*, 217–28. Boston: G. K. Hall, 1982.

Brent, Jonathan. "The Unspeakable Self: Philip Roth and the Imagination." In *Reading Philip Roth*, edited by Asher Z. Milbauer and Donald G. Watson, 180–200. New York: St. Martin's Press, 1988.

Cohen, Joseph. "Paradise Lost, Paradise Regained: Reflections on Philip Roth's Recent Fiction." *Studies in American Jewish Literature* 8 (Fall 1989): 196–204. In *Epilogue: The Prague Orgy* Roth "salvages the trilogy and even justifies its excesses."

Cohen, Sarah Blacher. "Introduction: The Varieties of Jewish Humor." In *Jewish Wry*, edited by Sarah Blacher Cohen, 1–15. Bloomington: Indiana University Press, 1987. A survey and analysis of different kinds of Jewish fiction.

———. "Philip Roth's Would-be Patriarchs and Their *Shikses* and Shrews." *Studies in American Jewish Literature* 1 (Spring 1975): 16–23. Reprinted in Sanford Pinsker, ed. *Critical Essays on Philip Roth*, 209–16. Boston: G. K. Hall, 1982. On women in *Goodbye, Columbus, Portnoy's Complaint,* and *The Breast,* and the "petulant" young men who blame their "Yiddishe mommes" for their powerlessness.

Cooper, Alan. "The Jewish Sit-Down Comedy of Philip Roth." In *Jewish Wry*, edited by Sarah Blacher Cohen, 158–77. Bloomington: Indiana University Press, 1987. "Roth's comedy is not romance; it reaches no happy endings, only surcease of pain."

Denby, David. "The Gripes of Roth." *New Republic*, 21 November 1988, 37–40. An extensive review of *The Facts* in the context of Roth's fiction.

Feldman, Irving. "A Sentimental Education circa 1956." *Commentary*, September 1962, 273–76. Reprinted in Sanford Pinsker, ed. *Critical Essays on Philip Roth*, 32–36. Boston: G. K. Hall, 1982. Notes various literary influences on *Letting Go,* especially Flaubert's *A Sentimental Education.*

Friedman, Melvin J. "Jewish Mothers and Sons: The Expense of *Chuztpah*." In *Contemporary American-Jewish Literature*, edited by Irving Malin, 156–74. Bloomington: Indiana University Press, 1973. On the mother-son confrontation in *Portnoy's Complaint* and other novels and on Roth's literary techniques.

———. "The Schlemiel: Jew and Non-Jew." *Studies in the Literary Imagination* 9 (Spring 1976): 139–53. On the background of the type and its appearances in many modern works.

———. "Texts and Countertexts: Philip Roth Unbound." *Studies in American Jewish Literature* 8 (Fall 1989): 224–30. On *The Facts* in the context of Roth's fiction.

Girgus, Sam B. "Between *Goodbye, Columbus* and Portnoy: Becoming a Man and Writer in Roth's Feminist 'Family Romance.'" *Studies in American Jewish Literature* 8 (Fall 1989): 143–53. On *When She Was Good.*

————. "The Jew as Underground Man." In *The New Covenant: Jewish Writers and the American Idea*, 118–32. Chapel Hill: University of North Carolina Press, 1984. Roth's Jewish background provides an important source for creative literary and linguistic innovation.

Gittleman, Sol. *From Shtetl to Suburbia: The Family in Jewish Literary Imagination*. Boston: Beacon Press, 1978. Treats the themes of Jewish identity and traditional Jewish values in Roth's fiction, along with that of others.

————. "The Pecks of Woodenton, Long Island, Thirty Years Later: Another Look at 'Eli, The Fanatic.'" *Studies in American Jewish Literature* 8 (Fall 1989): 138–42. Roth's values have not changed much since his earliest work.

Gray, Paul. "A Surprising Mid-Life Striptease." *Time*, 19 September 1988, 94–95. Review of *The Facts*, noting how it "inevitably shades into fiction."

Grebstein, Sheldon. "The Comic Anatomy of *Portnoy's Complaint*." In *Comic Relief: Humor in Contemporary American Literature*, edited by Sarah Blacher Cohen, 152–71. Urbana: University of Illinois Press, 1978. On Roth's adaptation of stand-up comics' "spritz" and other techniques.

Gross, John. "Marjorie Morningstar, Ph.D." *New Statesman*, 30 November 1962, 784. Reprinted in Sanford Pinsker, ed. *Critical Essays on Philip Roth*, 40–43. Boston: G. K. Hall, 1982. Review of *Letting Go*, noting its readability but "overblown size."

Guttman, Allen. "Jewish Humor." In *The Comic Imagination in American Literature*, edited by Louis D. Rubin, 329–38. New Brunswick, N.J.: Rutgers University Press, 1973. Roth rivals Saul Bellow as "a master of subtle irony."

————. "Philip Roth and the Rabbis." In *The Jewish Writer in America: Assimilation and the Crisis of Identity*, 64–76. New York: Oxford University Press, 1971. Roth's stories and the novels *Letting Go* and *Portnoy's Complaint* show his sensitivity to the problems of assimilation.

Howe, Irving. "Philip Roth Reconsidered." *Commentary*, December 1972, 69–77. Reprinted in Sanford Pinsker, ed. *Critical Essays on Philip Roth*, 229–44. Boston: G. K. Hall, 1982, Roth's work has declined since the early stories, and his fiction has become vulgar, especially in *Portnoy's Complaint*.

————. "The Suburbs of Babylon." *New Republic*, 15 June 1959, 17–18. Praises Roth's "unique" new voice in *Goodbye, Columbus*.

Hyman, Stanley Edgar. "A Novelist of Great Promise." *New Leader*, 11 June 1962, 23. Reprinted in Sanford Pinsker, ed. *Critical Essays on Philip Roth*, 36–40. Boston: G. K. Hall, 1982.

Kartiganer, Donald. "Fictions of Metamorphosis: From *Goodbye, Columbus* to *Portnoy's Complaint*." In *Reading Philip Roth*, edited by Asher Z. Milbauer and Donald G. Watson, 88–89. New York: St. Martin's Press, 1988.

Kazin, Alfred. "Tough Minded Mr. Roth." In *Contemporaries*, 42–44. New

York: Atlantic/Little, Brown, 1962. Praises the stories in *Goodbye, Columbus*, but calls for more "delight in life for its own sake."

**Kundera, Milan.** "Some Notes on Roth's *My Life as a Man* and *The Professor of Desire.*" In *Reading Philip Roth*, edited by Asher Z. Milbauer and Donald G. Watson, 160–67. New York: St. Martin's Press, 1988. "Infinitely vulnerable in his sincerity, Roth is infinitely ungraspable in his irony."

**Lee, Hermione.** "Kiss and Tell." *New Republic*, 30 April 1990, 39–42. Review of *Deception*.

**Lewis, Cherie S.** "Philip Roth on the Screen." *Studies in American Jewish Literature* 8 (Fall 1989): 205–11. On the film versions of *Goodbye, Columbus* and *Portnoy's Complaint*, with an extensive bibliography of other criticism on the films.

**Lyons, Bonnie.** "'Jew on the Brain' in 'Wrathful Phillipics.'" *Studies in American Jewish Literature* 8 (Fall 1989): 186–95. Focuses on *The Counterlife* and on questions about Jewishness and what it means to be a Jew in relation to other themes.

**Mitz, Lawrence E.** "Devil and Angel: Philip Roth's Humor." *Studies in American Jewish Literature* 8 (Fall 1989): 154–67. On various aspects of Roth's humor.

**O'Donnell, Patrick.** "'None Other': The Subject of Roth's *My Life as a Man.*" In *Reading Philip Roth*, edited by Asher Z. Milbauer and Donald G. Watson, 144–59. New York: St. Martin's Press, 1988. Subjectivity is the topic.

**Rubin-Dorsky, Jeffrey.** "Philip Roth's *The Ghost Writer*: Literary Heritage and Jewish Irreverence." *Studies in American Jewish Literature* 8 (Fall 1989): 168–85. *The Ghost Writer* is the "most intricately patterned and exhilarating" novel in *Zuckerman Bound*.

**Shechner, Mark.** *After the Revolution: Studies in the Contemporary Jewish Imagination*. Bloomington: Indiana University Press, 1987. Acute analyses of many of Roth's characters and techniques.

———. "Zuckerman's Travels." In *The Conversion of the Jews and Other Essays*, 91–103. New York: St. Martin's Press, 1990. On *The Counterlife* and the other Zuckerman novels and their theatrics.

**Siegel, Ben.** "The Myths of Summer: Philip Roth's *The Great American Novel.*" *Contemporary Literature* 17 (Spring 1976): 171–90. Traces several of the background sources of the novel along with excellent analysis.

**Sinclair, Clive.** "The Son Is the Father to the Man." In *Reading Philip Roth*, edited by Asher Z. Milbauer and Donald G. Watson, 168–79. New York: St. Martin's Press, 1988. A perceptive essay on *Zuckerman Bound*.

———. "With the Playmates on the Oedipal Playmat." (London) *Times Literary Supplement*, 24 February 1984, 183. Review of *The Anatomy Lesson*.

**Spacks, Patricia Meyer.** "About Portnoy." *Yale Review* 58 (Summer 1969): 623–35. On the linguistic techniques of the novel.

**Watson, Donald G.** "Fiction, Show Business, and the Land of Opportunity: Roth in the Early Seventies." In *Reading Philip Roth*, edited by Asher Z.

Milbauer and Donald G. Watson, 105–25. New York: St. Martin's Press, 1988. Roth experiments in many of his novels with ways of incorporating American show business into his fiction.

Whitfield, Stephen J. "The Enchantment of Comedy." In *Voices of Jacob, Hands of Esau: Jews in American Life and Thought,* 115–39. Hamden, Conn.: Archon Books, 1984. On the origins and nature of Jewish humor, including Roth's, Bellow's, and others'.

———. "In the Big Inning." In *Voices of Jacob, Hands of Esau: Jews in American Life and Thought,* 172–79. Hamden, Conn.: Archon Books, 1984. Compares *The Great American Novel* with other books about baseball.

Wirth-Nesher, Hana. "From Newark to Prague: Roth's Place in the American-Jewish Literary Tradition." In *Reading Philip Roth,* edited by Asher Z. Milbauer and Donald G. Watson, 17–32. New York: St. Martin's Press, 1988. Roth tries to reconstruct a lost literary tradition, writing "a literature of retrieval."

Wisse, Ruth. *The Schlemiel as Modern Hero.* Chicago: University of Chicago Press, 1971. Cites Alexander Portnoy as an excellent example of the modern schlemiel.

# Index

# The Author

Jay L. Halio was born in New York City and educated at Syracuse University and Yale, where he received his Ph.D. in 1956. From 1955 to 1968 he taught English at the University of California, Davis. In 1968 he moved to the University of Delaware as professor of English. A member of the editorial board of the University of Delaware Press since 1975, he became its chairperson in 1985. He is the author of *Angus Wilson* (1964) for the series "Writers and Critics" and the editor of a volume of critical essays on that novelist for G. K. Hall's series on British writers. For many years he wrote a fiction chronicle for the *Southern Review*. A Shakespeare scholar as well, he is the author of *Understanding Shakespeare's Plays in Performance* (1988) and has edited *Macbeth, King Lear* (twice), and *The Merchant of Venice*.

# The Editor

Frank Day is a professor of English at Clemson University. He is the author of *Sir William Empson: An Annotated Bibliography* and *Arthur Koestler: A Guide to Research*. He was a Fulbright Lecturer in American Literature in Romania (1980–81) and in Bangladesh (1986–87).